BIRTH OF THE BINGE

CONTEMPORARY APPROACHES TO FILM AND MEDIA SERIES

A complete listing of the books in this series
can be found online at wsupress.wayne.edu

GENERAL EDITOR

Barry Keith Grant
Brock University

ADVISORY EDITORS

Robert J. Burgoyne
University of St. Andrews

Caren J. Deming
University of Arizona

Patricia B. Erens
School of the Art Institute of Chicago

Peter X. Feng
University of Delaware

Lucy Fischer
University of Pittsburgh

Frances Gateward
California State University, Northridge

Tom Gunning
University of Chicago

Thomas Leitch
University of Delaware

Walter Metz
Southern Illinois University

BIRTH *of the* BINGE

SERIAL TV *and* THE END *of* LEISURE

DENNIS BROE

WAYNE STATE UNIVERSITY PRESS
DETROIT

ISBN 978-0-8143-4597-9 (hardcover); ISBN 978-0-8143-4526-9 (paperback); ISBN 978-0-8143-4527-6 (ebook)

Library of Congress Control Number: 2018961790

Wayne State University Press
Leonard N. Simons Building
4809 Woodward Avenue
Detroit, Michigan 48201–1309

Visit us online at wsupress.wayne.edu

To Paris, the City of Light, which contributed in its own way to my seeing television differently.

To Bob Spiegelman, with whom I have shared many pleasurable conversations on television, film, culture, and politics and whose generous spirit regarding my work has constantly pushed me forward.

Contents

III: SERIAL AUTEURS AND THE POSSIBILITIES OF INDUSTRIAL RESISTANCE

ACKNOWLEDGMENTS

MANY CONTRIBUTED TO THE making of this book and to encouraging me along the way.

I was able to develop my ideas on television initially through teaching graduate classes in New York and Paris. Thanks particularly to Long Island University and its Media Arts Department and to the Sorbonne, Paris III, and its Department of Cinema and Audiovisual.

At LIU I would like to thank the LIU Library for its help in my research and particularly media librarian Rachel King. From the faculty, much love to Claire Goodman and Larry Banks whose always thoughtful encouragement aided me greatly as well as to the television-writing program headed by Norman Steinberg and to fellow professor Steve Molton. My students aided me greatly: in particular Frank Zagottis, whose master's thesis helped me immensely in clarifying key aspects of this book and who remained a thoughtful participant throughout; Fangchi Gato, whose lively participation and enthusiasm is always much appreciated; Brian Jackson, for his general thoughtfulness and appraisal of *Last Resort*; and Robin Lee Kelly for her intellectual curiosity and constant support. Finally, to the university itself for granting me the time and resources to complete the project.

At the Sorbonne, thanks to Guillaume Soulez, Martin Goutte, Kira Kitsoupanidou, and Maria Vezzoni for putting up with my French and allowing me to teach a graduate course in television studies, which also furthered my research.

My thoughts on television were also formed and expressed in various media outlets in three countries. Special thanks in the US to Prairie Miller of Pacifica Radio and WBAI's *Arts Express* for giving me free rein and allowing me to articulate my thoughts on the progress and meanderings of serial television. Thanks in France to Paris's *Art District Radio* and particularly to Didier Dippe and Julie Chaizemartin for their encouragement and help in launching my show *Breaking Glass* and my television series *TV on TV*. Special thanks as well in Britain to Garrick Webster and Maria Sophia of Crime Fiction Lover for their help with my Serial TV Crit and to Mike Quille and *Culture Matters* for their generous exposure of my television criticism. Thanks also to Diana Odile-Lestage and Forum des images for Series Mania which gave me an extraordinary entrée to both global television series and producers.

I was also ably supported by various writing groups. Of immense help were my primary group of Dan, Judith, and Mathilde, whose encouragement and enthusiasm for my work went far beyond any call of duty. Many thanks also to Jerry, Larry, Pat, and Nona. My writing career really began in earnest with my work with Jerry Mundis, the best friend and counselor any writer could have. A number of people were also helpful in weekly conversations about the work, and these include Alexis, Aviva, Laurie, and John.

A special thanks to Patrick and to Rich Kieling for their help in keeping me focused.

My parents, Joyce and Jim, supplied much needed funding for books and were always curious about my progress.

Many friends have contributed to this work, including Ed Levy, whose constant encouragement is a model of a committed friendship; Bob Spiegelman, whose conversation always inspired me; and Michael Pelias, whose intellectual elocution is only matched by his kind heart. In Paris I would like to thank James, Ying Ying, Jay, and Annemiek for their warm friendship and help in adjusting to a new city and a new life.

Finally, to my wife Sri, who taught me again what it means to work and, when troubles came, gave me the wise advice to "just let them go."

PREFACE

Oh! Williams!: The Rise and Fall and Rise Again of Television Studies

THE DISCIPLINE OF TELEVISION studies has made great strides in the last few years, including being integrated into the master's program at the Sorbonne, where I have taught, in a department that is now titled Cinema *and Audiovisual*. However, this still-emerging discipline, in some ways founded theoretically by Raymond Williams in the 1970s, at times veers too close to simply being an industry mouthpiece, which leads to a questioning of its legitimate status as an area of study. This book, an integrated multidisciplinary examination of the politics, economics, and aesthetics of contemporary television, is also aimed at broadening the theoretical basis of the field of television studies. The attempt here is to more thoroughly ground the field in part by stressing its interconnection to the established fields of philosophy, sociology, psychoanalysis, political economy, aesthetics, and art and literary theory while also establishing the crucial differences that are a part of its own media specificity, differences that are especially prominent and striking in the age of Complex or Serial TV.[1] One underlying aim of the book then is to contribute to enlarging the discipline so that in effect its academic acceptance, and appropriateness for undergraduate and graduate study, might continue to match the significant strides in an increasingly sophisticated media practice. The advances of Serial TV makers need to be accompanied by equally profound scholarly practices that explicate and keep pace theoretically with the aesthetic and industrial complexity of contemporary television while maintaining a theoretical and analytical distance.

Of course one of the major characteristics of the field is that it is made up of television aficionados captivated and captured by the medium since childhood, of which I am one. That early imaginary and the fond feelings it evokes nevertheless needs to be analyzed so that those warm and fuzzy memories, part of what Bernard Stiegler calls the memory outside ourselves fashioned by the medium (and some of my own best memories of childhood are of being left with my siblings at 11:30 a.m. to watch reruns of *The Dick Van Dyke Show* [1961–66]), are themselves scrutinized rather than simply overlaid with an adult critical intelligence. These earlier "tertiary retentions" are memories that are both collective in the sense of positive shared experiences but also fashioned by a commercial medium where desire is both enlarged (this gave me access to an outside world I craved) and channeled (I accepted the perfect Rob-and-Laura-Petrie household as a substitute for my own far-from-perfect one).

The other, though related, constraint in developing the discipline is television's increasingly more crucial role in the media landscape and media's more crucial role in the overall US and global economy. An Ernst and Young 2015 forecast saw cable channels and networks, satellite TV, and broadcast television outdistancing not only film production but for the most part also interactive media, electronic games, and music as areas of profit. (The recent trend in disconnecting from cable is necessitating a shift in the mode of distribution but likely not a decrease in profitability for television as a whole.)[2] In 2017 the US media industry accounted for a projected $712 billion, generating more profits than such pillars of the Fordist factory economy as the automobile, aerospace, and consumer-goods industries.[3] This frantic acceleration of profits of course heightens an accumulationist mentality and is part of the pressure that media creators (and media scholars and critics) are working under. Potential limitations on the discipline are both the popular and academic notions that (a) the subject matter is not to be taken seriously (when I said recently I was teaching television studies, one wag responded, "What's that, how to use a remote control?") and (b) that those who write about it are simply adjuncts to the industry where often "trying to understand" furthers the industry's goals or superficial criticism of series substitutes for actual analysis.[4]

This book then attempts to interweave the political economy of a dominant media formation with a structural, formalist, and narratological analysis of its products. These products are both conditioned by their place in the industry but also, through the work of the artists of the medium, striving to escape their positioning as pure product. The best instances of the work of television artists act as critical vehicles commenting on both the medium of television itself and on the challenges and failures of the virtual world, of which this medium is a part. These efforts may both compensate for capital's on- and off-line rapacious dynamism and in a dialectical manner, from inside the belly of the beast, point the way to a more human on- and off-line world that works in harmony to restore and reset the inequality and destruction that this frantic level of accumulation in both worlds has promoted and encouraged.

INTRODUCTION

Down the Rabbit Hole of Seriality, Narrative Complexity, and Quality Television

SOMETHING VERY DIFFERENT STARTED to happen in television at the dawn of the Reagan years and the birth of neoliberalism. This change then made a significant leap forward over a decade later and now has become the series dominant, or at least has forced each series to define itself in relationship to it. That something we will call "Serial TV" or "seriality," though it also goes by the industry term "Quality TV" and by another critical term "Complex TV" (Mittell 2006). What appeared in embryo in the early 1960s in *The Fugitive* (1963–67), began officially, perhaps by happy accident, with *Hill Street Blues* (1981–87),[1] took a giant stride with *The Sopranos* (1999–2007)—and now defines the brave new world of cable, online streaming services, and many network series—is a blend of multicharacter narratives, overlapping time periods, and most prominently a circumvention of the contained episode in favor of a sustained story arc lasting an entire season (*True Detective* [2014–]) or even an entire series (*Lost* [2004–10]). The dominant element in this mix is the continued story, the serial, which has been borrowed from a long history in literature, movies, and radio (to say nothing of art and music) but which is now imbued with a density that teases, enervates, and hooks audiences into one of the new modes central to digital entertainment. Surely, in its purposely addictive nature, seriality is a mode of digital engineering but may also be, in the way it challenges the commercial imperative, a model pointing toward liberatory viewing.

The model has grown up at a moment where capital accumulation, particularly in the digital realm, has intensified. Capital has in many ways reached its capacity, or continues to brush against its limits, in areas such as its contamination of the planet and its exhaustion of sustainable energy. As the economic system, accelerated by the 2008 Great Recession—which for many has yet to end—circumscribes a "real" world that is more and more unequal and more and more needing to be reinforced by new forms of militarization, the digital "virtual" world becomes capital's (sole?) hope and beacon for its promise of abundance and the site of its last pretensions to equality. Television seriality is an integral part of that strained abundance.

This book is an examination of this now-dominant mode of television-series narration, both in the US and across the world. The rise of seriality, of a new sophisticated mode of the continued story, and the consumption of this seriality, in a new mode of reception called "binge watching," is emblematic of larger changes not only in television and in the media industries as a whole but also in the very form and content of patterns of both work and leisure in this rarefied age of capital accumulation that Bernard Stiegler and others have termed not post- but *hyperindustrialism*. Television seriality and binge watching have developed as part of this new model of perpetual productivity, or integrated work and leisure, which Jonathan Crary terms "24/7," and which countries outside the Anglo-Saxon world in which this mode has developed sometimes refer to as "non-stop."[2]

This new mode of production, these new forms of luring the spectator central to capital's new virtual accumulation, Jonathan Beller and others have termed "the attention economy." Stiegler (2008b) further describes this "manufacturing of an audience," this new kind of technics and prosthesis, or machinic apparatus interacting with the human, as accomplishing an "indus-trialization of memory." These phenomena are written onto the narrational patterns of contemporary television seriality, a new complexity sometimes deployed in the service of training workers in skills needed for the virtual economy through the lure and promise of leisure and relaxation and under the rubric of what Steven Johnson terms "problem solving."

Fandom in this model, as in the example of Facebook, while perceived as leisure, is also of course integral to building product recognition and the brand of the networks associated with a series. Fans are not only being worked on (and worked over), but they are also working; their labor is crucial in building this commercial structure. For Theodor Adorno, the Fordist culture industry reproduced the pattern of the assembly line (through, for example, the routine aspects of genre repetition) in such a way that workers never got a break from that industrial process. Likewise, hyperindustrial products in the era of the

Early serial multiple protagonists in *Hill Street Blues*.

mobile computer are a deadening imprint of the process of virtual accumulation. Thus in TV seriality, "narrative complexity" may simply be a duplication of technological complexity where the stress, rather than on making sense of the world, is on tracking increasingly intricate but also highly repetitive patterns. Beyond that, these media are also, in a function now inherited from the education system as a new component of Althusser's ideological state apparatuses (ISAs), a mode of hierarchizing, training, and manufacturing workers in the new economy.

Finally, this new seriality, which Stiegler (2008a, xii) characterizes as "portals to forms of addiction and unseen kinds of toxicity," engages addiction directly in its acceleration of older narrational tropes. Thus, for example, the cliffhanger becomes the multicharacter cliffhanger. The form attempts to accentuate the compulsive nature of viewing acknowledged by the industry in its term "binge watching." This has reached the point where, in light of Adorno's characterization of the media industries as replacing use value with exchange value, fans now boast not about *what* they have viewed in watching a full season of a series but instead of the feat of accomplishing this viewing over a short period of time, often consuming the series in a single weekend. Raymond Williams's (1974) concept of television "flow," the blur of images that confront the viewer in succession, has in the Serial TV era been internalized. Flow, in the unhooked era, where television series present themselves not as single units but as part of a wider agglomeration, is now the serial flow itself within the series as well as the imperative to then "pick up" another serial series.[3]

However, there is an opposite side to this "industrial manufacturing of an audience" (Stiegler 2008a, xii), to the addictive quality written into the narrative processes that has caused even twelve-step groups to refer to the consumption of television's new seriality as akin to "morphine drip." Derrida's (1981) revival of Plato's concept of the *pharmakon*, the substance that is both poison and cure—and both at the same time—is useful in describing a potentially resistant side to seriality. The form has meant a new assertiveness for television writers against the budgetary pressures of the absolute dumbing down of television that is "Reality TV." Here, artist and audience do indeed fetishize complexity but as an antidote to a mind-numbing form of mass celebrification. Serial TV itself has challenged the old commercial constraints of having to tell a story in one episode so that the series can be syndicated as a stand-alone entity. Instead serial producers have spun a complex story that relies for its impact on consistent and more active viewing.

The serial form has attracted auteur directors such as David Lynch (*Twin Peaks* [1990–91, 2017–]), Lars Von Trier (*The Kingdom* [1994–97]), and Jane Campion (*Top of the Lake* [2013, 2017]) and sometimes induced a kind of lucidity in their creations not seen elsewhere.[4] The form has also produced its own "television auteurs," most prominent among them Joss Whedon and J. J. Abrams who in series such as *Dollhouse* (2009–10) and *Fringe* (2008–13) began by respecting the anthology, single-episode, format and then threw off that commercial yoke entirely and experimented with pure seriality even as their respective series were being shunted aside by the networks. If the impetus for contesting the industrialization of memory must grow out of the machine itself, Whedon's *Dollhouse* proposes a new kind of identity formation for its rebuilt feminist heroine, who is able to fashion the means to overthrow the corporate Dollhouse through absorbing the multitude of identities implanted in her, and not via a simple return to a privileged era of activism before the machinic.

Finally, following the militarization of American television after 9/11, where the model has become the single-episode *policier* (*CSI: Crime Scene*

Investigation [2000–2015], nearly every hour-long drama on CBS), it has been the serial model that artists have most often employed to oppose television's domestic "War on Terror." Thus the protagonists in both J. J. Abrams quickly canceled series *Revolution* (2012–14) and *Believe* (2014) and Joss Whedon's *Firefly* (2002–3) are on the run from various manifestations of the security state. It is this form that has added nuance to a simplified media good and evil, seen most strikingly in the re-viewing of Reagan's Cold War pyrotechnics from the Russian perspective in *The Americans* (2013–18). In this characterization of seriality, narratological complexity begets ideological complexity.

This book then views television's new seriality, now a globally popular form, in the wider contexts of its philosophic relation to the hyperindustrial epoch; its sociological relation to the changing nature of work and leisure; its psychoanalytic relationship to both addiction and to new kinds of hyper-engagement where forms of autism may now be described as a social metaphor; and its changing relation to new contemporary television modes of production, distribution, and exhibition, most prominently those of the "streaming studio," streaming video on demand (SVOD), and the mobile screen. The book explores each of these areas to see how they are written onto the form of this new narrative complexity while also delineating the history of the concept of seriality itself as taken up by Nietzsche and Sartre. Also explored are previous forms of seriality in painting, music, and literature (we now have Shakespeare serialized for television in the *Game of Thrones*-ish [2011–19] *The Hollow Crown* [2012, 2016]) and in television and its evolution from the radio and film serial. Lengthy analysis of several series, ranging from *The Big Bang Theory* (2007–) to *Silicon Valley* (2014–) to *Orange Is the New Black* (2013–) argue that this contemporary form continues to be part of both the mind-numbing conformity that Stiegler (2008a) terms *télécritie* while at the same time itself commenting on and critiquing this conformity in a way that points to a potentially liberatory path forward into what Stiegler likewise terms the *televisual*.

The book is divided into three parts (as was all Gaul, in Julius Caesar's description of a previous *analog* empire). The first part, "Metaseriality," concerns the overall social, economic, political, and industrial structures that have nurtured the new seriality and into which it inserts itself; that is, how seriality fits into the totality of capitalist production and accumulation. The second part, "Serial Specificity," focuses on first a cross-aesthetic and philosophic tracing of the concept and then on television narrative in particular. The third part, "Serial Auteurs and the Possibilities of Industrial Resistance," is an analysis of two serial creators, concentrating on how the television work of Joss Whedon and J. J. Abrams has surpassed narrative-cinematic conventions to the point where television is now one of the factors dictating cinematic form.[5] This section illustrates as well how the work of "authors in discourse" may counter and rework the accumulationist impulse.

The first chapter, on the hyperindustrial epoch, characterizes the present moment of capital accumulation not as decentralizing but as accelerating a frenetic, never-before-seen scramble for profits and an attempt, particularly relevant to television, to control and manage time. Adorno's concept of leisure in the Fordist culture industry as simply a reinforcement of the stultifying pattern of the assembly line is updated to suggest that hyperindustrial modes of leisure are not just reinforcing the digital mode of production but are actually tutoring its participants in how to reproduce that mode. This is being done through the new dominant ISA of the media, which, to update Althusser, works in conjunction with the previous apparatus of the school to both indoctrinate workers and hierarchize their relative levels of participation in this new economy.

Chapter 2 describes changes in American and Western industrial-work patterns that have, as Thomas Piketty (2014) argues, accelerated income inequality and effectively eliminated or substantially modified the concept of leisure. It was this concept that network television was formerly based on; that is, the practice of families gathering around the television set each evening from eight to eleven at night, in what used to be termed "prime time." In the era of two breadwinners, with each working two to three jobs while going to school to attempt to retain a middle-class lifestyle, as described by commentators like Rick Wolff (2012) and Robert Reich (2010), television has altered its mode of delivery to accommodate either the new prime time of eleven at night to two in the morning or, more likely, to make itself available in the "flex" off-hours, which may simply be on the way to and from work. In the process, the mobile screen has also undercut the place of the television as centered on and centering domestic life, and as such it has also undermined the ISA of the family. Leisure in this reading has disappeared and become instead "leisurality," a hypercondition that connotes the stealing of a few minutes here and there in a time when even the digital "slacker" is now busily at work on various social platforms furthering accumulation in the era of reduced expectations that has brought us the "staycation."

Chapter 3, on psychoanalysis, explores two forms of pathology in both their literal and metaphoric levels as they intersect with television seriality. The chapter first considers how forms of autism centering on Asperger's syndrome are a metaphor for the hyperindustrial condition where market social organization now validates the replacement of human contact and where understanding of human relationships is replaced with technical expertise. This condition, becoming a dominant as "geek culture" enters mainstream culture, is seen on television in the now-acceptable form of the character of Sheldon, the theoretical physicist who cannot communicate in *The Big Bang Theory*, and in its hyper form in *Silicon Valley*. The chapter then considers the way that the serial pattern attempts to induce addictive watching through amplifying narrative tropes such as the cliffhanger and through heightened and more quickly shifting scenes to attempt more rigorously to hook an audience to stay tuned or to consume the entire series at once. The chapter illustrates how *24* (2001–10), a seminal series in this regard, employs hyper forms of Roland Barthes's codes of constructing a text to accomplish this aim.

Chapter 4 outlines the shift from network to cable to online streaming services where the series is never even scheduled to play on television. Though the industry parlance proclaims this era is about flexibility in programming for diverse audiences, the television power structure remains in place, with networks and the older film production companies producing series and branching into production for the more diversified audiences of cable and online streaming. The series themselves are examined for the way that they brand their own networks and modes of delivery and the way this branding is written into the series logic. This is accomplished through a comparison of the situation-comedy form as it manifests on network television (*The Office* [2005–13]), cable (*The Larry Sanders Show* [1992–98]), and online-streaming services (*Orange Is the New Black*) showing how each still adheres to the principles of that form, noting as well that narrative patterns in part established by advertising demands still linger and define shows that are financed by subscription rather than advertising. The term "quality television" is also described as a commercial-branding mechanism rather than a prima facie designation of aesthetic worth.

The next chapter, on the nature of seriality, first explores philosophical considerations of the term, ranging from Nietzsche's eternal return to Sartre's treatment of seriality as capitalist mundanity and expression of everyday class patterns of interaction and finally to a resistant seriality that recalls Hegel and Marx's totality. The chapter then goes on to explore the history of seriality in various art forms as it reproduces these philosophical positions, including the serial movement in music (Steve Reich / Philip Glass) and art (from Monet's wheat stacks and Rouen Cathedral to Warhol's postmodern Marilyns). Finally, the chapter then develops the direct lineage of seriality from newspapers and literature (Balzac, Zola) to radio to cinema to its persistence as a mode in television production, concluding with an examination of an early political use of serial totality in *The Fugitive*.

Chapter 6 defines the cluster of narrative tropes that combine to form the new seriality, including an acceleration of genre hybridity; multiple time frames, consisting of flashbacks, -forward, and -sideways; and layering of the narrative that may include reflexivity in the service of a continuing meta-narrative, or metadiegesis, that dominates the individual story, or diegesis, of any single episode. Season 2 of *Justified* (2010–15) is examined for the way that it either integrates or sidelines many of these elements to create a coherent whole that challenges the dispersed use of the same elements to simply further addictive viewing.

The first of two chapters on the potential resistance of serial auteurs begins with a consideration of the auteur and the television showrunner not as creative genius but as "author in discourse" who mediates between television codes and his or her own social reality. The chapter briefly recounts the path of film auteurs attracted to the potential of the long form of storytelling on television and whose work in that medium has pioneered and furthered the new seriality. These include David Lynch (*Twin Peaks*), Lars Von Trier (*The*

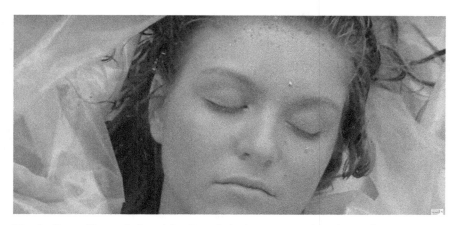

The finding of Laura Palmer's body and the beginning of modern television seriality in *Twin Peaks*.

Kingdom [1994–97]) and Jane Campion (*Top of the Lake*—the first radical-feminist series on television). The chapter then goes on to describe the work of the television writer/auteur Joss Whedon in a trilogy of series beginning with the post-Cold War feminist series *Buffy the Vampire Slayer* (1996–2003) but concentrating on his extended use of seriality in his immediate questioning of the 9/11 ethos in *Firefly* and his rebuilding of a feminism fractured within postwar 9/11 militarism in *Dollhouse*.

Chapter 8 details how the ultimate serial auteur, J. J. Abrams, has used the form to rupture and critique the increasing militarization of television accomplished largely through the episodic, or stand-alone, form employed in the post-9/11 return of the police procedural. Two resistant series deploying the serial form, both canceled after short runs, *Revolution* (2012–14) and *Believe*, are examined as attempts to use that form to disrupt the post-9/11 television "consensus." *Revolution* criticized Bush-era neocons in the guise of the "Patriots" who ravage the postapocalyptic landscape of a world without electrical power, and *Believe* critiqued military-industrial experiments in mind control employed by the American equivalent of the Nazi Dr. Mengele.

A short conclusion summarizes how serial totality both promotes and combats the fracturing of consciousness that Stiegler has described. This conclusion, along with a critical appendix of seminal serial series broken into periods, argues that with the potential overthrow of net neutrality, and the corresponding mergers that is necessitating, the second golden age of television, that of Serial TV, may have already passed in the US. However, the impulse that began that era is active in the way that foreign series are modifying, deepening, and challenging American dominance in the new era of Global Serial TV.

The central question this book poses is whether this new form of television narration, which springs full blown—depending on your perspective—either from the belly of the beast or the head of Zeus, is anything more than the detritus of that belly or the electrons of that head and whether this new poison contains within it the antibodies to also effect a cure. Is it possible that, as Marx originally claimed at the conclusion of the Communist Manifesto in referring to industrial capitalism's development of the proletariat, even one of the talismans of this new, accelerated form of hyperaccumulation, Serial TV, may have produced a hypercritique that will point us in directions that may yet transform and liberate these new forms of cyber dispossession?

I

METASERIALITY

Hyperindustrialism, Hypernarrativity, and the Home Screen

THE SCOPE AND SCALE of television series changed dramatically beginning in 2004 with *Lost*, which presented an ever-shifting world/island that seemed to alter the rules of time and space in a narrative cosmos that likewise with its fractured continuity and continuing development across six seasons altered the face of the series, bringing to network television what had already begun in cable. In the next ten years, the *Lost* model would push beyond cable and even beyond the traditional television screen to the point where these new serial series are not watched but streamed, with the online service Hulu, in what is now becoming commonplace, contracting two of the biggest names in network television, J. J. Abrams and Amy Poehler, to shows that will never air on a television or cable network and with Netflix now enlisting ABC's primary showrunner, Shonda Rhimes.[1]

Television studies' descriptions of this epoch most often begin with a narratological summation of this new televisual model, which I call Serial TV or seriality and whose features include season- and series-long arcs; ever-expanding (and expendable) casts of characters and plots built around them; and a kind of audacity around narrative and storyworld leaps that is the equivalent on the small screen of big-screen special effects (Mittell 2015). Instead, we will back up a bit and first consider the overall philosophical context in which the political economy of this model developed, looking at changes in the social landscape in which these new narratives and this new, now-portable, technology came into practice. In that way we are first integrating this new hyperseriality into its industrial epoch, which Bernard Stiegler (1998) has termed hyperindustrialism.

We will then consider the ever-shifting tropes of seriality, including its hypergeneric combinations and its consumption pattern—binge watching—as part of an ever-increasing role for these series in the culture industry (Adorno and Horkheimer 1972). Finally we will look at the serial mode as a new, perhaps now-dominant, component of what is termed the ideological state apparatus (Althusser 1971) and its role in socializing and reproducing (segmenting and training) new generations for positions in an ever more precarious and ever more cognitive (or mental) economy. The conclusion of this chapter will illustrate the way the complex serial form may combat these tendencies through an examination of the final episode of *Lost* as both exhibiting and critiquing this new brave new world by contrasting the digital and virtual world's utopian promises to what Slavoj Žižek via Jacques Lacan called "the desert of the real."

The sociopolitical background against which this heightened seriality emerges, with its much more intense luring of an audience into a more complicated and extended fictional world, is one of a seemingly ever more powerful capitalist system centered in the Anglo (American and British) world (Gindin and Panitch 2012), as are the television series that circulate out from it. This system has, on the one hand, no limits, no recognizable opponents, as it continues to expand and commodify all aspects of everyday life. But in the real world, capital is all the time surging against boundaries and destroying them at its own peril. The earth itself is in grave danger as the energy and resources needed to power the capital-technological revolution (oil, fracked natural gas, radioactive minerals strip-mined for communication devices) are rapidly destroying the planet.[2]

Meanwhile, inequality both in the US and globally now stands, as Thomas Piketty claims, at a level unseen since 1913, when the world was on the brink of two world wars. Private wealth in the US now equals nearly seven times the gross domestic product for a single year while 20 percent of the population now lives near or below the poverty line.[3] The Great Recession of 2008, brought on by the greed of (financial) capital, only amplified that condition, and the solution was not a (green) new deal in which the needy were put to work but a raw deal in which central-bank "quantitative easing" ensures that money fresh off the presses is used to restore the liquidity of banks, which now partially function as global casinos, and is then invested in the stock market. The result is that financial capital profits from its own miscalculations while those below suffer the consequences, even as they are blamed for bringing on the crisis.

The repressive state apparatus is everywhere apparent in maintaining this inequality both at home in the US, as the police become a highly militarized force waging war against the (black) victims of poverty, and abroad, as the US is now perpetually on the brink of provoking a war with Russia over its push to bring the Ukraine into the US-led NATO and resituate the European economy under its hegemony.[4] At the same time, the US state, the caretaker of capital, also continues to rain bombs while its drones practice assassination in the Middle East and now in Africa as well as this rapacious capital continues its resource grab under the name of a perpetual war on terrorism. The US populace is asked never to think of the root causes of this war as the homeland is protected by the home screen, which itself drones on endlessly about both the "terrorist menace and the Russian threat."[5]

It is not barbarism or civilization but rather barbarism *as* (capitalist) civilization, with its promotion of endless civil wars by playing the race card at home and around the world with a persecution of the poor under the code words "Muslim" or "Arab" as the West's never-ending need for the resources to power its technologically advanced lifestyle continues unabated. The world is becoming a much uglier place as the unfettered reign of capital "progresses" nearly unimpeded.

Nevertheless, there is a refuge, a place of plenty where the capitalist promise of abundance can still be fulfilled, and that is in the digital or virtual realm. That realm may operate through what Adorno (1972) designates as desire unfulfilled and Stiegler (2013) characterizes as the process of reducing the object of desire to "a calculability,"[6] but it nevertheless promises infinite pleasure and at an affordable price. (Thus, while the price of education, health care, and food from 2005 to 2014 has increased in the US by anywhere from 20 to 40 percent, the price of cell phones, toys, mobile accessories, computers, and televisions has fallen 40 to 100 percent, suggesting the poor, and increasingly elements of the middle class, while being denied basic needs and ways of advancing, are being offered the virtual world as a compensation.)[7]

Television seriality is entirely bound up in that promise. TV pilots present the lure of dark unsolved mysteries, with the series burrowing ever deeper into uncharted realms, though often the end game of these series disappoints fans for not answering the questions the series posed, as many complained regarding the ending of *Lost*. Other times the series too obviously let their wires show. In their apparently complex plotting, serial series posit what Roland Barthes would call a lure as an actual event in the lives of the characters and then a few episodes later resolve the embattled state in a way that showed that the supposed deep-seated conflict was only a way of prolonging the series. Season 5 of *Glee* (2009–15) featured a short arc in which the fiery Santana blazed with anger and envy at Rachel's success on Broadway, a contrivance that was quickly and arbitrarily resolved a few episodes later as another false crisis arose to animate the next segment of a show that had long since lost its purpose.

Think Greedily, Distribute Locally

Against the postmodern, postindustrial description of a world splintered into local production units in which workers are free to pursue "flex hours," Stiegler (1998) characterizes this as a "hyperindustrial" age, in which the drive toward capital accumulation, toward profit, is if anything more intense than in the previous "industrial" age. The drive itself is more centralized but is satisfied by catering to highly specialized demographics in a supposedly more "democratic" marketplace that in effect is often simply a reiteration of the same formula in slightly different bottles. In this way singularities become *particularities*, the difference being that the singular has been transformed into a quantity that is now calculable and programmable (Stiegler 2015, 78). One size no longer fits all, but that single size is now carved up into three or four sizes with these minute variations now defining "individuality" in the hyperindustrial age, just as Adorno's moustache or French accent were the bearers of a previous marketized individualization in culture in the industrial age.

Stiegler's characterization of hyperindustrialism also gives the lie to the postmodern slip of logic wherein globalized production is presented as decentralized, as fracturing into fragments with no recognizable whole. The television industry, for example, would seem to be a perfect illustration of this postmodern sleight of hand, with its proliferation first of cable channels, each challenging the power of the networks, and then of streaming services, now transforming themselves into streaming studios, so that television is so decentralized that it is no longer even seen on a screen. While all this is true, the proliferation of networks, channels, and streaming services also conceals the overall organization of an industry that is still largely run by the four major networks and the remnants of the old Hollywood studios who either own the majority of the predominant cable channels (Anderson 2005), produce the shows for the new streaming services, or serve as the site of apprenticeship for producers who have now thoroughly integrated ancient network formats.

Thus, for example, a show that looks entirely "modern" like Netflix's *Orange Is the New Black* seems to have a representational pattern never seen on television before in its mix of comedy and drama set in a women's prison with a predominantly minority cast. The show, though, was created by Jenji Kohan who comes out of a standard situation-comedy training and is best known for the Showtime series *Weeds* (2005–12). There is an episode in season 1 of *Orange Is the New Black* that has to do with "juvies" coming to the prison, with the inmates supposed to show them prison life to change their views. On the surface, the episode looks like nothing ever seen before, but in fact it follows a standard sitcom plot of kids visiting the place of employment of the main characters—used for example in an episode of *The Larry Sanders Show* (1992–98) where students visit the show's set. Yet viewers fail to recognize these fairly transparent "transformations" that remain trapped within similar stock story ideas, and fans are utterly shocked when *Orange* is described as a standard example of the genre that sifts multiracial representation through a very traditional and leaking sitcom sluice.

Rather than starting from an industrial framework in terms of the monetizing of perception in the attention economy (Beller 1994), Stiegler starts from a phenomenological perspective in characterizing media beginning in the twentieth century as hyperinflating "tertiary retention." Stiegler engages Edmund Husserl's understanding of perception as situated in time and taking place in two dimensions, with primary retention being essentially sense perception and secondary retention the filtering of that sensation through immediate memory (Stiegler gives the example of perception of a single note in musical listening being primary retention and perception of melody, which involves the memory of previous notes now organized in a linked chain and taking place over time, being secondary retention). To this conceptualization Stiegler adds another, now more dominant, mode of longer-term memories constructed outside immediate perception and separate from both experiential memory and from species evolutionary (or epigenetic) memory. This external memory—of a past that we ourselves have not lived—is delivered to us through culture, through "technical objects that embody the knowledge of our ancestors, tools we adopt to transform our environment" (Howells and Moore 2013, 3). A dominant earlier method of transmitting these cultural memories through technical means is writing, part of the overall process of recording and transmitting memory that Stiegler's philosophical mentor Jacques Derrida (1981) termed grammatization. This historical progression of transformed memory transmitted through the ages is treated by Stiegler, not primarily for its literary or cultural quality but for its technical quality, as the expression of an evolving technics that has been a crucial component in the species life of humans.

With the advent of recording devices in the nineteenth and twentieth centuries, including the photograph and recorded music, the potential for the "the sedentary processes left by the production of tertiary retention" (Stiegler 2013, 62) to influence and in fact to create memories increased. Indeed with the advent of analogical processes, these technologies of memory have gone from being techniques of transmitting knowledge to being an increasingly important part of the industrial economy. This has reached the point where today they are "integrally submitted to the imperatives of globalization and the mechanics of work" (22). This development was a major victory for capital and a major moment in its encroaching on not only the economic life of the populace but also on consciousness itself as the control of these memory-making devices was subsumed by capitalist investment (95) and as consciousness itself came to be seen as an "object of systematic exploitation" (58).

Beginning after World War II, with the advent of television and the spread of the power of US multinationals, this process intensified as advertising then viewed consciousness as merchandise, as a "disposable resource." The mastering and the systematic exploitation of this "resource" became a condition of capitalist development so that "businesses no longer make products but now make memories" (Rifkin quoted in Stiegler 2013, 59).[8] The advertising-and-attention onslaught was noted in its initial flowering in the consumerist moment of the 1950s by Vance Packard (1959) who described the "grandeur" of the US as bound up in "the creation of needs and desires, the creation of disgust for all that is old and outmoded."[9]

This process reached yet another level of intensity in the moment at the beginning of the 1980s of the change from analogic to digital that allowed a kind of hyper-reproducibility and corresponded to the moment of the triumph of neoliberalism, with its attendant unfettered and largely unregulated global-ization of capital. Stiegler calls this epoch "hyperindustrialism" to signify that the new digital age is primarily neither a postmodern, information-economy, nor postindustrial age. The factory system, which in part defined modernity, has not been exceeded but rather intensified so that this continuation of the industrial age into the virtual world is driven by capital and involves the "industrialization of all things" where calculation reigns supreme. This "dom-ination of nature by the technical" (Stiegler 2013, 78), as Heidegger (1954) feared, has had disastrous consequences—for the planet and for first- and third-world working peoples, who are the detritus of this process—but has accelerated capital's profits to the point where US stockholders in the period *after* the 2008 crisis, have seen their dividends, when adjusted for currency fluctuations, increase 10 percent.[10]

Today culture has not only been absorbed into the economy of capitalism but plays a crucial part in capital's imperative to constantly expand. The har-nessing of psychic energies now takes its place in the virtual world alongside the exploitation of forms of physical energy (Stiegler 2008a, 194). The intensi-fication of this mental fracking, or "the assault on everyday life," began in the period of the Reagan and Thatcher counter-revolution in the 1980s with the rise of the personal computer and the dismantling of the systems of social pro-tection (Crary 2013, 70). The intensification was dictated not only by market imperatives but also ideologically by the need for modes of compensation as the income gap widened and it became apparent that neoliberalism's promise that a "rising tide lifts all boats" instead elevated only yachts on the crest of the waves while everyone else's waterlogged rafts and dinghies were engulfed in their wake.[11] It is precisely the neoliberal period and the birth of this new technology that has seen the rise of Serial TV in the early 1980s with *Hill Street Blues*.

The importance of tertiary retention in this account is that the vast accumulation of memories created outside ourselves pattern a conscious lifetime and where "images I see and the sounds I hear are less different from my neighbors, so my consciousness is less different" (Stiegler 2013, 19). Tertiary retentions may become the dominant mode of memory, so that as each of our relationships to these images and sounds increases and intensifies as the media industry increases its reach and grasp, our pasts become less and less different. "We love them [pop songs] in perhaps the same way as we have loved them already" is the way Stiegler characterizes the assembly line quality of this affection (55). The problem in this assault on memory or "aesthetic war" by the "societies of control" (Deleuze 1992) is that prior primary and secondary retentions based on group solidarity—what cultural studies called the raced, classed, gendered spectator—are being erased or downplayed by this "manufacture of the one as phantasm of the all" (Stiegler 2013, 21).

Of course the idea and desire of creating these memories is not new. It goes back to Saint Ignatius of Loyola's Jesuitical dictum: "Give me a boy until 7 and I'll have him for life."[12] What is new is the mass-market technology of ever increasing and refining this manufacturing of memory, from Disney's own application of Loyola's principle with its attempts to promote its brand over generations to Disney subsidiary Marvel's activation of its comics' imaginary by patterning comic book worlds that seem to be complete in themselves. In this vein, a *Le Monde* critique of *Avengers: Age of Ultron* (2015) showed how Marvel within the film had created its own left (the New Deal Captain America) and right (the Trump-like entrepreneur Tony Stark). The important point being not the creation of an actual left and right but that that political spectrum could exist and be subsumed by the Marvel world in an attempt to convince us that these tertiary memories are complete and sufficient unto themselves. Stiegler highlights the danger in a "lifetime value" where the individual "I" is subsumed under an attachment to a "we" fashioned "entirely by a line of products and services" (Stiegler 2013, 102).

Glee, for example, attempts to fold all our high school experiences, often very painful, into one high school experience where controversy is mentioned then quickly evaporated. One chorister, Sam Evans, exhibited a significant trait of being poor—a trait that disappears from the story line after his secret is revealed and he is then reabsorbed into the group, with the class condition not resolved but ignored. This industrialization of memory also calls for us to rethink one of the primary characteristics of Complex TV (Mittell 2015), self-referentiality. The hyper-referentiality of series like *Lost*, where ABC—in an attempt to clue viewers into the layers of complexity—reran episodes with popups that explained the multiple references to previous seasons, is itself part of a way of structuring memory that in its thickening is as much about "zapping consciousness" (Stiegler 2013) as it is about expanding our consciousness through complex gameplaying (Johnson 2006).

Time Is on My Side

Along with this simple exploitation goes a deeper alignment of consciousness that is specific to television: the mapping of the time of the life process to the media itself as more and more of our hours are taken up with being plugged in. The mobile phone and its apps have enlarged, rather than canceled, television's previous programming of the time of the American workforce in the Fordist-factory era "prime time" routine. This routinizing and chronologizing of leisure, rather than being limited as it was in the era of simply turning off the traditional television, has expanded as television adapts itself to the new destruction of leisure and makes itself available 24/7 to fill up the workers' last remaining moments while journeying from one job to another or exhaustedly falling asleep after two jobs and school in a frantic effort to outpace their own automatization.

Television is uniquely in the business of selling time, that is, networks sell advertising time to sponsors guaranteeing the delivery of a manufactured audience and the synchronization of consciousness. The product they sell is indeed the audience they produce (Wu 2016). This extended synchronization taking place across digital media as a whole is now affecting a change in time in an attempt to overlap the two concepts of time as envisioned by Henri Bergson (2001). That is, the media industries attempt to convert pure time or duration—actual time, which is also the time of reflection—into mathematical time divisible into units or intervals, a description of time previously seen as artificial.[13] Stiegler (2008a) uses this conception in his distinction between the behemoth of *télécritie*, the mediatic synchronization of time and subjectivity, and "the televisual," which contains the potential for restoring the more social elements of duration and reflection to the machinic domination of regulated time.

Capital of course has always attempted to control the rhythms of time and to submit them to the rigor of capitalist production, to "domesticate time" (Leroi-Gourhan 1945). To accomplish this goal capital has regulated basic processes such as transport, has adopted life to the rhythm of the assembly line, and has submitted "leisure" time to the rhythms of programmed film and pop songs and the more constant programming of radio and television. (As the pop song attains and affects all the ears, television "attains all the eyes" is the way Stiegler describes the process [2013, 53]). The result of this domestication is an entirely synchronized society and a "liquidation of the social" in this attempt to align duration with mathematical time and eliminate the time of reflection (Stiegler 2013, 118).

Thus, what Raymond Williams (1974) first termed the "flow" of television —claiming that it is this flow which must be studied not its individual moments—is in this sense an attempt to colonize time so that time under Stiegler's *télécritie*, the continual televisual flow, is the time of the market. Under hyperindustrialization, the time of consciousness becomes the 24/7 of the metamarkets, where the natural system of the seasons as well as the time of memory is submitted and synchronized to the global system of production of consumer goods and financial products (Stiegler 2013). Memories which have now become "temporal industrial objects" (52) are then part of this global network, themselves manufactured in a production system that, far from having overthrown the Hollywood dream factory of the golden age of the 1930s to the 1960s, has expanded it to all areas of cultural production.

Williams's "flow," which contemporary television critics claim has now been superseded since programming in the streaming era may now be determined by the individual viewer (Lotz 2014, 989), in fact has been reestablished in a more interior, subjective fashion. Television flow is now the addictive, relentlessly forward momentum of Serial TV while the series is being binged, which is followed by the imperative—highlighted by streaming algorithms that suggest like-minded series—to quickly begin again a new serial flow. Television flow now also integrates itself into internet and mobile activity at the time of watching. This activity either relates to the series and potentially—though not necessarily—enhances it or does not relate at all and distracts from it.

How does contemporary television seriality, a part of these media objects that are not only specific to but also determinant of time, extend this conception? The episodic series presented television by appointment for a specific duration. At the end of that duration the series world ended, most often to pick up the next week at a place where even the events of the previous week seemed obliterated. (The famous joke from *The Simpsons* [1989–] about this format is Mr. Burns every week not knowing the name of Homer Simpson, whom he likely had had a painful interaction with the week before.) In that sense series respected mathematical time and did not suggest themselves as pure time or duration. With the stress on continuity between episodes and an evolving "storyworld" (Mittell 2015), the serial series attempts to create a parallel world of real or pure time that itself synchronizes with the viewer's time. Older-style cliffhanger endings are utilized less in this model because they suggest the artificiality of quantified time. Thus, many of the episode conclusions on *The Walking Dead* (2010–) rather than suspense cliffhangers are instead announcements of character changes that seem to coincide more with actual personality changes in a real world that has now itself become corporate. The penultimate episode of season 5 ends with the series' nominal and very troubled hero, Rick, now the sheriff of a gated—meaning sheltered from the zombies—community, brought "to heel," in a mild reversal of Hilary Clinton's racist term, by Michonne, the black female warrior whose broad brimmed hat announces that there is a new sheriff (or project manager?) in town. [14]

The new mode of temporal consumption of serial series, binge watching, is an extension of the industrial era, but with a goal of completely seizing time. The series are designed to be consumed over a short period. They are usually ten to thirteen episodes of an hour or less in duration for a season, taking approximately that many hours to consume, and so the ideal time to "binge watch" is the weekend, with viewers often boasting that they "accomplished" watching the series' season in that time.[15] This is a dramatic further extension of mathematical time to where it breaks the boundary with pure time and dominates the life process. Binge watching is also an integral part of the digital world of "shopping, gaming, working, blogging, downloading or texting," and while one cannot be engaged in these activities in every moment, the new flexibility of television series means they are a part of a world in which there is never a moment when one cannot "shop, consume or exploit network resources," all part of this "non-time of 24/7" which results in the "annihilation of the singularity of the place and the event" (Crary 2013, 31).

The Price Is Right: Gaming Participation

Adorno made lack of participation a central principle in his chronology of the overall technical process of development of mass media when looking at that development in the 1940s in the US. He noted the degradation of the level of involvement in the movement from the telephone to the radio, with the earlier actively encouraging, in fact demanding, participation and the later producing more passive "audiences." Stiegler claims the onslaught of contemporary media goes farther in destroying or channeling desire so that instead of a driver of new expansive experiences this nonparticipatory, false desire becomes a "circuit of the given" as the feeling, sensitive, desiring body is "transformed into a consuming body" as part of a mass production of "the industrial ecology of the spirit" (Stiegler 2013, 35–36).

Desire itself in this market model is manufactured along the model of Hollywood genre production, with the spectator knowing exactly what rewards are promised with each genre, what specific chain of desires are activated (love in the rom-com, exhilaration in the action film) and the formula then guaranteeing a variation slight enough to seem novel but not significant enough to disturb the genre's underlying routinized promises. These now-dominant forms of grammatization, different from the earlier processes of writing,[16] are the result of tertiary retentions being confiscated by the "technologies of control" (Stiegler 2008a, 236). They lead to a "logics of dissociation" that do not bring people together but further entrench them in their own isolated hell (which is no longer, as with Sartre, other people but rather other people's devices) all the while destroying the "desire of the future" (28–32).

This lack of participation is also part—and perhaps a culmination of—a massive deskilling of society, which in the symbolic realm Stiegler (1998) calls the "proletarianization" of the consumer, a major characteristic of hyperindustrialism but also a somewhat false distinction, since the consumer is also still and always a worker. Capital has for a long time harbored the ambition of routinizing human productive knowledge and programming it into a machine, a trend since the beginning of industrialization. This general weakening of know-how has resulted in an age of precarity in employment and a gradual disintegrating of workers' communities at both the skilled and nonskilled levels. Stiegler claims that the accompanying "intensification of the flow of goods and people" has been complemented on the virtual level by an "intensification of the flow of symbols," which as a result of the market organization of this new never-ending flow that is constantly assaulting us results paradoxically in "a massive desymbolization" (Stiegler 2008a, 81), or as Fredric Jameson once put it at an earlier stage of this development, the inability to grasp one's place in these hyperaccelerated sign systems (1991).[17]

This pacification of workers, extended to their position as consumers, certainly also contains an element of compliance as, in the post–World War II era, US workers led the way for the rest of the world in defining a workforce "sleepwalking down the corridors of history" (Broe 2009). This workforce gave up claims to be able to define the nature of work in exchange for salary and other benefits in a Fordist-Keynesian compromise that produced the welfare state. With the rise of neoliberalism, beginning in the Reagan Years, there has been an acceleration first in prescribing the mechanics of performing tasks so they could be outsourced and then, with what Martin Ford (2015) terms "the rise of the robots," in transferring those tasks to machinic memory. This transfer has progressed to the point where a 2013 Oxford study predicted 47 percent of the jobs in the US could potentially be automated,[18] including, as Ford notes, massive coming automation not only in the service industry but also in many professional services, including the medical industry, legal industry, etc. (Amazon warehouses already function as centers of advanced robotics with human intervention only needed in some cases as quality control at the end point as an order is being shipped.)[19] The drive toward artificial intelligence, while suggesting a melding of human and machine as depicted in series such as *Altered Carbon* (2018–), is also in the logic of capital a frantic effort to move automation from unemploying workers in the service industry to also unemploying highly skilled workers such as surgeons.

Stiegler (2015) periodizes this process in the symbolic realm by linking it to moments of grammatization, with the industrial age proper being about deskilling in terms of *savoir-faire* (knowing how to make things); the analog era, with its use of recording to aid in the mass manipulation of leisure, as prompting the decline of *savoir-vivre* (knowing how to live); and finally the digital era as being the attempt by capital to eliminate *savoir-theorie* (or knowing how to know, to think, to conceptualize). Similarly, *Wired*'s Chris Anderson has claimed that the arrival of Big Data eliminates the need to theorize, substituting massive statistical facts for conjecture (Stiegler 2015). This general level of nonparticipation comes at a time when active participation is more than ever required to face the challenges of automation, of rapidly accelerating income inequality, and the degradation of the planet and global health.[20] Serial television does promote a kind of active participation and increased audience acuity in making sense of its complex stories. However, whether it is encouraging or disrupting levels of apathy is one of the crucial questions in evaluating the form.

Destruction of the Collective: The We as Disoriented "Us" and the I as "Your"

The result of this generalized deskilling and pseudoparticipation for Stiegler is the destruction of the "we" (*nous*), the collective that could challenge this system, and its transformation into a mediatized and impersonal "us" or "one" (*on*). This destruction is made possible because of the annihilation of the "I" (*je*) necessary to form this more collectivized identity. The condition is the result of a system that "destroys the attention it captures and engenders inattention" and "absolute distraction" (Stiegler 2013, 105). Under hyperindustrialism, this synchronizing of all consciences to the time of the media market "short circuits the process of transindividuation" (Stiegler 2008a, 157) or the coming to consciousness over time of a more genuine "I" that can then embrace a collective.[21] Stiegler's new "us," or the "I" transformed into a "your" (your beverage, your film, your TV series), is an ominous characterization of the media and contemporary television spectator as similar to the Borg, the Star Trek (*The Next*

Generation 1987–92) half-human, half-machine enclave hooked into a single "hive." The Borg motto "Resistance is futile" perhaps describes a society where corporate control has reached a level where individuals not only interiorize the culture of business but also where business now promotes, through devices like complex gameplaying and serial television, the production of the capacities it needs for the industrialization of everyday life (Stiegler 2013, 110).

Television has a particularly dominant place in this system with roughly 45 percent of babies now having televisions in their bedrooms and 90 percent of the population regularly watching some form of recorded device by age two (Stiegler 2008a, xv). Further along in the life cycle, students are now going to sleep at night later to stay on mobile devices, with a quarter of college students keeping the device on throughout the night, which can cause sleep deprivation.[22] Stiegler considers television a process rather than a device, one which for him is a kind of continuation and intensification of the cinema in the home, whereby the goal is the massification of publics in their formation as audiences or artificial crowds from which springs "processes of regressive individuation unknown previously" (217). Television itself then is for Stiegler, in a kind of Foucauldian reversal of accepted logic, not a device but a system whose purpose is the creation of "ephemeral crowds" constituted for the sole object of obtaining their attention, which is then monetized as ratings (and now as personalized data) to sell to advertisers (142). The device for binding and "channeling" the time of this collective disposable mind (and globally installing the "American way of life" and product-oriented lifestyle as Hollywood films accomplished starting in the 1920s and '30s)[23] is the television program either as a single entity or as a television flow experienced often as generalized zapping that "annihilates the self" (xvii). In the contemporary case Serial TV audiences, ephemerally associated with each new and highly tailored show, are then industrially organized "flash mobs."

This pursuit has been heightened in the era of mobile television and of the individualized and serialized television series. Here the idea of the niche audience with its attendant fans and system of fandom becomes the substitute for collectives organized around actual needs. This hypersegmentation and patterning of the "we" into delusional singularities based around ephemeral brands (Stiegler 2013, 107) (like the biker-wannabe audience that constitutes itself for *Sons of Anarchy* [2008–14]) is sold as a new freedom not only to watch shows developed "for you" and "your lifestyle" but also the "freedom" to watch at any time, to choose your own package of what were formerly cable channels; that is, to constitute "your own network." In Stiegler's framework, the more the audience is deluded into thinking they have control and "freedom," the more controlled they are.

Back to the (Frankfurt School) Future: "Training" Replaces "Entertainment" in Hyperindustrial Leisure

As opposed to Walter Benjamin's (2006) belief in the potential democratizing ability of mass media and equally opposed to Siegfried Kracauer's (1995) 1920s formulation in "The Little Shopgirls go to the Movies" that mass media provided a needed diversion for the pressured life of the worker, Adorno, with Max Horkheimer (1972) in "The Culture Industry: Enlightenment as Mass Deception," extended Marx's critique that capitalist industrial society not only produced goods but also reproduced the workers necessary to make these goods. Adorno argued that what was taking shape in front of him in the midpoint of the twentieth century was the rebuilding of the worker as a consumer and the refashioning of needs in a diversification and segmentation that would fit the market. This process, as Stiegler would later describe it, was nothing less than "the refunctioning of the aesthetic dimension of the individual according to the interests of industrial development so that he adopts the habits of consumption" (Stiegler 2013, 19).

Adorno's phrase about this encroachment of the factory process into consciousness was "the might of industrial society is lodged in men's minds" (Adorno and Horkheimer 1972, 127). Rather than being a release from the pressure of the working day and the monotonous grind of the factory, the products of the cultural industry bore the imprint of that process, carrying in their own repetition and formulas "the stamp of industrial production," in a way that "amusement under late capitalism is the promulgation of work" (137). There was now a seamless circle in which the factory system, originally the creation of human thought, is abstracted from that thought and then subsequently reproduces thought and desire itself not only at the factory but now in the leisure time that was supposed to be the time of reflection and separation from that process.

Adorno's formulation is today more apt than ever, and the process has in fact accelerated as Steven Johnson (2006) (partly unwittingly) attests in his description of the process of contemporary media and of television seriality in particular in *Everything Bad Is Good for You: How Today's Popular Culture is Actually Making Us Smarter*. Johnson's claim is that gaming and complex television alike are intellectually demanding exercises, freed of moral (meaning social or political) content, and are performing a benefit for society; they constitute a "cognitive workout" and instill in players and viewers a "set of cognitive tools" (300–302). Johnson's description of the process of playing and comprehending these forms, though, makes that process sound very much like work, the particular work that is necessary under hyperindustrialism where the factory and profit system have engulfed all areas of physical and cognitive being. His description is a cataloging of the particular type of work necessary in the symbolic economy, where linear coding has replaced reflection and conceptualizing.

"The dirty little secret of gaming," he tells us, "is how much time you spend not having fun" (Johnson 2006, 403–4), so that the process becomes the completion of a sequence of tasks "more like chores than entertainment, something you have to do, not something you want to do" (425). Johnson is then describing entertainment today not as continuation of the work process but *as* the work process, with gameplaying along with tracking complex and serial television being a kind of training for work in the hyperindustrial world. "You have to probe the game's logic to make sense of it . . . by trial and error . . . by following hunches" (595–96). The player then forms a hypothesis and "reprobes the world with that hypothesis in mind seeing what effect he or she gets" (619–23). Gaming then is digital coding made fun and it teaches or conveys a particular view of the world as symbolic cognitive entity, stripped of political and social values, whose primary purpose is to reduplicate the symbolic economy and to induce the participant in his or her supposed hours of leisure to learn and perhaps master the rules needed to survive and prosper in this economy.[24]

Thomas Elsaesser (2009), in discussing mind-game or puzzle films such as *Memento*, which require a degree of cognitive acumen similar to computer games and serial television, notes, following Johnson (2006), that this training amounts to American mass media "fulfilling their historic role in adapting the working population to the social technologies that promise their economic survival, maintain civic cohesion, and assure America's hegemonic position in the world." They accomplish this, in a hyperindustrial framework where "training and learning are now a lifelong obligation," by fashioning a "(post-bourgeois) self" that is "flexible, adaptive, interactive and above all . . . [knows the] 'rules of the game'" (Elsaesser 2009, 33–34).

Johnson equally proposes serial television, which he studies at its inception in the 1980s and 1990s, as being a part of the integration and immersion of the viewer in the codes and regulations of the symbolic economy. His claim is that serial television has equally become training for cognitive development through the "parsing of narrative threads" (Johnson 2006, 796–97) and the increasing demands put on the viewer to make sense of a continuing narrative. Thus *The Sopranos* connected multilayered plot lines that each built on events from previous episodes (850–53) while *The West Wing* (1999–2006) was filled with such opaque information that it altered the usual narrative framework from posing the question of what is going to happen to that of what is happening right now (921–23). Meanwhile, *ER* (1994–2009) immersed the viewers in so much medical information that the task became deciphering what was important to the narrative thread in cases where "you have to know what you're not supposed to know" (850–53). Again, viewed in this way, Serial or Complex TV is simply a direct extension of work in the hyperindustrial world. Far more sinister than Adorno's reflection of the work process that invades the worker's leisure time, Johnson's cognitive exercises amount to a training and inducement through leisure in the cognitive patterning necessary for work in the symbolic economy.

Media as Dominant Ideological State Apparatus: Althusser in the Age of Symbolic Reproduction

In this way media has become, to revive Louis Althusser's term, the dominant ideological state apparatus (ISA) acting in concert with—though at the moment also locked in mortal combat with—the educational apparatus, with both now utterly transcending the prior, and still circulating, modes of the family-church. (A friend from a traditional society with a very strong family structure within a dominant religious context watches her niece's fascination with my friend's iPhone and sees the child's constant desire to be experimenting with it as her primary form not only of play but also of education.) ⟶

Althusser concentrated on the school as the dominant form of a social indoctrinating apparatus, but Johnson explains how instead much of the education for the hyperindustrial economy is being conducted by the products of that economy; the complex modeling of gameplaying and tracking of narrative threads is education for participation in the symbolic economy of a kind that is "not happening in classrooms or museums; it's happening in living rooms and basements, on PCs and television screens" (Johnson 2006, 244–51). Stiegler, on the other hand, characterizes this onslaught where "brands invade the schools as privileged terrain of viral and tribal development" as a process that ultimately aims to "destroy all the forms of social attention" (Stiegler 2008a, 112) and replace it with an attentional process that is "hypersynchronized, regressive, instinctual and without conscience" (175).

There is a particular way in which Althusser's analysis of the school system in capitalist industrial society, as being developed not for universal education but for making sure that each reaches and does not exceed the level that is useful for industrial development, is relevant to today's media in which both school and media manufacture consciousness in a way that reaffirms an ever more unequal class system. Althusser points out that the division of learning into subjects is either " 'know-how' wrapped in the ruling ideology (the subjects of French, arithmetic, natural history, the sciences, literature) or simply the ruling ideology in its pure state (ethics, civic instruction, philosophy)." He then notes three class distinctions or levels at which the education apparatus deposits or dumps its charges: those who drop out of high school and are immediately "ejected 'into production'" (workers); those who endure, who finish high school, and today college, destined for the posts of "small and middle technicians and executives, white-collar workers and small business people" (middle class); and finally those who reach the education summit of PhD and several graduate degrees, destined if they are artists perhaps for semi-employment, but more likely fulfilling the role of "agents and managers of exploitation" or "professional ideologists" (upper-middle and upper class) (Althusser 1971, 155).

There is a sense in which there is an equal management for the hyperindustrial economy where media itself attempts to find, apportion, and manufacture its own creative and class levels. High school dropouts now injected into service-industry production (flipping burgers at McDonalds) are equipped with the most rudimentary media skills, and for them these advanced media function as a diversion, as something that presents itself as infinite variety as opposed to the monotony of their existence. These are simply the consumers of video games, mobile devices, and serial television for whom other forms of education barely exist. For the next level, the skills imparted by the media become part of the interaction at their job or the skills needed to make it in the cutthroat world of the small entrepreneur, and there is a level of enjoyment in those skills, but also a nonmastery of the apparatus, which seems foreign to them, as well as a succumbing to the addictive aspects of the devices.

The final level includes those who do the programming of the devices or, on the narrative level, the creation of the shows, as well as those who become managers or apologists for the hyperindustrial mode. At this level, the important distinction is that media is either thoroughly absorbed and mastered or it is integrated into former aspects of the educational apparatus and kept in perspective, that is, enjoyed but not addictively, which is part of the mastery. Thus Johnson's (2006) "technical training" accommodates itself to the hyperindustrial class system and becomes also a kind of sieve that, similar to and along with the educational system, not only trains but also makes the separations necessary for work in what is becoming an increasingly hardened class society with fewer and fewer making it to the third level or finding work there.

Lost, "The End": Seriality and the Desert of the Real

Thus far, we have painted a fairly bleak picture of the hyperindustrial economy of which serial television is an integral part. But, as with Derrida's concept of the pharmakon where the poison may also become the cure, so too the critique launched by aspects of media and of serial television may point to a way of both illuminating our present condition and of halting "the machine from producing the worst" (Stiegler 2008a, 220). We are now going to look in this last section at the way these teletechnologies may, through their critique of their own place in this media and its symbolic landscape, "invent new forms of social links" (35) while mapping the aftermath of a society in which the market has imposed its control and has attempted to replace all forms of social bonding.

This illumination is nowhere better in evidence than in a moment at the height of the serial form: the 2010 last episode of *Lost*, a series that through its serial complexity transformed the television landscape and forced every subsequent series to incorporate aspects of a continuing and more complex plotting. The finale focuses, through a technique of *flash-sideways* that had been deepened in the sixth and final season, on a contrast between two different and parallel worlds. The first is the world of the island—where the major action of the series had taken place—a deteriorating world of primitive emotions and catastrophe, which may be read as exhibiting the structure of feeling of life under the capitalist neoliberal order where civilization and the natural world are breaking down. This is a world, as Stiegler says, where the collapsing of social boundaries "replaces desire with instinct" (Stiegler 2008a, 84) and where the "loss of expertise and knowledge of the world" (the primitive state of the island) promotes "a kind of despair" over the prospects of the future (118).

The alternate world, constructed in the final season and brought to fruition in the show's finale, is a perfect world where the differences of the plane crash survivors are surmounted, where all wrongs are righted, and where the characters are restored to a pristine (and luxurious) state. This world in the show's purveyance is seen as a kind of "purgatory" before "crossing over" to an actual paradise, but it might equally be read as the world of abundance and plenty—the virtual world where capitalist contradictions and inequalities are resolved (or repressed). This is the world Johnson (2006, 522–23) describes as the world of the gamer, where "reward is everywhere. The universe is literally teeming with objects that deliver very clearly articulated rewards: more life, access to new levels, new equipment, new spells." The show, though, chooses to close on the image of lead-character Jack's solitary death on the island; a reminder that the contradictions cannot truly be effaced.

The series pilot, in 2004, opened in the chaotic aftermath of a plane crash, recalling the panic and pain of 9/11—the moment when the colonial and imperial history of the US "returns" in a devastating way—and was in its casting and its multiple protagonists at least an attempt to project a global consciousness onto the survivors of the island. This consciousness though is not that of the plenty that was promised by neoliberal globalization. Instead the constant dangers on the island and the contorted histories of its multiple protagonists define it not as tropical paradise but as an emotional landscape expressing the perils of life in a world where fellow-feeling is breaking down.

In the main character clash on the island, Jack Shephard, the rational surgeon and leader of the survivor flock, opposes John Locke, who argues for the instinctual as his namesake had argued for the primacy of sense perception (while also founding the economically liberal principle of the contract). That the two cannot reconcile on the island indicates the dilemma of contemporary capitalism, where its own hyperrationalism is also—in the way it subjects the world to the rigors and tempestuousness of the profit system—highly irrational. This system also constantly separates rational and irrational and dreads the consequences of a questioning of the aims of the system, which might result in the melding of head and heart. The series finale is centered around a fight to the death between the two, with Locke, now in a different guise as the Man in Black, boasting to the seer Desmond in regards to the two lovers Kate and Jack, "I'll kill them both right in front of you" and emphasizing as he draws his machete, "I'll make it hurt." Jack responds with an equally brutal, "I'll kill you." Ultimately Kate shoots Locke, and Jack throws his body over a cliff, after Locke had boasted that all Jack's efforts were in vain, that "You died for nothing." Rather than the triumph of good over evil, the battle seems to resolve in a kind of nihilism, the rational order wins but irrationally, through violence, and separates itself from feeling.

On the island, Jack and Kate's love is impossible, disrupted through the competitive triangle that also includes the Southern bad boy Sawyer or simply because there is no time, since both are dealing with the contingencies and emergencies of the island as one (capitalist) disaster after another threatens their existence. Finally, just prior to Jack's death on the island, Kate kisses him

Lovers united and reunited in the digital paradise in the finale of *Lost*.

and both say "I love you," but these are their parting words and the first time they have expressed the sentiment. The series is also filled with a dawning consciousness of the looming ecological disaster of which we are now fully aware. In the final episode, Jack descends into a hole at the center of the island and saves the entire ecosystem by plugging the hole and thus restoring life to the island. The precarious nature of the "plug," which is only after all a finger in the dike, more than hints at the ecological disaster that is now our world and that can no longer be halted by stop-gap measures.

Jack is the nominal (white, Wasp) hero of the series,[25] and though his heroism is constantly called into question in a way that will be further elaborated in the even more problematic "hero," the sheriff Rick in the next apocalyptic serial series, *The Walking Dead*, it is still his death, alone on the island, that ends the series, as his eye closing recalls the series beginning shot of his eye opening.[26] The loneliness of his death, in the "desert of the real" (Žižek 2002), contrasts strongly to the reunion in the other perfect world that takes place just before this shot. This nothingness and isolation is also social, as Jack's utility to the project of saving the survivors of the island—he watches the plane carrying Kate and Sawyer depart—is exhausted. Jonathan Crary might almost be evoking this moment when in *24/7* he claims that, "Death in many guises, is one of the by-products of neoliberalism: when people have nothing further that can be taken from them, whether resources or labor power, they are quite simply disposable" (Crary 2013, 44).

The alternate world, a world of plenty where in the end all the lead characters are in evening dress and suits ostensibly attending a funeral, series showrunners Damon Lindelhof and Carlton Cuse were at pains to defend as equally real. They differentiated the ending of *Lost* from its serial forebears and from other famous endings, citing respectively the finales of *St. Elsewhere, Newhart* (1982–90), and *The Sopranos*. In *Lost*, they claimed, there was a definite ending in an existing world rather than "a snow globe, waking up in bed, it's all been a dream, cut to black kinds of endings."[27]

In this perfect world, one of (capitalist) bounty and plenty, Sayid, the Iraqi Red Guard, is reunited with Shannon, the blonde Southern California–type beauty queen; Charlie, the heavy-metal-band bass player recovers from a drinking- and drug-induced fit to assist Claire at the delivering of her baby; and Jin, the South Korean mob bagman, not only becomes a loving husband to his wife, Sun, who has also just delivered a baby described as "perfect in every way," but also speaks English, the language of the digital and idyllic virtual world. Kate and Jack reunite in the church; Jack, the surgeon, operates on and saves Locke's legs; and Locke forgives the evil Ben who had killed him on the island. It must be said this is not just a world where relationships are restored to perfection. It is also visually not—say for example—a Boschian purgatory with distorted figures in sadistic poses but rather the predestined world of Southern California, of Hollywood glitz and glamor. Desmond and Kate show up for the funeral in tuxedo and black evening dress, more arriving on the red carpet for the Oscars than readying themselves for the afterlife, reminding us of the role of the film and television industry in the creation of this perfect virtual world. The afterlife here is not a beyond but the parallel life of digital plenty, which, as the showrunners claim, in the digital age has the weight of the actual world.

The contrast between the two worlds, of capitalist destruction and capitalist abundance, is stressed in the episode through a very striking series of cuts from one world to the next. There is Kate in the luxury vehicle with Desmond who is taking her to the church contrasted in the next shot with a beat-up Kate on the island with her face muddied and her hair messed; there is the

Jack's lonely death in the desert of the real.

frightened Hector on the island who says about the confrontation between Jack and Locke, "I got a bad feeling about this" versus the confident Hector as spiritual guide in the other (virtual) world who says to Sayid, "Stick with me, you'll be happy you did"; and finally there is the couples reunion in the church with Jin and Sun, Charlie and Claire, and the ultimate couple, Jack and Kate. The beauty of the light in the church conceals and covers Jack's death alone on the island in the darkened hues of that desolate moment.

These flash-sideways emphasize that the two worlds exist next to each other and are distinguished from other forms of narrating time in the series, which included the more traditional flashbacks in the first two seasons; the flash-forwards at the end of the third and following in the fourth season; and time travel in the fifth season. The flash-sideways are in many ways the most sophisticated of the series' inventions for dealing with time (and extending the series' location off of the island) and the one that points to the contrast between the perfect virtual world and the disruptive, collapsing physical world.

Finally, the series also tentatively proposes at its conclusion a reconciliation between the two worlds, as Stiegler maintains that the only way beyond the delusion of the promise of plenty in the capitalist virtual world is through that world itself. In the perfect world Jack asks his father, Christian Shephard, whose name is heavily religiously coded, where they are. Christian replies that they are in "a place you all made together so you could find each other. The most important part of your life was the time you spent with these people; you needed all of them and they needed all of you, to remember and to let go."[28] It is possible, as Stiegler says, that in the midst of the betrayed promise of fulfillment is the hint of the actual promise. The passing over at the end of the series is that hint, the suggestion of a new industrial model, of a "political economy of associated milieus developing . . . in dynamic exchanges produced by and in these associated milieus" (Stiegler 2008a, 180). In this way the crossing over of the characters, which Jack's father describes as their next step, is the hint at the potential of fulfilling the promise of the digital world not by separating it from the actual world of torment and misery but by fusing the two in a way that will, in Stiegler's term, "reenchant" both worlds.

THE MOBILE SERIAL TV VIEWER

Prime Time Begets Flex Time Begets No Time

Each time that I have gone out, I have walked the great suburbs
of Paris and I have seen the roads covered with beat up cars,
little motorcycles or two-seat bicycles, with worker couples clad
in assorted sweaters who demonstrate that the idea of leisure
gives in them rise to a naturally playful behavior . . . one has
created within them some hope.

> Leon Blum on the effects of the Popular Front law
> decreeing paid holidays

INSTEAD OF BEGINNING WITH the industry concept of the audience, produced and manufactured for the purpose of ratings and data mining, we will begin this sociology of the television viewer by seeing him or her first as a worker and secondly as consumer. We will trace the position of workers in the US (and advanced capitalist societies) initially during the episodic period of television, roughly coinciding with what in France is called the Trente Glorieuse, the Thirty Glorious Years, and in the US the Great Prosperity of 1945 to 1975 (Reich 2010), which in television conformed to the dominance of the network era from 1950 to 1980. This is the period of the establishment of a predictable normality in viewing that centered around the prime time appointment from 8 to 11 p.m. in the family living room in an episodic television format whose outstanding feature was its stability from week to week.

What follows as television seriality is being developed is a period of rapid change as wages stagnate for approximately 30 years and the middle-class family, which Robert Reich (2010, 404–5) defines as the middle 80 percent and which also accounts for the vast television audience, attempts to cope in various ways (more hours worked, more members working, more debt) with the ending of the Fordist-Keynesian (industry and government) pact that had promoted and secured the gains of the welfare state. With wages stagnating there were less means to pursue the demanding lifestyle of the consumerist economy. Also, the pressure brought on partly by the ever more conspicuous consumption of the rich now enjoying an ever-expanding part of both wages and wealth accelerated anxiety and depression. This pressure was increased by the fact that it was never a subject of conversation in a newly consolidating corporate conglomerate media that was more than ever saturated with and desperate for products to validate this ever-shrinking lifestyle. Not much of this erosion ever became the subject of network television, and we will look particularly at the way one of the most popular and prized shows at the end of this transition period, *Modern Family* (2009–), is not so modern after all and relies on nostalgia for the bygone era of the Fordist stable family and home for its popularity in a quasi-retreat from the serial format.

We will then look specifically at the neoliberal era of the 1990s to mid-2000s, where the concept of leisure, divorced from work, begins to erode and where work becomes the permanent condition that not only dictates time but also infiltrates personal relationships. Industry and postmodern theory terms this new freedom "flex time," but that term takes on a kind of cruel aspect when tied to the fact that, though hours may be less circumscribed, more workers are working more hours to compensate for stagnant or lower wages, and it perhaps better goes under the term "precarious labor." Television distribution begins to accommodate to this "flex time" by less centralized modes of delivery. In this era—which boasts a vast expansion of seriality—the advanced rhythm, rupture, and flow on display in the form of the serial series is akin to the structure of feeling of a middle class under enormous pressure. Serial TV in this sense is a narrational mode that allows this class to cope with the continual changes of flex time or precarity. The form itself expresses some of the grace under pressure the audience exhibits. Here we will look at *The Big Bang Theory* as representing a new kind of permanent labor where the apartment, formerly a domestic space in the situation comedy, is now equally a site of work.

Finally, we will look at the Great Recession of 2008 and the resulting collapse of the American dream as seriality accelerates and now becomes a dominant mode of series creation. The result of the crashing of this phase of the neoliberal era is that by 2015 more than half of all American workers were approaching or below the poverty line. The majority of those workers made less than $30,000 per year, while almost 40 percent of them made below $20,000 in a country where the poverty level for a family of five is $28,410.[1] And yet, in the corporate media this is seldom acknowledged, and so there has been—in a way that has been highly validated in the serial television sphere—a frantic acceleration of the neoliberal praxis of every person for themselves and all against all in a world where power reigns supreme (*House of Cards* [2013–], *Game of Thrones* (2011–), *Wolf Hall* (2015), *Billions* [2016–]).

With Western capitalist audiences now forced to work, or think about work and survival, in every moment of their existence, the concept of leisure has disappeared to be replaced by the hyperindustrial condition of "leisurality," a frame of mind that replaces the former "slacker" mentality where it was possible to hide in the nooks and crannies of capitalism. Here capitalism plasters and fills the nooks and crannies of everyday life. Leisurality amounts to enjoying whatever free moments exist, usually very late at night. In this new regime, 11 p.m. to 2 a.m. replaces the former family leisure period of 8 p.m. to 11 p.m. "Free time" exists in moments of travel between jobs or between jobs and school in the era of not just reduced but obliterated expectations that has brought us the "staycation," a leisurality moment that makes a virtue and fetish of no longer having the time or money to travel. Conversely, when they do travel, workers remain online so that a vacation is now increasingly coming to mean putting "our bodies somewhere beautiful while we work" (Turkle 2012, 165). Television delivery methods have accommodated to this condition as have narrational patterns, and we will look at *Silicon Valley* as demonstrative of this new period where leisure and interpersonal relationships are utterly subsumed under labor.

Stagnation and the *Modern Family*

The two most salient economic facts of the Trente Glorieuse, or the Great Prosperity of 1945 to 1975, were persistently rising wages and a narrowing of the income gap so that more income went to the middle 80 percent and less to the top 10 percent (with the poorest 10 percent, highly disproportionately blacks and other minorities, hardly progressing at all and mostly "invisible" [Reich 2010, 710–12]). From 1947 to 1972 hourly wages rose 75 percent while weekly wages rose 61 percent (Wolff 2012, 1876–79), promoting a general feeling that life in the US and in the Western economies as a whole was steadily improving. Conversely, national income for the 1 percent steadily declined, falling each decade after the high of 23 percent in the pre-Depression year of 1928 all the way down to 8 to 9 percent in the 1970s (Reich 2010, 297–99). This was an era of increased production and consumption, and one of the markers of that abundance was the move from the television set being first a communally watched device—with neighbors gathered at the home of the first family on the block to have one at the beginning of the 1950s—to being owned individually by most families by the end of the decade (Reich 2010). Broadcasts were initially in black and white and then color by the mid-1960s, beaming the affordable products of the consumer society into the American home.

This era boasted an employer-employee pact, initially instituted in the Henry Ford factories and often referred to as Fordism, whereby workers, now more strongly represented by unions (over one-third of all workers by the mid-1950s [Reich 2010, 667–72]), were both less likely to disrupt production with costly strikes and themselves the main consumers of the goods they were producing, so that the increased wages were for the most part reinvested in purchasing the goods promoted as the miracle of the society of consumption. In return they received such benefits as time and a half for over forty hours of work, a minimum wage that improved workers' pay at the bottom, a pension system that guaranteed their retirement, and unemployment benefits to tide them over if the economy slowed (638–42). "Business is coming more and more to assume the shape of the government civil service," noted a textbook written at the time titled *The American Class Structure* (667–72).

The (US) government played an active role in promoting the pact, following the dictates of economist John Maynard Keynes, who had suggested the state be an enabler of prosperity and an income leveler. It did this by issuing unemployment benefits, disability insurance, and Social Security to complement retirement packages and in 1965 instituting, through Medicare and Medicaid, health insurance for the elderly and poor, which consequently dropped the poverty rate among the elderly by half. Besides instituting a welfare state, the government's role was also to bolster the security of the pact, which it did by encouraging home ownership by offering low-cost mortgages and decreased interest on mortgage payments (Reich 2010, 667–72). The government also acted to ensure future security by widening access to higher education through the GI Bill, which paid college costs, and by expanding public universities so that by 1970, near the close of the era, 70 percent of four-year students were in public universities and colleges, which averaged an affordable 4 percent of a median family income (687).

This security and stability was also in part paid for by taxing the rich so that even under the conservative and procorporate administration of Dwight Eisenhower in the 1950s, the top tax rate increased from 79 percent during World War II to 91 percent (Reich 2010, 710–12). The close of this era of expanding middle-class prosperity was presided over by another procorporate president, Richard Nixon, who nevertheless purportedly declared, "We're all Keynesians now" (634–35).

In this era the television set was the fulcrum and beacon of stability in the American living room, where it was most frequently watched during the leisure hours of 8 to 11 p.m., in some sense not only participating in but also dictating the form and mode that leisure would take. The dominant genre which the television set broadcast was the weekly episodic series—likewise a beacon of stability, where the same actors appeared each week from series opening to closing in narratives with prescribed beginnings and endings that presented hermetically sealed worlds that seldom referred directly not only to the world outside the show but also to other series on television. The stability of the Fordist-Keynesian pact was ratified and reinforced in the viewing and structure of the episodic series.[2]

THE BREAKING OF THE PACT AND BEGINNING OF THE DISRUPTION OF TELEVISION FLOW

The next thirty-plus years, from 1975 to 2008—let's call this period the Great Stagnation—saw the gradual dismantling of the pact and a switch from stability to disruption as wages stagnated, well-paying jobs diminished (and lower-paying jobs increased), and workers made frantic but losing efforts to compensate for the decrease in wages and the dismantling of industry and government benefits that went by the name of neoliberalism. This era of disruption and spontaneous coping methods gave rise to new television viewing patterns and to the beginning of the serial series, a less stable narrative form, which by the end of the era was itself reflective, with its sudden deaths of lead characters and its more strident references to the turbulent world outside of television, of the interrupted flow and rupture of middle-class life.

The major change in this period was the decline in workers' wages resulting from several factors that included an attack on unions (declining from 24 percent of contracts in 1973 to 12.5 percent in 2005), industries moving abroad, and a transformation from heavy manufacturing to lower-paid jobs in the new service economy. From 1973 to 2005 hourly wages for the 80 percent of workers in nonmanagement jobs increased for the entire thirty-two year period by only thirty-four cents an hour (from $15.76 to $16.11) and, because work hours declined, weekly wages fell 6.5 percent (from $581.67 to $543.65) (Wolff 2012, 1843–47). At the same time other costs rose, particularly for health care and education, the costs of which went from an average of $2,340 per year in 1978–79 to $16,584 by 2009, increasing three times faster than the average consumer item and necessitating student debt of between $15,000 and $20,000 by 2005 (471–73).

Accompanying and supporting this decrease was the changeover for the rich from a predominantly manufacturing economy to a much more prominent financial industry consisting of banks, Wall Street, and other areas of speculation as well as the burgeoning virtual and communication industries. With government deregulation of banks, which facilitated the rise of more highly speculative trading instruments, finance became the fastest growing sector of the US economy, accounting for more than 40 percent of corporate profits by 2007. Even the Ford Motor Company, the pillar of the former pact, accounted for over one-third of its profits in the same year by earnings in its financial division (Reich 2010, 808–9). Meanwhile the majority of jobs migrated from factories to the lower-paying areas of health care, restaurants, school systems, and what was left of increasingly hollowed-out government agencies.

Neoliberal administrations, beginning with Reagan's 1981 attack on the air traffic controllers, promoted this antiworker shift by allowing companies to bust unions, deregulating and privatizing industry, increasing the cost of public higher education, and cutting the safety net so that by 2007, for example, only 40 percent of those without work were eligible to collect unemployment insurance. Government also cut tax rates, claiming to aid the middle class but predominantly returning ever more money to the wealthy so that the top income tax rate fell from its low end of 70 percent during the Trente Glorieuse to 25 percent. Government also allowed income to be treated as capital gains and thus be written off, and it shrank the inheritance tax to allow wealth to be more easily perpetuated (Reich 2010, 808–9).

The net effect of this neoliberal economy was a transfer of wealth from the lower and middle 60 percent to the richest 10 percent, with the middle 30 percent attempting to cope with stagnation in various ways. From 1967 to 2001 income for the bottom 60 percent fell from 32 to 27 percent of national income while income flowing to the top 5 percent increased from 18 to 22 percent (Wolff 2012, 287–92). Many members of the former "aristocracy of labor" were now forced to work for wages of $10 an hour, a way of disciplining a proud labor force. The share of national income for the top 1 percent rose from its low range of 8 to 9 percent in the Great Prosperity to 23 percent by 2007 (Reich 2010, 297–99). CEO salaries rose to three hundred times that of the typical worker's as opposed to (only?) thirty times greater in the previous period, with the salaries of financial executives and traders following suit (808–9). The other measure of disparity besides income, ownership of wealth, also worsened for the majority. By 2005, the top 5 percent owned almost 60 percent of total wealth in the country, with the bottom 50 percent owning only 2.8 percent (Wolff 2012, 287–92).

LIFESTYLES OF THE STRESSED AND PRESSURED
During this roughly thirty-year period resulting in a revising of the Great Prosperity downward to make it a Great Prosperity for the few, production increased, flooding society with consumer goods that, because of the lower wages, were now less affordable. At the same time, corporate media ignored the condition of the average consumer who was now less able to buy, blacked out discussion about this dramatic changeover, and instead trumpeted the conspicuous consumption of those benefiting from the shift in income and wealth as beacons for the rest of the society to follow (*Lifestyles of the Rich and*

Famous [1984–95]). And follow it did as consumption increased to 70 percent of GDP as wages fell (Wolff 2012, 548–51). The end result was workers who frantically felt pressure to maintain what was now the façade of prosperity by continuing to acquire the goods that constituted the American dream without having the means to pay for them. Several coping mechanisms were employed by this new "modern family."

The first was working more hours. The forty-hour work week by the mid-2000s was more likely to be a fifty-hour week for men and more than forty hours for women. It was also not unusual for workers to work two or three jobs each of twenty hours a week. By the end of this period the American family put in five hundred additional hours of paid work (not counting unpaid household labor), or twelve full weeks more, than in 1979 (Reich 2010, 881–82). As wages continued to stagnate and prices climbed, workers sometimes found there was just not enough time to work to make up the difference. These changes were taking place globally as well. "Burn out," with 3.2 million employees "in a situation of work that is excessive and compulsive," was identified as a major problem in France in a discussion before the National Assembly.[3] In Japan two major contemporary problems are "death by overwork," known as *karoshi*, as eighty-hour-work weeks have become more common,[4] and persistent loss of sleep because of fear of the economic situation.[5]

The second coping (or survival) mechanism was to send more family members out to work, which most prominently included a mass entry of women into the paid labor force as part- or full-time workers, the vast majority of whom began their sojourn into the workforce in low-paying entry-level positions that put much more pressure on child rearing. In 1966 just 20 percent of mothers with young children worked outside the home, but by the late 1990s, a majority of those women, 60 percent, were working (Reich 2010, 873–74).

When both of these mechanisms failed to halt the downward trend, the final gambit was to borrow. Workers began to accumulate massive personal debt, including borrowing on their homes and cars and using multiple credit cards. Savings decreased and debt increased beginning dramatically with the "Reagan Revolution." During the Great Prosperity working families saved approximately 9 percent of their average net income, but by 2006 that figure in real terms lowered to −1.5 percent (Wolff 2012, 1762–65). Conversely, debt during the earlier period had averaged a little over half of family income, but by 2007 this had almost tripled, and family debt reached 138 percent of income (Reich 2010, 906–7). That much accumulated debt, where families owed more than they made or could pay back, took its toll in the pursuit of other ways of coping by the middle class, such as drugs, alcohol, and shopping in the megamalls that dominated suburban landscapes, so that consuming, one of the factors driving the debt, became one of the ways of avoiding thinking about it. Another way of coping was television, as the era of seriality—a far more involving form of television billing itself as more than simply *divertissement*, or diversion, which began with *Hill Street Blues* at the beginning of this onslaught in the Reagan era, continued apace with ever more compulsive ways to lure audiences into tranquil oblivion.

A particularly insidious form of debt that became prominent by the end of the thirty-plus years of decline following the thirty years of prosperity was the reverse mortgage. Here, often to compensate for a lack of retirement benefits as pension funds were defunded and IRAs and other government-savings plans became sites of speculation, homeowners, instead of paying off mortgages and eventually owning their homes, mortgaged their futures to borrow on homes in which the banks then owned increasing equity to the point where they would—if not in this generation, in the next—own the home. Homes then, under these reverse mortgages, "doubled as ATMs" (Reich 2010, 906–7). In 1990 only 150 reverse-mortgage loans were engineered, but by the end of this massive period of speculation in 2007, 120,000 such loans had been signed (Wolff 2012, 527–28). This mortgaging of the future, and the anxiety it would bring for homeowners who had now borrowed on the last object of value they possessed and would eventually lose that object, was the exact opposite of the happy ending of the American dream that had marked the Great Prosperity's march to home ownership.

The result was that the television audience of American workers became the people in the (Western) world with "the least number of days of vacation," "least number of sleeping hours," and the largest numbers of jobs and side businesses to try to eke out compensation from an economy that was now organized against their succeeding.[6] The typical American worked 2,200 hours a year, 350 hours more than workers in Europe, and more hours even than those pillars of industrious labor, the Japanese (Reich 2010, 881–82).

Not so *Modern Family*

The sitcom *Modern Family* won five Emmy Awards for best comedy from the 2009–10 to the 2013–14 seasons, as, after the 2008 recession, the middle-class family floundered in debt and anxiety (to use the synecdoche). The series was justly valued for its new social and sexual wrinkles on the traditional American and sitcom family, with nuclear, step, and same-sex branches of a more multicultural clan that included a Colombian second wife and a Vietnamese daughter. However, given the way that most middle-class families lived in the worsening conditions of the postrecession period, the show evoked not a modern but a nostalgic sense of family that was part of a television myth. The show's popularity (it finished many weeks as the top scripted series in the 18–49 age group) perhaps resided in its idyllic evocation of a family life that was now defunct. The extended grouping in this family had three male breadwinners who earned enough to support each family unit. Their income guaranteed regular leisure hours and vacations, allowed them not to go into debt, and permitted them to own secure affluent homes in suburban LA whose ostentation defined their (upper-middle-class) lifestyle. The trio of families were unhindered by and protected from economic crisis, seemingly unaffected by the stagnation of wages and the attendant anxiety that had provoked major work and lifestyle changes in the previous thirty-five years. The show is sometimes compared to *The Cosby Show* (1984–92), another kind of idyllic family representation, which was as far from the experience of the majority of black households under siege by Reagan's slashing of social programs as the Pritchetts and Dunphys are from the equally under-siege middle and working classes in the era of the 1 percent.

Jay, the *Modern Family* clan patriarch with a second family, has no money worries because of his business manufacturing designer closets; Phil, the nuclear or traditional sitcom-family head, is a successful real estate agent; and Mitchell is a corporate lawyer. Each support their immediate family in a job that seems to require no extra hours (though there is an episode in which Mitchell refuses a job at a more pressured and time-consuming law firm).

Their mates do not need to work, though this raises some anxiety, particularly in Phil's wife Claire, not because the family needs the money but out of guilt—perhaps that everyone else in the society is working. A comedy writer in a tweet asked, "If *Modern Family* is so 'modern' then why don't any of the women have jobs?"[7] In a fourth-season episode, "Flip Flop," at the conclusion of a multi-episode arc, Claire—who in the first four seasons also ran for public office and in season 5 did get a job (albeit working in her father's company)—says that she bought and fixed up a house to "flip" it (to immediately put it back on the market) because she wanted to contribute something to the family, but there is no pressure for her to do so. Her flipping of a house also marks her as flippantly benefiting from those who have lost the kind of home Claire appropriated.

Jay's wife Gloria is not employed. Mitchell's partner, Cameron, positioned on the show somewhat as a more traditional "wife"—at least economically—is multitalented and does stints at the high school as a choral and football coach, but for much of the show's tenure these were more whims than steady and necessary gigs and were treated as such. *Modern Family* is cunningly aware of the pressure on the American home and sublimates that pressure in its humor. As they are trying to sell the house, Luke, the Dunphy boy—in this episode a budding capitalist—asks, if he finds a buyer for the house, "What would that be?" "Adorable," Claire replies, ignoring that Luke is seeking his own commission on the house in a way that flirts with the idea that children in actual modern families are often compelled to work. Tensions between the "80 percent" and the lower-10 percent are also evoked when Cameron in solemn appreciation thanks Paco, the house renovator, for his work in a way that makes Luke ask if he is dead. "No," Cameron replies, "he's on the roof fixing it"—an answer that both acknowledges and deflects the class tensions that enable the middle class ensconced in the living room below with champagne to benefit from the work of a rapidly increasing itinerant underclass.[8]

For each of the show's families, the home—far from "doubling as an ATM," in an era when many families after gambling on their homes through reverse mortgages were forced to part with them—is the stable landmark of family life. The living room is the central location of each family, and each of these rooms is elaborately furnished—seemingly without the family acquiring credit card

The Dunphys flipping houses while others lost theirs in *Modern Family*.

debt and certainly without them working extra hours because salaries are stagnating or declining. The housing crisis that resulted from the 2008 recession is acknowledged in that in "Flip Flop" there are no buyers for the house they are attempting to flip, but this modern family rather than experiencing the anxiety of having a home in jeopardy is on the winning end of putting one up for sale.

Here family life within the home is also stable, and dysfunction, including what might be labeled emotional incest, is glanced over so that in the same episode, when Gloria feels she is losing the affection of her son, Manny, to her ex-husband's new girlfriend, Jay tells her she has nothing to worry about: "He may never form a healthy attachment with another woman after you." To which she replies, proudly, "Aw, you're just saying that."

Though called a modern family, implying this might be a median middle-class family, this is a family with every confidence in the American dream, which formerly was sometimes defined as owning a house and two cars. The parents on the show are homeowners who believe life will be better for their children, though—after forty-plus years of declining lifestyles, paychecks, and employment opportunities—this is not the case for most American families, for whom "the new American dream is to have a job."[9] The *Modern Family* lifestyle, while touted as average, is really much closer to that found inside a gated community in California, not exactly that of the 1 percent but more like the "think they haves" (Wolff 2012), those higher than the bottom 75 percent, who saw those below them floundering while the superrich above them engaged in "consumption orgies." This group "borrowed their way up to taste the lifestyles of the top 1 percent, pressed their children to aspire to a good hedge fund job, and comforted one another with assurances that rising incomes and home prices would assuredly keep them solvent despite mounting debts" (672–77). Minus the anxiety and the borrowing, this description accurately depicts the lifestyle of the Pritchetts and Dunphys, who are posing as an average family.

These are families with plenty of time for each other—the ethical distinguishing mark in the series—as part of a generalized pattern of leisure which harkens back to that of the years of the Great Prosperity. They have the time not merely, as the series constantly reaffirms, because they care about each other but also because family members are not compelled to work or, if they do, to work overtime. Phil's main goal as a father is not to provide, which is a given, but to be loved by his family as a "cool dad." A season-1 episode titled "Coal Digger" features the other two families coming to Jay's house to watch football in his den, a very typical leisure activity. However, that typical outing for the actual modern family is upset particularly in its most traditional instantiation, at Thanksgiving, when more and more families interrupt both football and their meal to either participate in person or online in store bargains for the upcoming Christmas season in a compelled consumerism where the two holidays collide to impinge upon and attack a formerly sacred family gathering. In "Flip Flop," Trish, Gloria's ex-husband's fiancée, reveals herself to be jealous of Gloria's physique. "That body, how many times a week do you go to the gym?" she asks. "Who has time to go to the gym?" Gloria replies, in a way that cleverly plays off of the actual middle-class pressure of women who are both homemakers and breadwinners, though she, who really does live a life of leisure, is only the former.[10]

The drive and pressure toward ever-accelerating levels of consumption as a badge of honor distinguishing the middle-class family is also playfully hinted at (or sublimated?) in the show. In "Flip Flop," when Phil's son Luke may have found a prospective young buyer for the house, he describes him to his dad as "an adult with money" but one who "drives a nicer car than you," hinting at the pressure these families feel to keep up.[11] Since Luke's "friend" is in his twenties, this is also in disguised form discussing the particular structure of Hollywood, where young executives and creatives are constantly threatening more established members of the industry. Meanwhile, in reality, in order to respond to the pressure to maintain the façade of an ever more abundant lifestyle, it was becoming much more common and acceptable post-2008 for actual modern families to shop at Walmart or other low-end temples and bargain basements of consumption (Wolff 2012, 668–70).

The form of this series, which has been credited with restoring life to the traditional family sitcom, is, like its content, a patina of "modern" seriality concealing a more traditional episodic series. In a break with the classical sitcom, the show is shot single camera without a laugh track; is framed as a "mockumentary" about the family's lives, with them talking straight to the camera; and follows multiple lead characters, twelve in all, and several recurring characters as well. However, the series is largely framed episode to episode, has the required numbers of JPM (jokes per minute), features only slight character development outside of the traditional mode of children aging and adding characters through births, and has moral or ethical lessons—post-*Seinfeld*, less heavy-handed, lessons, but lessons no less—that involve family loyalty. In "Flip Flop," while the families' efforts to control the sale of the house fail, their togetherness eventually helps them weather the economic storm, and Phil, the "cool dad"—where cool really just means caring—triumphs over the ferociously greedy broker who is forced to capitulate because his client wants the house.

In its nostalgic evocation of the American and sitcom family grounded in the economic reality of the Great Prosperity of the 1950s to the 1980s, *Modern Family*, which claims to represent the new American reality (of multiculti and same-sex families) is in another sense concealing and sublimating actual middle-class anxiety in its refusal to directly acknowledge that anxiety and its lived consequences. In that way the show is following, aiding, and abetting the trajectory of corporate media as a whole, which for the most part refused to discuss the "social problem of a society suddenly ending a century of rising real wages" (Wolff 2012, 131–42) and facing increased pressure to pretend that change was not occurring.

Precarity and *The Big Bang Theory*:
Work Hard *while* You Play Hard

If *Modern Family* essentially dissolved middle-class contradictions in a nostalgic haze, *The Big Bang Theory* did reflect a more modern approach to the new, postrecession condition of endless work and leisurality, that is, leisure being filtered through and fitted to work. This change was concomitant with an increased level of seriality in general, which began to function as a middle-class way of maintaining composure and grace under stress.

With the generalized debt crisis of 2008 the Great Stagnation turned into the Great Recession, and not stability but precarity became the order of the day. The result of the layoffs that followed the housing and lending crisis in the US and the government-debt crisis in Europe was that, in the US particularly, those threatened with being laid off from their jobs "accepted lower pay and benefits as a condition for keeping them" (Reich 2010, 944–45). New jobs created between 2008 and 2013 paid less than those lost in the recession, with predictors for the following decade claiming seven of ten growth occupations would be "low wage."[12] This "growth" was taking place mainly in service-industry jobs, which replaced manufacturing jobs after companies moved overseas in the globalization of the 1980s and 1990s. Workers in these jobs today are particularly vulnerable to automation, which is reducing even factory work. Reich, for example, reported christening a factory during the Clinton presidency, whose construction was subsidized by state-government funds, that was "humming at full capacity" on the outside but inside only employing a few workers in a sea of machines. "This factory marks a major millstone, er, milestone" is the way a slip of his unconscious then described what the opening actually signified (753–54).

Those jobs, now paying less and often involving fewer hours, became more demanding as the trend toward increased productivity, an aspect of the Great Stagnation, accelerated in the age of precarity, with workers "pushed to work harder, faster and with ever more [complicated] machinery" and threatened with losing their jobs if they did not comply in an era when unions continued to shrink (Wolff 2012, 1216–18). This resulted in greater gains for employers, whose conspicuous consumption continued to set the standard for the society. The worker's plight was hardly acknowledged in the products of media conglomerates, which were growing ever larger. Workers were now hopelessly unable to catch up to or even afford the shell of the consumerist lifestyle but still told they were "losers" if they could not (867–69).

Post the 2008 crisis, household savings were largely exhausted, and acquiring new debt became more difficult. Banks, after being bailed out by the government in order to stimulate the economy, curtailed lending even as households were "deleveraging" (or abandoning) their homes to get out from under the debt they had accumulated (Reich 2010, 956–58). Meanwhile, as tens of millions of baby boomers approached retirement age, they were finding depleted or exhausted company pension plans (so that by 2003 even Ford, the pillar of the Great Prosperity, owed well over ten times the total worth of the company to its pensioners [Wolff 2012, 1716–18]). They were also finding the "nest eggs" they had been convinced to speculate on had disappeared in the stock market crash of 2008 (50 million workers in 2009 lost $1 trillion in their 401K plans [Reich 2010, 956–58]) and they subsequently had to postpone or cancel their retirement even as work at their age became more challenging and harder to find. This description accounts for the middle 80 percent, but alongside this increasing anxiety went a bonanza for the top 10 percent, who added insult to injury by stowing away $1400 billion from 2008 to 2014 in both on- and offshore tax havens (can you say Delaware and Wyoming?).[13]

The psychological import of these changes was fatigue and stress from increased work as well as increased worry about how to keep up with the Joneses, who now were also shopping at Walmart, all of which resulted in higher rates of divorce and greater use of legal and illegal drugs leading to increased dependency (Wolff 2012, 841–46). This desperation was exacerbated by the notion dawning on the majority of Americans that, with their coping mechanisms now exhausted, they could no longer afford to live as they'd expected in the era of the Great Prosperity nor as they had been living after the end of that era by borrowing or working extra hours (Reich 2010, 906–7).

MIDDLE-CLASS HIP-HOP; FLOW, LAYERING, AND RUPTURE

These changes in the period of the Great Recession and its aftermath were concomitant with the development and rapid advancement of a television seriality that could function, in a way analogous to legal drugs, as a sedative to soothe this anxiety. The form of Serial TV, though, also suggested a way of coping with rapid and overwhelming changes in the (now blatantly neoliberal, meaning procapital, antigovernment) structure of the society and with an underlying, though seldom-acknowledged feeling by these beleaguered households of being under assault.

Tricia Rose (1994) in "A Style Nobody Can Deal With: Politics, Style and the Postindustrial City in Hip Hop" compellingly claims that the form of hip-hop expressed in music, dance, and art was conditioned by a response to (black) spaces that were delimited and under attack in the 1970s. This phenomenon glaringly affected New York's South Bronx, where manufacturing jobs deserted the city to be replaced by lower-wage jobs, if such jobs remained at all. These underpaid jobs in technology and service industries were part of a declining social space that consisted of "limited housing, a shrinking job market and diminishing social services." City government itself was under siege and losing autonomy (exemplified in the famous *New York Daily News* headline "Ford to New York: Drop Dead") as landlords in the Bronx participated in their own "urban renewal" by setting fire to decaying buildings to rebuild them as high rises.

Rose then argues that the series of blows suffered by black youth accounted for their creation of a coping style (in the art form of hip-hop) whose characteristics consisted of discontinuous rhythms (in rap music), jerky movement passed from one body to another (in freestyle dance), and visual discontinuities (in graffiti). All these types of layering incorporated in their form the breaks their creators were feeling on the social plain in communities "ruptured by the dislocation of the post-industrial [which we might today term neoliberal] city." Hip-hop culture then was a way of fighting back, "a counter-dominant narrative . . . against a mobile and shifting enemy" (Rose 1994, 82) (i.e., corporate capitalism), and a way of absorbing the series of shocks leveled at these communities and continuing and persisting in everyday life, so that rupture is layered (absorbed) and transformed into (a herky-jerky kind of) flow.

What was done to black America in the 1970s has now expanded to include the (Western) middle class as a whole in the wake of a "collapse in the institutional forms of representation of workers, such as trade unions, which . . . in the past served to give some coherent shape and social visibility to these [worker] identities" resulting in a "largely uncharted landscape in which jobs are created and disappear with great rapidity, often without even a concrete designation . . . [and in] a pick-and-mix combination of 'skills,' 'aptitudes,' and 'competences'" (Huws 2014, 48). This disruption produced new forms of both distribution and narration in middle-class television. Distribution patterns moved away from the stationary household television set to on-the-go viewing on mobile phones, tablets, and portable computers. Two 2016 surveys found that nineteen-to-thirty-two-year-olds, a very sought-after demographic, stream as their favored mode of television watching.[14] In the same way the stable distribution of series, with broadcast networks scheduling openings in the fall and spring and a set season of twenty-two episodes, has undergone a rupture as well. Many series are now offered in variable lengths of both time and number of episodes, and they begin and end at different times of the year on cable television or, on SVOD (streaming video on demand), where they are rolled out continuously throughout the year and all at once.

The major element of rupture within flow, though, is the serial form itself, where multiple characters come and go, are added and die, while the series itself extends beyond the former boundary of the single episode to arcs only somewhat limited even by the single season. The sitcom, the most stable of episodic forms in the period of the Great Prosperity, has itself become densely layered with more characters and season and series arcs. *The Big Bang Theory* illustrates this premise by later in the series even adding two (female) characters to its five main characters, all seven then with developed plot lines. (In so doing, the series passed from a more limited male audience to a wider audience so that by its fourth season it was TV's highest-rated comedy.)

However the main area in which seriality has developed in the sitcom is in that genre's rom-com (romantic comedy) element, in a movement from Sam and Diane's tumultuous relationship in *Cheers* (1982–93)—which in an ode to feminism never permanently bonds its fated-to-be-mated couple—to the never-secure-until-the-finale relationship of Ross and Rachel in *Friends* (1994–2004) to Leonard's pursuit of Penny in *Big Bang* through nine seasons (2007–15), which ends most conventionally of the three in marriage at the start of season 10. The Penny-Leonard story is dominant but is still only one of four serial romantic arcs in the series, the remaining involving the other three main male characters: Sheldon, Howard, and Raj, each of whom have serious relationship problems that the series exhibits and then moves to resolve. The constant clashes within the romantic relationships of these three series, well known to series fans (Sam and Diane's pattern of persistent breakups with casual passersby in the bar telling them they were not right for each other; Ross's famous cheating on Rachel because he thought they were "on a break"; and Penny's answering Leonard's first "I Love You" with "Thanks"), were often followed with moments of persistent and deeper couple unity. Here, the flow and layering within these most celebrated television rom-coms sustained continuous moments of rupture in a history that straddles the Great Prosperity, the Great Stagnation, and the Great Recession.

THE RECESSIONAL QUANTIFICATION: PRECARITY, SUBLIMATION, AND *THE BIG BANG THEORY*

The Great Recession erupted during the first season of *Big Bang*, 2007–8, and the show hit its stride in the aftermath of the recession. *Big Bang* does not directly seem to be concerned with the effects of this momentous occasion on the television viewer, but in its approach to work, the show radically alters the former "workplace" sitcom and in a dramatic way presents a new kind of continuous work that now invades the home and relationships as the distinction between work and leisure are dissolved in postrecession desperation. Previous workplace sitcoms, such as *Murphy Brown* (1988–2008) and *The Larry Sanders Show*, featured a clear demarcation between work and home, with each at pains to create a—mostly facile—home life for their characters. *Friends* and *Frasier* (1993–2004) marked the changeover to the new work economy, with the café functioning as an alternate site to the apartment at a time when cafés were becoming more prominent work sites—or hyperindustrial factories, where coffee, the neoliberal addiction, allows the worker to keep producing. *Big Bang*, which is at great pains to delimit the workplace designation of each of its characters (Sheldon is a theoretical physicist, Leonard an experimental physicist, Raj an astrophysicist, and Howard an engineer without a PhD), often sets work in the home and begins to utterly dissolve the distinction between the two as it also dissolves the generic boundary between workplace sitcom and TV rom-com.

The paradigmatic figure in the collapsing of leisure is Sheldon, who in an episode titled "The Einstein Approximation" (S3E14) has been up all night in his and Leonard's apartment trying to solve a physics problem. One might say his work is a nonalienated creative expression of his being, but equally it could be argued that it is ubiquitous and perennial. Though all four scientists work at Cal Tech and are sometimes shown at work, Sheldon in his obsession is seen working much more often in his apartment or in the Cal Tech cafeteria, another site of leisure, rather than in his office. Penny finds Sheldon staring down an equation on a blackboard when she enters the living room. The blackboard is simply a visually more engaging remonstrance of the computer, the ubiquitous screen that follows workers everywhere, never giving them a break, and functions as site of both work and (streaming site) of leisure.

The apartment has now replaced even the café as work site in the postrecession economy, where work is becoming constant and habitual. Although nominally the primary tension in the series is the romantic one between the geek Leonard and the cheerleader-type Penny, it could be argued that the more pronounced tension is between Penny, who has a pre-recession idea of the separation of work and leisure, and Sheldon, for whom that separation is highly tenuous. When Penny asks Sheldon what he is doing eyeing the board so early in the morning, he answers, "I'm attempting to view my work as a fleeting peripheral image so as to engage the superior colliculus of my brain." She replies, "Interesting, I usually just have coffee," a response that positions her as a worker who must "get ready" for work as opposed to Sheldon's conception of a worker who never ceases work. (In another episode Penny evokes what Marx calls "manufacturing" or family industry by converting the guys' apartment into an earlier model home factory complete with assembly line to produce barrettes called "Penny Blossoms.")[15]

Sheldon's mode of leisure is, as Steven Johnson argues, not so much a break from work as a prolongation of it, with he and the other three geek scientists constantly engaged in either various types of games that test their mental agility either on- (*Age of Cohan*) or off-line (*Dungeons and Dragons*) or creating a mentally competitive atmosphere around their enjoyment of geek art, so that

Sheldon and Penny's alternate modes of work in *The Big Bang Theory.*

Sheldon for example praises the Joss Whedon series *Firefly* but disapproves of Leonard's liking *Babylon 5* (1994–98). In "The Einstein Approximation" while "trying to figure out why electrons behave as if they have no mass when travelling through a graphene sheet" Sheldon spreads marbles, which connote play, on the apartment floor to model protons and neutrons, tripping up Penny and Leonard who are returning from the conventional leisure activity of roller skating and surprised to see the apartment transformed into a laboratory. Sheldon later steals away to a ball pit for children in a mall in search of bigger electron models, in both instances converting leisure spaces and objects into work sites and tools. This obsession with work, or 24/7 capitalism, is a sublimated way the sitcom discusses the pressure ordinary workers are feeling both to heighten productivity and to compete for dwindling, low-paying jobs.

The empowered high-tech workers at Cal Tech, and Sheldon particularly, contrast sharply with Penny, who performs service work as a waitress at the Cheesecake Factory, a deskilled work which Stiegler describes via Peter Sloterdijk as a "domestication of being" in a sphere in which more and more knowledge is being passed to machines and the "worker has no need of knowledge" (Stiegler 2008a, 179). Penny's job and her lack of a satisfying work is a subject of anxiety for her and often makes her an object of ridicule for Sheldon, who in "The Einstein Approximation" shows up at Penny's restaurant to "take a menial job like yours" so that his mind has the space to conjure the physics problem, just as Einstein worked at a patent office in solving relativity.

However, the salient point perhaps is not Penny's deskilling but Sheldon's persistent overcompensation—his desire to win the Nobel Prize, meet science celebrities, publish in the most prestigious journals, all of which is revealed in a later episode to not even have been enough to secure him tenure at the university. Driving him also, in a way the series cannot quite acknowledge, is the specter of the fall from grace back perhaps to his lower-class small-town Texas roots if he does not strive persistently. He likewise, in sublimated form, is filled with the new anxiety over work.

Sheldon's machinelike efficiency at work also carries over into his personal life, where, in a Taylorist scientific model of labor adapted to the hyperindustrial era, he attempts to ritualize personal behavior—both his own (sitting on the same spot on the sofa, knocking on Penny's door three times, and depersonalizing even his most intimate acquaintances by always addressing them by their first name) and that of others, who he attempts to control through capitalist contractual arrangements such as the "roommate agreement" with his best friend, Leonard, and the "relationship agreement" with his girlfriend, Amy. Relationships for him also are defined around work status, so that he never tires of making fun of Howard, an engineer, for not having a PhD or of Leonard for being an experimental, not theoretical, physicist. Thus in this atmosphere of intense competition, personal relations and personal care and conduct are devalued and Taylorized, becoming themselves scientific instruments for furthering the interpenetration of (a capitalist mode of) work into daily life.

Sheldon in fact begins to pattern himself after the new worker, the machine, and this patterning—which in *Big Bang* is seen as an aberration—a few years later in *Silicon Valley*, as the anxiety over work increases apace, will become the norm. There is a series of jokes in the Einstein episode positioning Sheldon as nonhuman in his 24/7 obsession with work, exhibiting characteristics that are animal-like, monstrous, and ultimately robotic. Leonard tells Penny on finding Sheldon working until dawn that "If you don't put him in his crate at night he just runs around the apartment." He is later described as Frankenstein-like in his midnight trip to the mall, "escaped and . . . terrorizing the village." Finally in a sort of *Wall-E* (2008) slapstick joke, Sheldon is described as so obsessed with problem solving that he has taken to using "a stick of butter as deodorant," to which Howard replies, "Have you tried rebooting him?" Sheldon himself says about his obsession, "I don't need sleep, I need answers." In this episode particularly, but throughout the series, Sheldon represents the spectacle of the worker machine, where leisure is dissolved into work, a sublimated marker of the anxiety all workers feel in the postrecession as jobs disappear while demands for increased production accelerate.[16]

We're All in Plastics Now: *Silicon Valley* and the Permanence of Neoliberal Work

The collapsing of work and leisure in an acceleration of the efficiency and ruthlessness of now-permanent work, *one of* but not *the* central focus of *The Big Bang Theory*, is taken up in the acerbic satire of the neoliberal ethos refracted through once-rebellious internet creators in *Silicon Valley*, the best sitcom of the last twenty years. Not since *The Larry Sanders Show* (also on HBO) has a sitcom so viciously and systematically mocked the ostensibly moral underpinning of an industry. The former series brutally but hilariously pointed out the hypocrisy of supposedly psychologically sophisticated "entertainers," who at heart were driven simply by pride and profit, while the latter's social satire is constructed around the gap between the enlightened humanitarian and democratic good intentions of the early internet founders who still see themselves as creating a different form of enterprise expressed in Google's original slogan "Don't be evil" and the now-ruthless corporate mega-entities these companies have become. Apple is now the most profitable company in the world while Amazon CEO Jeff Bezos claims that Amazon (along with Apple and Microsoft) makes $2,000 a second,[17] a claim that is indicative itself of the hyperindustrial age, with its fetishized monitoring of time. The *Silicon Valley* creator/showrunner Mike Judge (*Beavis and Butt-Head* [1993–2011] and white-collar film satire *Office Space* [1999]) had worked in the 1980s at a Silicon Valley startup, where he termed the participants "Stepford Wives," "true believers in something and I don't know what it was."[18] There is a similarity between the insularity of the techies in *Silicon Valley* and the stay-at-home misanthropes of *Beavis and Butt-Head*, the difference being that these technical Beavis and Butt-Heads are now taking over the world.

The series has the density of both language and industry experience that marks HBO's other, more celebrated comedy series *Veep* (2012–),[19] but unlike that series *Silicon Valley* does not simply wallow in cynicism that in the end (in the case of *Veep*, owing partly to the Julia Louis-Dreyfus character/casting/persona) we are supposed to ultimately find endearing. *Silicon Valley*, like all good satire, is finally about exposing and changing the ruthlessness of this capitalist industry rather than forgiving it for its supposedly endearing smarts, as *Veep* forgives the vacuousness of neoliberal politics.

PERMANENT WORK AS NEOLIBERAL ETHICS

Two factors distinguish work in the post- (or rather enduring) recession period after 2008, both accentuated by a frantic drive to increase global productivity to make up for the loss of worker's wages. The first factor characterizing the changing nature of labor is the permanence of work as the digital revolution is now extended in time to a twenty-four-hour work situation and in space so that for some workers, including those on *Silicon Valley*, there is no distinction between home and office. The second characteristic is the precarity of work, as seen by the fact that in 2009 in the US there were 15 million out of work, 8 million more than at the onset of the recession.[20] More workers were also being replaced by an ever-faster implementation of automation, with the prediction being that in the decade from 2015 to 2025 unemployment will begin to oscillate between 24 and 30 percent (Stiegler 2015, 15). This anxiety fuels the sublimated content of the show, where what underlies the intensity of the show's description of 24/7 work subsuming all personal relations is the fear of no work at all.

In the twentieth century factory, managers decided workers would be "more effective and sustainable producers" if they were allowed time off (Crary 2013, 14). In France, in the 1930s, workers were granted two weeks of unpaid vacation in August, and one of the major gains of the Popular Front era was winning pay for those two weeks.[21] However, with the erosion of unions and effective corporate regulation, rest and recuperation has been increasingly viewed as "too expensive to be structurally possible within contemporary capitalism." This "bioderegulation" has attempted to sync the 24/7 of deregulated markets with human rhythms, seeking ways to surpass physical limitations

(14). In the global neoliberal model, the planet becomes a "non-stop work site" with "one's personal and social identity . . . organized to conform to the uninterrupted operation of markets, information networks, and other [revenue generating] systems" (9). The world is also an "always open shopping mall" (17) either real or virtual (the Apple iPad and iPhone screens are after all a personal, portable mall). Here, leisure is defined purely in terms of consumption, that is, as an adjunct to profits and production This drive toward the 24/7 personal and portable mall where consumption never ceases defines the new SVOD model of broadcasting, where series are mobile and available on all devices at all times.

This new post- (or really permanent) recession world, the world of 24/7, "has the semblance of a social world, but . . . is actually a non-social model of machinic performance" (Crary 2013, 9) and is a further extension of Sheldon's robotic world in *Big Bang* but now encompassing all the *Silicon Valley* characters. Mike Judge's is a workplace sitcom where the home is an office. Far from being no distinction between the two, the home is eviscerated and is instead simply a living space that fledgling entrepreneur Erlich Bachman sets up for Richard and his coworkers to develop their start-up business.[22] The "camaraderie" of the start-up team in the home is supposedly contrasted to the ominousness of Hooli CEO Gavin Belson's regimented cubicles, with Belson himself seen as the greedy corporate-tech head. He despises Richard's tiny outfit and, as Bachman says, "wants to make sure no other investor offers you a dime." However, the personal relations of the tiny, independent band are equally shot through and defined by the same greed and competitiveness as Hooli. So, for example, the two rival engineers Dinesh and Gilfoyle in the episode "Two in the Box," when pressed to define their roles in the company, each claim they should get more equity than the other. In the end, is Hooli's Death Star–like corporate complex more threatening than the encroachment of the work ethos into the home, that former staple of the sitcom, where the new family—and it is said that all sitcoms are family sitcoms—is now a band of techies in a start-up, and does this signal the end of domestic space?[23]

In this subsumption of all human activity and personal relations under the sign of work, even sex becomes simply commodified leisurality that, rather than offering a diversion from work, is expressed in the same terms *as* this work. The opening of "Two in the Box" has Bachman hiring a stripper for the guys to celebrate their getting funding from an investor. Gilfoyle, on being told to alter the atmospheric mood, commands his computer, "License to Kill 9, Change the lighting to something erotic," and a black light floods the room, so that mood and desire are simply alterable and programmable logics. The team deserts the room, leaving only Nelson "Big Head" Bighetti, who tells the dancer, "You seemed like someone I could fall in love with," in reply to which the sex worker Mochachino asks who is going to pay her. On being asked if she accepts American Express, she replies, "You're damn right I do," and produces a portable card reader in a way that indicates this is a purely business transaction and that the street, where greed is on the surface, is a direct reflection of the suite, where the same greed appears in an only slightly more disguised fashion.

SERIALITY IN THE POSTRECESSION SITCOM

Silicon Valley is a serial series with a strong and overriding arc, but that arc is not the traditional one of the romantic comedy or even of personal character change. The arc in the show is constructed on the success or failure of the start-up and each week tracks a different moment in its development. The story of securing funding and moving the company forward and the rivalry of Richard's independent small company and the tech megalopolis Hooli replaces the character change and romantic ups and downs of the traditional sitcom (with Pied Piper and Hooli taking the place of Sam and Diane, Ross and Rachel, and Penny and Leonard). There is a romantic relationship developing between Amanda, who works for the Pied Piper investor Peter Gregory, and Richard, in whose idea she strongly believes. But this is clearly a minor plot that in no way dwarfs or subtracts from the start-up main plotline and which proves that the sitcom form can, by overlaying and revising the skeleton of the romantic comedy, serve as a formidable satirical vehicle.

Thus, while *Big Bang* ends its first season with an episode about whether Penny and Leonard should go on a date, with both agonizing about where it would lead and finally agreeing to go out at the end of the episode, *Silicon Valley* instead ends its first season with Richard, at a development convention in danger of losing out to Hooli's reverse engineering of his code, up all night concentrating on the company's compression feature and being mobbed by investors the next day, after his successful presentation. The anxiety over dating is replaced by the anxiety over losing funding, and the fulminating that in *Big Bang* is aided by Sheldon's explanation of the principle of Schrödinger's cat, which says there is no way to definitively know an outcome until an event is attempted, is replaced by Bachman's discourse on masturbating each member of the audience—which leads Richard to realize the actual personal content of his company. The investors mobbing him at the end of the season replaces Penny and Leonard's successful date. The overlay itself suggests the subsumption of romantic relationships into the world of work and finances.

BEING EVIL: CORPORATE CAPITAL INVADES THE VALLEY

The underlying persistent theme—and main joke—of the series is that tech companies, supposedly started to help humanity and still somewhat clinging to that rhetoric, have become instead ordinary capitalist enterprises, now laying claim to being "the new center of economic gravity in the Unites States," with all the greed and double dealing maintaining that position entails.[24] Google, which pretends to be a neutral information deliverer, is now spreading its tentacles through all industries and is currently attempting to outmaneuver German car manufacturers and the German system of union participation and low unemployment in heavy manufacturing by making its own smart car. Meanwhile, Amazon's Jeff Bezos, who has boasted about working toward being able to lay off 50 percent of his employees, has engineered an almost entirely automated warehouse system in which humans only participate at the end of the warehouse chain, in verifying quality control—a job the company is also now looking to mechanize.[25]

Investment financiers and programmers have been deserting Wall Street and going to work for tech companies. This exodus has been led by the chief financial officer of Morgan Stanley, the US' largest bank. This direct overlay indicates that the Valley is eager to embrace its position not merely as a technological leader of capital but now as a financial leader as well. The Wall Street "brain drain," which also includes high-level programmers on whom the financial industry has become dependent in its rush to develop new investment tools, has so worried financial institutions that, in 2014, two months after the trend was reported in the *New York Times*, Morgan Stanley's CEO James Gorman felt compelled to answer the charge in a somewhat desperate "Lunch with the *Financial Times*," claiming in his retort that "banking's a sexy industry! Creative, it's dynamic, it's global, it's fast-moving, you bring a lot of talented people together!"[26] His underlying message then was that Wall Street banking is *as* sexy as the new center of both technical and financial innovation, Silicon Valley.

The digital philosophe Evgeny Morozov claims that tech companies are still being thought of theoretically as not primarily capitalist but rather as democratic enterprises, according to which issues such as "net neutrality" are not considered for their primarily economic effect as part of an industry under "the angle of imperialism, of financialization, or neoliberalism." Morozov concludes, "I do not see why a world in which Google offers its services in exchange for our data or its own publicity will be better than a world in which all will be billed by . . . Siemans [the largest engineering company in Europe, a sort of European Halliburton]. There is no credible response [to the tech industry and its new dominance] without rethinking capitalism."[27]

Underlying this move of professionals from one center of finance to another is perhaps a moral revulsion by potential employees over the supposition that banks helped create the 2008 crisis. However, the move is discussed in a *New York Times* article simply in terms of dynamism and efficiency, so that a Goldman Sachs deserter who joined a start-up because he wanted to be a part of "a software revolution" claims, "Smart people go to where they feel there is the most growth."[28] In the same article, a Silicon Valley recruiter describes how his young clientele views banking as "a regulated industry where it's increasingly difficult to innovate" as opposed to the world of the more freewheeling and dynamic tech giants. In the 1970s, after Watergate, young graduates flocked to journalism because they felt they could "make a difference," that is, they followed an ethical and moral imperative. In the neoliberal era, the stated motivations have only to do with dynamism and efficiency, which is this era's ethics.[29]

It is in these polluted waters that the characters of *Silicon Valley* swim, and the series charts the increasingly rapid transformation from an industry that began with a great deal of egalitarian rhetoric—about an open internet—but rapidly turned into a site where personal relationships, lifestyle choices, language and class differences are subsumed into a corporate ethos of efficiency and profit.

In the episode "The Cap Table," relationships are recentered around corporate streamlining. Richard hires a Chief Financial Officer, Jared, from Hooli, who in a typical neoliberal corporate move quickly assesses the team members' roles to see who can be let go, deciding the dead weight on the team is Richard's "best friend" since childhood, Nelson "Big Head" Bighetti.[30] Richard refuses to make this concession to the efficacy of the company and is told by another member of the team that "the CEO of Microsoft does not have a paid best friend." Richard is chided by Bachman and instructed that as head of the company he needs "to be an asshole." Instead, Richard takes a principled stand in retaining Big Head, who then tells him that he has been offered a huge contract by Hooli, who we later find out wants to pick his brains to reverse engineer Richard's compression program. "I went out on a limb for you," Richard exclaims in astonishment, to which Big Head replies, "This is huge for me, I can move out, get my own place." In the neoliberal world, ethics, principle, and fellow feeling are constantly outmaneuvered by profit and personal gain.

The episode ends with Richard dismissing Big Head, and Bachman then complimenting him by remarking that he was "kind of an asshole back there." Personal relations are utterly transformed into business relations centered not around any idea of fellow feeling that might lead to a true collectivity but only on the efficiency of the company and the dynamism of the corporate team. The cutthroat nature of this supposedly humanitarian business becomes more apparent as the series progresses. Thus, when Gavin Belson, after the failure of his Nucleus reverse-engineering team, discovers the team's employee contracts are invalid, he fires them without severance, and—more crucially in the world of the corporate start-up in which profits accelerate quickly—takes back their unvested stock options. In the end of season 2, Richard, in a stockholder revolt, is fired as the head of his own company.[31]

In terms of language, while *Big Bang* introduced a highly technical scientific language to the sitcom, *Silicon Valley*, while not skimping on the technical language of software development, is even savvier about the burgeoning dialect of venture-capital investment engulfing the tech industry. This linguistic confluence demonstrates the way that the technical and financial are inter-acting, or rather the way the technical is being subsumed under the financial, documented on the show at the moment this change was taking place in the Valley. In Richard and Bachman's initial meeting with the investor Peter Greg-ory, Gregory inducts Richard—creative but a business neophyte—into the world of technical finance: "What is this company? What did I buy? . . . The algorithm is the product of the company. What I'm asking about is the com-pany itself. What do they do? . . . Are they essential?" He then reacts sharply to Bachman's share in the company profits for his sheltering of the team: "Ten percent, I'm paying you 200,000 for 5 percent and yet you're giving this man twice that in exchange for a futon and some sandwiches." Thus, reproduction, securing the worker's physical state to ensure their ability to produce (Marx 1977), is here utterly reduced to its financial value. This reduction initiates a later, more ruthless exchange where the language becomes more brutal. Bach-man demands, "Are you going to fire Big Head or not? Richard, stop being a fucking pussy and start being an asshole." Finally, there is a merger of the stark efficiency of the neoliberal business model of bottom line and profit above all and the technical proficiency of the programmers, as Gilfoyle describes Big Head (while he is in the room) as "as pointless as *Mass Effect 3*'s multiple endings." In *Silicon Valley* there is a density in the merger of the technical and business languages that is integral to the satirical thrust and which conveys the way the two are merging in reality.

The show also seizes on the gap between the '70s California "me genera-tion" and alternative cultures that were part and parcel of the growth of the tech industry and their present use as simply sustaining a new rapacious form of capitalism. The California tech industry is defined by and lauded for "relaxed dress code, better weather and more freewheeling culture" as opposed to New York finance, where Silicon Valley recruiters conjure up the negative image of "walking into a tall building in a suit or high heels" and into an industry with "more hierarchical decision making and standardized processes" (Popper and Dougherty 2015).

However, the series illustrates the way "personal growth" is itself made to conform to an increasingly more strict business model. Gavin Belson (whose name conjures the San Francisco real-estate developer Gavin Elster, whose attempt to murder his wife sets in motion the events of *Vertigo* [1958]), addressing his guru Denpok—who in his infinite wisdom has decided to stand for the entire summer as a means of enlightenment—says, "I hate Richard Hendricks, that little Pied Piper prick. Is that wrong?" The guru acknowledges that yes, "in the hands of a lesser person" this can be wrong, but "in the hands of the enlightened, hate can be a tool for great change," thus rationalizing a crude competitive business sentiment by couching it in the language of caring and understanding. Belson then orders his office Siri to "Play John Lennon's 'Imagine,'" and the voice responds, "Cuing John Wayne in a mansion," demonstrating that the tech world does not escape more traditional and conservative meanings in its attempt to present itself as grafting alternative lifestyles onto the drive toward ever-increasing accumulation.

Finally, class differences, which the tech ethos of freedom and alternative living often claim to dispel, are emerging in the Valley itself and are highlighted on the show. San Francisco rents have climbed in the years following the 2008 recession to four times the national average, and this is largely due to newly wealthy tech company employees as the companies become publicly traded while at the same time receiving government subsidies. "They should be ashamed," said a forty-year, just-evicted, resident at a 2014 send-up of the tech awards the Crunchies called the Crappies. Protests that year centered around private luxury vehicles using city bus stops to usher employees out to Cupertino with the (largely minority) luxury-van drivers forced to wait unpaid for the tech workers to finish their shifts to drive them home. "It's an attitude of entitlement, of arrogance that's coming in," said one resident (Popper 2014).[32]

In the opening of "The Cap Table" Mochachino, the black woman hired to dance for the team, on finding they are for the most part either too shocked (Dinesh's "I don't like getting an erection around people I work with") or challenged (the nerd Gilfoyle's "I entice the flesh, I don't pay for it") by her up-front sexuality while arguing over who will pay for her performance, says—in a line that is especially emphasized because it closes the show's opening sequence and introduces the credits—"I hate Palo Alto." This sentiment is a strong registering of the feelings elicited by residents of San Francisco, and more pointedly of the largely minority city of Oakland, locked out of the Valley's instant profits. Later after Big Head leaves the apartment to figure out what will become of him, he's found by Richard at Mochachino's house. There, she is transformed from her role as fetishistic object of desire in the Valley to poor mother of two kids, whom she's cooking for in the kitchen (though we never learn her actual name). When Richard arrives she says to Big Head, "Your ride is here"—a wonderful moment where she's humanized and one subtracted from the wealth, status, and competitiveness that defines the Valley that Big Head will be returning to with Richard.

Silicon Valley sublimates, as does the society as a whole, the concern of the new worker about the rapidly changing nature of work into a comedy about 24/7 work, but in the process, in employing the serial mode, it satirizes these new relationships by illustrating how they are in fact the seeping through into this brave new world of the old detritus of ruthless capitalist accumulation.

THIS IS YOUR BRAIN, THIS IS YOUR BRAIN ON SERIAL TV

Autism and Addiction as the (Psychoanalytic) Hyperindustrial Condition

The web allows us to borrow cognitive strengths from autism and to be better infovores.

Tyler Cohen, *Create Your Own Economy*

It's like the people who make potato chips. They know how to put the right chemicals in there to make you want to eat the next potato chip. Our goal is to make you want to watch that next episode.

Lost showrunner Carlton Cuse

THIS CHAPTER EXAMINES AUTISM and addiction, first, together, as psychological states that each promote a kind of retreat from the social world and as modes fostered by Serial TV's method of delivery and narrative construction. Each is then examined separately, taking as an example of autism Sheldon Cooper's brilliant but emotionally challenged physicist on *The Big Bang Theory* and as an example of narrative inducement of addiction the structure of the Fox series *24*.

Autism and addiction are both branded as pathologies, in part to erect a false boundary between them and "normalcy." Indeed each, with a clinical definition that is all the time moving toward stressing them as nonaberrant, is embedded and imbricated in kinds of inducement and representation in hyperindustrial capitalism in general and in television seriality in particular. They are a kind of social metaphor for the destruction of the personality in this epoch, so that we are now all on the autism and addiction spectrums. Rather than seeing the branding of each as stigmatizing, one might suggest that social media in general, and the mode and narration of television seriality in particular, are participating in producing a kind of acceptable social disconnectedness. The twin features of this change are a correspondent validation of abstract conceptualization over relational skills that may be thought of as "social autism" and the promotion of a kind of regularized "social addiction" that goes under the name of "binge watching."

The autistic condition is often celebrated in contemporary television in a corporate-utopian imagining and distortion of its high-level manifestation, Asperger's syndrome, of which a primary representative is Sheldon Cooper, the brilliant, supremely competent, but interpersonally inept theoretical physicist in *The Big Bang Theory*.[1] Sheldon's technical skill suggests that relational aptitude really is a thing of the past, while the Adonis physique of Dr. Reid on *Criminal Minds* (2005–), which accompanies his six university degrees and disinterest in relational communication, suggests that brains and looks really are all that is necessary under contemporary capitalism.

There is also a sense in which the representation of autism and Asperger's on television has a strong class dimension. Autism, withdrawal from the social world, is in general not represented in the media—though an approximating of an autistic condition is everywhere induced and thus is more and more subliminally implied as an appropriate response to the intolerable conditions of the contemporary conjuncture (mass unemployment, vast income disparity, global climatic destruction), especially to those most vulnerable, who now are left with only their social media as laxative. In fact the retreat into the home is known in media-marketing circles by the neutrally or slightly positive term "cocooning." Meanwhile those more highly educated, better-off economically, are led toward the image of an idyllic and distorted Asperger's where technical competence is accompanied by an equal retreat from the social, sanctioned by a glorified image of how this distortion plays out in ordinary life—that is, suggesting that the problems posed by interactions with others are surmountable and easily dispensed with and in the end need not affect productivity.

On the addictive side of this conjuncture, the imperative to "hook" an audience (a much more contemporarily relevant term than David Bordwell's (1989) industrially neutral "cuing"), always prevalent in television in the era of the individual episode, has been amplified in the moment of seriality and in the presence of instantaneous online delivery systems so that there is now a hyperactivation of Roland Barthes's codes of reading that structure a narrative (outlined in *S/Z*), amounting to a rigorous intensification and refashioning of the codes to support the new industrial imperative of addicting rather than simply attracting an audience. A crucial moment in the transformation of the viewing process into one of pure addictive adrenaline was the Fox flagship series *24*. That series will be examined to show how it participated in transforming Barthes's codes in areas such as the season and weekly cliffhanger and sudden deaths of its characters for the purpose not of disrupting the codes, as was the case with earlier avant-gardes, but of heightening and reinvigorating them in a commercial frenzy.

The *S/Z* of Social Media and Serial Television: Seduction/Zapping

> By antagonism, I mean in this context the unsocial sociabili-
> ty of men, that is, their tendency to come together in society,
> coupled, however, with a continual resistance which constantly
> threatens to break this society up.
>
> Immanuel Kant

There are two parts to the autistic and addictive process: one is mode of delivery, let's think of it as hardware, and the other is the content, or the software the delivery system carries. SVOD acts as a kind of always available method for continually and persistently delivering the addictive content of Serial TV, the form of series television that has emerged with this new method of delivery. That is, Serial TV attempts, as Carlton Cuse has pointed out, to induce binge watching so that the entire series is consumed in one sitting, episode after episode. The liberal debate on this phenomenon sees on the negative side the "social value" of television (anticipating future episodes, sharing both the anticipation and the recapping of the last episode with friends) eroding and on the positive side compares indulging in "Complex TV" (*The Wire* [2002–8], *Breaking Bad* [2008–13]) to "reading more than one chapter of a novel in one sitting."[2]

However, there is a darker, or more commercial, reading of the link between online streaming and serial television where this form of television itself becomes, similar to the acceptable addiction to coffee peddled in the hyperindustrial workshops of cafés where work is indistinguishable from play, a way of coping with a 24/7 work- and lifestyle.[3] One recent study noted that "the functional overlap between substance misuse and television addiction is striking." Binge watching, itself an addictive term coined from food addiction, is referred to in some Alcoholics Anonymous circles as akin to "morphine drip" (Moran and Sussman 2013). In addition, the class differences built into the inducement to binge make its effect even greater and more subtle. Thus *24*, popularly available on network TV via the Fox network, which is notorious for doing anything to court ratings, might be thought of as a serial equivalent of "crack" (a street drug) whereas *Homeland* [2011–], the more nuanced cable series from Showtime with some of the *24* writers and a more refined use of tropes such as the cliffhanger, is the more upscale Serial TV "cocaine."

Television has always attempted to induce viewers to return the next week, but the more intense form of viewing that is bingeing got its start with series marathons, originating in the 1980s around the Labor Day holiday in the US, as a primer for the opening of the regular TV season. Bingeing now constitutes part of the lure of the streaming-video services that no longer release on a week-by-week basis but rather all at once. As French scholars note, though this new form is incredibly complex, it is also a part of a commodity interchange, with television series as consumer products, which, like products of the food industry, "can trigger cravings." Carlton Cuse's comparison of the similarities in the manufacture of a binge food (potato chips) and Serial TV binge programs indicates a preconception, know-how, and intent on the part of the manufacturer to "cause dependence" by fine-tuning the "ingredients" that "are most likely to generate and maintain their show's addictive quality" and as such might be compared to revelations about the knowledgeable inducement of addiction by the tobacco industry (Paquet-Deyris et. al 2016). The dominance of a more addictive form of television also takes place in the context of over- and under-the-counter-drug addiction, where almost two hundred people a day died of overdoses and where the use of antidepressants increased by 65 percent from 1999 to 2014 in a country that President Obama noted was a place where "we use medication to resolve numerous problems."[4]

The social addiction of television facilitated by online streaming is a part of the gradual remaking of social relationships as a whole as more and more life is lived online. One result of this migration is a retreat and isolation into an inner world (though of course this virtual reality at the same time also enhances relationships) and an inducement of an interpersonal paralysis. Here, autism and Asperger's and the lack of connectedness that they imply becomes a kind of metaphor for society as a whole, replacing earlier modern and postmodern conditions of alienation, ennui, and irony (Jameson 1991) by stony retreat or disaffected brilliance. Thus, *Big Bang*'s nerds, who in the teen films of the 1980s were on the margins of society, are now moving to the center and in the new symbolic economy are becoming its power figures so there is a now either a little or a lot of Sheldon in all of us.

There is another aspect to this gradually disappearing affect. There is in serial television a new heightened form of violence, as in shows such as *The Walking Dead*, that suggests that the accelerated emotions which that show and other series exhibit are, rather than semblances of a more violent world, instead or at the same time, the memory of and nostalgia for a former, more emotional life lived in direct confrontation and physical exchange with others.[5] There is a similarity to the way, 150 years ago, the Impressionists' views of nature were about capturing, in the midst of the onslaught of industrialization, a disappearing peasant landscape, as Van Gogh did at Auvers. In the Impressionist example the disappearing landscape is physical; in the case of serial television—with its excess of violence, of sexuality, of annihilation—it is emotional. As one French tome put it, "The more our world becomes immaterial and virtual the more we insist on creating a culture which valorizes sensuality, eroticism and a hedonistic existence" (Lipovetsy and Serroy 2013, 475).

There is again also a class component to this disappearance, since what is being lived vicariously in serial television is often a working-class life that is disappearing from the West but still dominant in the third world and particularly in Asia. Thus, while serial television adds drama to the globalized Western life migrating more and more online,[6] third-world life, though it has an online component, is much more lived on the daily level of a physically experienced brutal exploitation,[7] as seen in the frenzied production culminating in suicide in the factories and sweatshops ringing the Chinese industrial center of Shenzhen where Foxconn, which manufactures Apple's gateway to the virtual, is centered.[8]

The mandatory and compulsive increase in sex and violence in Serial TV is of course also a result of the increasing competition for audiences. Pay-per-view companies pioneered nudity and an increase in violence, both highly visible in HBO's trendsetter *Game of Thrones*. Both add to the addictive quality of the series and have been widely duplicated, with critics remarking that Netflix's *Altered Carbon* (2018–) fills a nudity gap for the streaming service. Meanwhile, globally, as German series attempt to compete with their American competitors, a scene in that country's series *Bad Banks* (2018–) that exoticizes a female Asian banker is simply pornographic. Cable has long used an increase in violence to distinguish it from network television, which—though constrained—attempts to follow suit in a way that recalls the competition among filmmakers for gore in the decade beginning in 2002 in what was called the "Splat Pack." Thus TNT's *The Alienist* (2018–), set in New York in the 1890s, updates and makes contemporary its period setting with the introduction of various graphic illustrations of mutilation by its serial killer antagonist while Fox's *Gotham* (2014–) modernizes its timeless noir city by the sadistic acts of its villains, in particular the offhand brutality of the Penguin and the serial-killer amorality of the Riddler. The general increase in the level of sex and violence in network, cable, and streaming services enhances the addictive effect by tapping patterns of desire that are the unconscious equivalent of the more conscious narratively addictive tropes.

Social Autism: The Hyperindustrial Condition

If it is possible that forms of autism are emblematic of and being fostered by the hyperindustrial age, then characteristics of the autistic personality ("self-sufficient"; "like in a shell"; "happiest when left alone"; "acting as if people weren't there"; "perfectly oblivious to everything about him"; "giving the impression of silent wisdom"; "failing to develop the usual amount of social awareness"; "acting almost as if hypnotized" [Kanner quoted in McGuire 2016,

30]) could be read in parallel with behaviors promoted and encouraged by the internet and so-called "social" media. Thus, a new more antisocial though extremely productive, partly because focused on work alone, personality becomes the hyperindustrial worker par excellence, a complement to the machine logic he or she now replicates.

The history of the diagnosis of autism suggests a more general application of the condition. Bruno Bettelheim in the early 1970s importantly suggested that autism was not simply a genetic disorder but had a social origin and could be "caused by early childhood experiences" (McGuire 2016, 39). The 1970s and 1980s saw more people being diagnosed with the disorder (44) and a movement toward defining the autistic spectrum as a continuum so that in the fifth and latest edition of the *Diagnostic and Statistical Manual of Mental Disorders* (*DSM-5*) four of the autistic subtypes are replaced with a central diagnosis of "autism spectrum disorder" consisting of "social communication deficits (combining social and communication problems) and restricted/repetitive behaviors." All this may indicate that the "disorder," now debated as potentially being socially produced, is becoming more widespread, or rather, that there is a continuum between "normal" and "autistic," rather than an unbridgeable gap (Vivanti, Tenison, and Vivanti 2016).[9] There is even an intelligence measurement known as the "autism quotient" which sets computational and relational skills on either end of a spectrum and values mathematical problem solving, the high end of the spectrum, over ability to understand based on reading emotional cues, the low end (Johnson 2006, 1190–95).

The change that serial television helps precipitate in both its method of distribution and its mode of narration is part of a wider change in neural conditioning and in relational patterns being effected by online life as a whole. In the chapter's opening quote, the economist's favorable description of modern internet users as autistic "infovores" suggests not a rational creature but a beast foraging with a snout that everywhere simply ingests information without digesting it. As Nicholas Carr (2011, 8) argues, the "calm, focused, undistracted . . . linear mind is being pushed aside by a new kind of mind that wants and needs to take in and dole out information in short, disjointed, often overlapping bursts—the faster, the better." What Carr is describing is a transformation of neural pathways to create a worker capable of scientific reasoning like a machine but whose social and relational skills and conceptual reasoning, less necessary for an increasingly technologically driven work process, are being devalued.

This transformation is reworking the fabric of society. "Whether I'm online or not, my mind now expects to take in information the way the Net distributes it: in a swiftly moving stream of particles," Carr claims (2011, 6–7). Thus for example, processing in serial television, as everywhere else in narrative, is sped up, and scenes are much shorter in sitcoms and dramatic series as the audience becomes both more readily able to grasp plot twists and less patient with longer character expositions. (One of the longest scenes in the entire series of Marvel and ABC's *Agent Carter* [2015–16] is an extended conversation in S2E9 between Carter and Jarvis, the butler who aids her, about whether they can trust each other, a constant subject of contemporary series TV in a world where trust is everywhere for sale and relational skills to determine authenticity are lacking. This intimate conversation between friends takes place with the two walking in the desert and is halted by the approach of two mob men who have come to kill them, illustrating that relational moments happen only under huge duress and only briefly in the new reality.)

Carr argues that this changeover of neural pathways, of our very being, is being effected for profit with, for example, internet-giant Google's earnings tied directly to the speed its customers absorb information and continue to click, since the more links and pages viewed, the more information about its users Google collects and sells in bundles to advertisers. This break in our concentration, disruption of attention, and attack on reflective thought is promoted and encouraged by companies who are in "the business of distraction" (Carr 2011, 156–57).

The voyeuristic, high-speed experiencing of our own lives, effected partly for the profit of others, creates "logics of dissociation" (Stiegler 2008a) or what Sherry Turkle similarly labels "narcissistic ways of relating to the world" (Turkle 2012, 179), which replicate the characteristics of autism. Online communications in general effect a distancing of emotions, with Turkle's interview subjects reporting that on the internet they appreciate not only the ability to avoid eye contact but also not having to experience, for example, when someone is upset "how hurt or angry they sound in their voice" (184). With texting, another subject notes how much simpler an online apology, where one simply types "I'm sorry," is since "you don't have to have any emotion, any believability in your voice or anything" (196). Relationships themselves become disposable and can be deleted as easily as emails. Subjects describe sending an email as having "taken care of that person" and suggest that, in the steady stream of communications mixing business and personal life that is the email bin, correspondence by friends and acquaintances are now viewed as messages "to be handled" or "gotten rid of," the language we use "when talking about garbage" (168). As one subject sums up contemporary communications, "I have a lot of people on my contact list. If one friend doesn't 'get it,' I call another" (177), a response that devalues intimacy and interpersonal communication but also views communication in a hyperindustrial mode, where one simply goes on to the next buyer.[10]

In this brave new digital world, television and particularly the more intimate, involved world of continuing characters that is Serial TV "can be used to compensate for a paucity of interpersonal 'connections'" (Moran and Sussman 2013). The predominance of the workplace and contemporary urban grouping in the *Friends*-type sitcom and, in the dramatic series, the predominance of work teams, albeit usually for purposes of surveillance (*CSI*), suggests an alternate life of companionship that is missing in the actual world of both work and now-more-autistic "relationships." "I log into Facebook and I feel less alone. Even when people are not there," Turkle (2012, 207) says, describing herself as a typical user. In the same way—in the more concentrated impact of Serial TV—we watch Leonard, Sheldon, and "the gang" (a term that is often used in contemporary sitcoms to foster feelings engendered by these false collectives) grapple with life situations such as career and marriage. These groupings simulate a companionship that may be lacking in non-virtual reality.[11] Says Turkle, summing up these autistic traces, "The ties we form through the Internet are not . . . the ties that bind [but] . . . the ties that preoccupy" (280).

In addition, the particular form of high-functioning autism that is lionized on contemporary television—a one-sided, high-end view of Asperger's stressing precocious and rapid intelligence—may be the hyperindustrial and neoliberal pathology par excellence, a condition that venerates efficiency over relatedness. Thus the ultimate value in this remade conception of time, promoted by "the interactions of globalization, neoliberalism and information technologies," is to be "physically, cognitively, psychologically, and metaphorically able to 'move fast.'" Hyperindustrialism is building its "new man" and woman who can "adapt quicker . . . think faster, understand immediately, innovate continuously, develop earlier, learn younger, look further, work more, produce more, consume more" (Hassan 2009, 19). This "need for speed" (and here we are reminded of Sheldon's short, clipped, loaded-with-technical-expertise bursts of communication) is imposed from outside the personality and "tied to the basic need for the capitalist to derive profit" in a world where time is understood as that quintessential commodity that puts us in touch with all other commodities since the efficient use of time allows us to "consume more [and] produce more" (19–20).

Thus television presents us with a gallery of characters in whom this substitution of neoliberal efficiency for relatedness is lionized in a distortion of Asperger's or its modification for market usefulness in treating the disorder as a "character quirk." Consequently, the "disorder" is becoming more and more a sought-after model of the hyperindustrial worker (Belcher and Maich 2014), where loss of relational capacity is deemed a fair trade-off for increased productivity. This avatar for a world that no longer values human interaction, the promotion of which we might call "corporate autism," is now a predominant character type, prevalent on contemporary television in both comic and dramatic modes in *Criminal Minds*, *Bones* (2005–17), *The Big Bang Theory*, *Grey's Anatomy* (2005–), *Fringe*, *The Bridge* (2013–14), and *Parenthood* (2010–15). Five of the characters in these shows are experts in their field of science, and all are viewed as "inspirational and exceptional," "intellectually stimulating geniuses who make us aspire to be like them" (1).

The series play down the negative side of the "disorder" or portray the serious lack of relational skills as "foibles" to be overcome, not as severe handicaps that persistently disrupt communication and inhibit interpersonal development. The disorder evolved on television beginning in the detective series in the 1970s, 1980s, and 1990s with *Columbo* (1971–2003) whose quizzical questionings and asocial aspect exhibited Asperger's tendencies. This representation then sprang forth full blown in the first decade of the current millennium with the brilliant obsessive-compulsive eponymous protagonist of *Monk* (2002–9) and was then normalized in the last decade as a series character with Dr. Reid on *Criminal Minds*, whose six university degrees and expertise in sociopsychological forensics is only occasionally tempered by his lack of social skills and disinterest in romantic relationships. That is, the model has gone from slightly aberrant and undiagnosed to near dysfunctional but effective to normalized, as a contemporary character like Reid is a functioning member of the *Criminal Minds* team. Similarly, in the social realm, the condition has been furthered, promoted, and manufactured by a society that everywhere demands its workers be less human and more efficiently machinelike and as relational skills take a back seat to technical capacity.

SHELDON COOPER (AND AMY FARRAH FOWLER) AS THE HYPERINDUSTRIAL NEW MAN (AND NEW WOMAN)

Although there are many examples of the validation and normalization of the traits of Asperger's on contemporary television, the most prescient and the one that has had the most cultural influence is undoubtedly *Big Bang*'s Sheldon Cooper (and his female avatar Amy Farrah Fowler). Sheldon is in many ways the most prominent character (one of the show's reviewers claimed the series would never have endured without him)[12] in a series whose ratings have increased as the digital and virtual economy has become more dominant in global society. In 2007, in its first season, the show failed to crack the top fifty highest-rated series. However, by its fourth season, beginning fall 2011, it was television's highest-rated comedy, and by its sixth season, beginning fall 2013, the highest-rated in the most crucial advertising demographic of eighteen-to-forty-nine-year-olds, a group that is also the most prominently involved in the digital explosion.

These ratings were boosted by the fact that it was the top-rated show in syndication the season before, that is, that it was being watched on a daily basis in an off-network form of bingeing. For the next three years *Big Bang* was the second-highest-rated series on American television. (During the show's rise in ratings, post the economic crash of 2008, the primary growth sector in the economy was its online component where, for example, investment in the high-tech sector alone rose to 46 percent of all venture capital investment.)[13]

The actor Jim Parsons has been nominated four times for the Emmy for best actor in a comedy and has won twice. There is now an asteroid named after the character,[14] and Sheldon's omnipresent expression "bazinga"—trademarked by Warner Brothers—has been appropriated in the natural world as the name of a newly discovered species of bee.[15]

Although the series co-creator Bill Prady denies it, Sheldon exhibits selective characteristics of Asperger's and autism in a way that overlaps general traits validated in what is termed geek culture, which itself has come to prominence with the predominance of Silicon Valley as motor of the new economy. A partial list of these traits, as described in the fourth and fifth editions of the *DSM*, include "repetitive patterns of behavior" (Sheldon's famous knocking three times on any door and saying the name of the person for whom he is knocking, usually his next-door neighbor Penny); "insistence on . . . inflexible adherence to routines" (his famous seat on the couch, the only place where he can sit in the living room and where he can detect any minute change in the conditions of this setting, as seen in episodes where Penny ruins the couch and it must be replaced and where Sheldon cannot accommodate to changing the furniture in the living room); "highly restricted, fixated interests" (Wednesday night is comic book night, and many other nights have a fairly rigid designation); and finally, "unusual interest in sensory aspects of the environment" (which necessitates Sheldon—in his first extended moments in Penny's apartment, in "The Tangerine Factor" (S1E17)—amalgamating "cushion densities, air flow patterns, and dispersion of sunlight" in order to figure out his permanent place to sit in a setting in which he is unfamiliar).

Most presciently, the condition expresses itself in a "general lack of humility and empathy" that results in "deficits in nonverbal communicative behaviors used for social interaction, and deficits in developing, maintaining, and understanding relationships." (American Psychiatric Association 2013) In "The Tangerine Factor," Penny asks Sheldon if he has a second—meaning some time for her. "A second what, pair of underwear?" he answers, which sets up an overall pattern in this scene of his misreading or disinterest in her verbal cues, illustrating his lack of involvement. Penny explains she wants to speak to him, they patter on the stairs, and she then asks him to come into her apartment. "We're not done?" is his reply. He then discourses on Leonard's lactose intolerance as emitting "noxious gas that could be weaponized," blithely unaware how he is impugning his friend in front of the woman with whom Leonard is madly in love. Penny then maintains that she and Leonard are, as Sheldon would say, "light years apart." "I would not say that," he counters, "light year is a unit of distance not time," unable or unconcerned with recognizing that Penny's analogy is an attempt to find common ground between her and Sheldon and to move the two of them closer as friends. In desperation she cries, "Do you have anything to say that has anything to do with what I'm talking about?"

However, in the series these deficits are seen as comic foibles, and they are outweighed and nearly negated by Sheldon's positive attributes, which ultimately are described in the series as potentially also useful in "solving" personal relationships. Sheldon is a theoretical physicist at Cal Tech with an eidetic memory and an IQ of 187, that is, his intellect, the most prized element of virtual and digital work, far outweighs that of the friends he mocks: Leonard for only being an experimental, not theoretical physicist; Raj for mastering the more obscure world of astrophysics; and most dramatically Howard, who has no PhD and is a lowly "aerospace engineer," someone whose material inscription in the work process summons the aura of the proletarian worker, otherwise entirely missing from the show.[16]

Sheldon is also the most verbally dexterous of the group. He has a command and linguistic fluidity with not only science but also pop culture (he describes Leonard's happiness at Penny's agreeing to go out with him as bringing to mind "the happy hippos in *Fantasia*"); literature (he negates Penny's description of Leonard having a little crush on her by claiming that would be like saying "Menelaus had a little crush on Helen of Troy"); and a (reflexive) knowledge of narratology and (sitcom) aesthetics (in his description of his friend's having driven Penny back into the arms of his rival: "Previously I felt sympathy for the Leonard character, now I just find him to be whiney and annoying"). Since the sitcom itself is built on verbal humor, characters with the greatest verbal skill redound as the most admired of the genre.

Sheldon's interpersonal defects are also partially mitigated by the fact that they are only a more exaggerated version of the glaring interpersonal deficits the other members of the gang exhibit. Howard is, in the early seasons of the show, a sex addict and pervert whose first reaction when Penny reports that her boyfriend has published an online account of their sexual activity is to hasten to the computer because "I have a blog to find." Raj is unable for the first five seasons to speak to women except when drinking, and in the later seasons when he overcomes this hurdle, he is drawn to unstable and asocial women. Leonard, the most "normal" of the group is terminally shy and unable to clearly state his feelings, continually resorting to scientific jargon, as when he neutrally rephrases the revelation by Penny's boyfriend that they have been engaging in sexual activity in public as a characterization of her as "open to expressing her affection in nontraditional locales."

In terms of the validation of Sheldon's autism, in "The Tangerine Factor" it is the physicist's logic and reasoning that solves the emotional and relational problem of whether Penny and Leonard should date. Both are hesitant, and Sheldon resolves the dilemma by first explaining to Penny the paradox of Schrödinger's cat, an analogy in quantum physics where a cat is positioned in a box with a sealed bottle of poison so that the cat may be thought of as alive or dead and "it is only by opening the box that you find out which it is"—the point being that Penny and Leonard will only know if they should be dating if they go on a date. In the next scene with Leonard, Sheldon simply, in order to "bring this conversation to a speedy conclusion," mentions the phrase "Schrödinger's cat." Leonard immediately understands the analogy and at the beginning of the date kisses Penny, who responds "the cat is alive." This episode is one of the most crucial in the series, the first time its lead romantic interests will date, and as such emphasizes that it is Sheldon's cold, scientific reasoning that resolves the interpersonal dilemma. (Nothing is made of the fact that the computational formula involves torturing animals, since that would culturally question the "reasonable" logic of the analogy.)

The serial aspect of the series concerns the overcoming of interpersonal handicaps by Sheldon and his friends so that over the course of several seasons their problems with human relationships are integrated into an overall trajectory of success as each pairs off and establishes permanent relationships with members of the opposite sex. But the most significant point of the series and its subtext would seem to be its validation of the brilliant aspects of autism in the form of Asperger's syndrome as beneficial and essential to success in the brave new virtual world of scientific logic. On *Big Bang* the interpersonal problems

Sheldon and Penny at cross-purposes in *The Big Bang Theory*.

that accompany that condition are downplayed, sidelined, and treated as so many foibles to be overcome on the way to the dominance of the machinic and the calculable in the human sphere.

24 and the Semiotics of the Addictive Text: Reading Barthes Reading Bauer

The attendant and complementary condition to autism in the digital age is addiction, that is, the deliberate manufacture of products that are not only distracting but that also prompt and program continual responses. This "addictive consumption" (Stiegler 2008a) turns its subjects into "lab rats constantly pressing levers to get tiny pellets of social or intellectual nourishment" (Carr 2011, 117). Serial television in both its mode of delivery and its method of narration incorporates concepts of the hyperlink, a crucial structuring device in the digital age. We are never reading a single text but always multiple texts that in different ways propel us out from the center with a multipurposing designed to "grab out attention" and to overvalue what is happening "right now." Thus, "we crave the new even when we know that 'the new is more often trivial than essential'" (Chabris 2008).

If "the Net is, by design, an interruption system, a machine geared for dividing attention" (Chabris 2008), serial television as a component of an overall online delivery system, duplicates this phenomenon. Streaming necessarily allows multitasking, so that, though the series may be more intricately plotted, there is now, as the corollary to the older moment of getting up and going to the refrigerator for food, a tendency to be working more than one device while watching. Viewers provide their own hyperlinks in researching actors, series locales, and commentary on the series as well as checking email or surfing the net on unrelated topics while the show is streaming, to say nothing of calls, texts, and social-media notifications that interrupt viewing.[17] Serial TV on streaming video on demand integrates itself into the overall neural-ecological digital environment in a way that promotes more intense concentration at the same time that concentration is, paradoxically, disrupted and splintered. The point often being to increase the addictive frenzy of immediate gratification that accompanies pressing buttons and having the world seem to respond to the individual's will and command, a pretend power in the face of increased actual social powerlessness.

Series are also being constructed in ever more addictive modes in ways their creators acknowledge directly. In a *Le Monde* article on French television *scenaristes*, Eric Rochant, creator of the French thriller *The Bureau*, talks about putting together a writer's room (a studio of writers), a new idea in France, to fashion series that are "better, denser, more complex, *more addictive.*"[18] In its series, Netflix often refuses to use the summaries, obligatory on cable and network series, of prior episodes that often begin with "Previously on . . ." *Daredevil* showrunner Steven S. DeKnight declares, "Why does that matter? People are going to binge-watch this."[19] Absorbing the hyperlink aspect of the internet in series narration has resulted not only in shorter scenes (and the scene is a more relevant measure in serial narrative construction than Barry Salt's [1992] "average shot length") but also in tracking more characters whose splintered presence rationalizes those shorter scenes in a way that is a kind of narrative adaptation of a hyperlink.

There are various methods of constructing these hyperlinked, multi-character narratives. A more archaic version, utilized by David Simon in both *The Wire* and *Show Me A Hero* (2015), was a novelistic dispersion of multiple characters and character groupings across a social landscape in often unrelated stories that together are employed to describe the fabric of a social setting—devastated Baltimore in the first series, racist Yonkers in the second. The fifth and sixth episodes, the concluding parts, of *Show Me a Hero* sharply contrast the decaying, suicidal career politician, who does not realize, as his friend tells him, that there is a difference between votes and love, and the ascending curve of the minority families who are starting life anew in court-ordered housing in the white districts of the city. Thus the frequent juxtaposing of scenes between the lone, failed politician and the four minority families have an easily recognizable thematic rationale for the frequent cutting between them.

In contrast a more contemporary series such as *Mr. Robot* (2015–) often features a number of characters besides the primary character, Elliot, whose battle in his head with the conspiracy theorist and literal battle with the tech corporation is the main thrust of the series. These other characters' plights— such as that of Elliot's sister, Darlene, a hacker herself who flits in an out of the series and his consciousness—relate obliquely to the thematic of the series about technological oligarchy and conspiracy. Thus these multiple story lines function as both critique of the digital life, which the lead character expresses verbally, but also validation of its powers of distraction as part of the new spectacle of the digital universe.

In this way Adorno's "effect," the isolated unit that predominates over the whole, becomes reified into an ever-multiplying cascade of dispersions for the purpose simply of dispersing, not only within the narrative but also among television and various other social media. That is, the former Hollywood effect was the startling stand-alone event—the explosion, the earthquake, the building collapsing—while the contemporary "narrative" effect relies less on the event itself than on multiple, more minor, events cascaded as so many windows open at the same time on the screen, where the effect is the distraction itself, no longer as spectacular diversion, but now simply as distraction.

BARTHES'S CODES OF READING AND SERIALITY: HERMENEUTICS HYPOSTHESIZED AS HAPPY HOUR

In *S/Z*, a book itself with a mysterious title, semiologist (that is, decipherer of the [social] science of signs) Roland Barthes dynamically "reads" Balzac's novella *Sarrasine* as a means to elucidate the codes that prompt and condition a reader's response, chief among them being the hermeneutic or enigma code, continually posing questions and positing enigmas that may or may not be entirely answered in the text. A text, Barthes argues, is not static, but dynamically produced in the process of "reading" or, we may say, viewing, as it operates in conjunction with its audience to create its effect. Barthes's reading is not so much concerned with the text as a whole, as systematized meaning, as would be a more Aristotelian reading that might trace the key moments of a plot's instigation, development, and conclusion (Lesage 1977). Rather his concern is with how moment to moment the text elicits its reader on a variety of levels, which he groups under five codes and which are enhanced in the hyperindustrial era to further addictive viewing.

Proairetic or action codes govern the simple who, what, when, and where of the plot itself, moving the story along and planting "seeds" in the plot which will ripen later (Culler 1976). The hermeneutic or enigma codes structure the unfolding of the plot, mainly through a series of devices that suspend and retard the story by evading the truth ("snares"), mixing truth and deliberate obfuscation ("equivocations"), providing partial answers, and proclaiming the mystery or circumstance is unsolvable ("jammings"). For Barthes, this is the heart of the narrative, a process of concealing the truth from the reader or viewer in an attempt to "arrest the enigma, to keep it open" (Barthes 1974), with the enigma codes working at cross-purposes to the action codes to retard the narrative. Serial television runs largely on the development of the enigma codes and has a new reflexivity about that development as witness the famous line from the pilot of *Veronica Mars*, "These questions need answers" (Mittell 2015, 68).

The semic or character codes govern the establishment of character by ascribing certain qualities and emotions (which Barthes calls "semes") to a character through mode of dress, dialogue, and ways others speak of the character. The referential codes "refer" to the cultural background of the text in the present or the past and summon up commonly understood references to the world outside the text. Finally, the symbolic codes govern the play of symbols and thematic readings of the text, which works often through antitheses, or opposites such as servants/masters, rich/poor, power/dependence (Lesage 1977) and which also may work against the text by transgressively suggesting that these opposites may be more alike than we imagine.

Barthes develops his method in reading and deciphering the construction of a classical text by Balzac, but it might equally apply to contemporary television and particularly to a show such as *24* with a highly addictive component that is not merely as David Bordwell (1989) describes "cuing" its reader but is from moment to moment, through the hyperactivation of the Barthesian codes, attempting to induce a more frenzied response in creating a perpetual mood of suspense or heightened anxiety by, for example, retarding forward movement by continually rerunning and reworking similar motifs over the course of the series. The show was conceived not only to produce an addictive text but also an addicted viewer. In season 1, the superagent Jack Bauer's wife, Teri, and daughter, Kim, are kidnapped and released or fail to escape retribution at least three times. Also in the course of the twenty-four hours and twenty-four episodes of the first season a terrorist cell emerges and is then crushed by Bauer three times . The show operates by employing the 12-step group's "definition of insanity" of "doing the same thing over and over and getting the same results," but its narrative process suggests that insanity is the normal rhythm of post-9/11 life.

24 and Hyperaddictive Narration

One of the key moments in the transformation to a more addictive form of television seriality was the implementation of these heightened techniques in Rupert Murdoch's Fox network's series *24* with its hero Jack Bauer.[20] It was a transformation that, not unrelatedly, took place within the context of the 9/11 attacks, since the series was scheduled to premier just after the attacks and was hastily rewritten to incorporate the moment's ethos into the first season.

The series itself was perhaps the first to highlight in its very title that the point was less the content of the series than the thrilling ride on which it was taking its audience. The title did not refer to any point in the plot of the series but rather emphasized the heightened narrative device of a season comprising a single day with each of the twenty-four episodes the screen equivalent of one hour. The show was Fox's big-budget, blockbuster attention grabber for the 2001 television season and was also, because of its densely layered episodes, almost impossible to just drop in on for a single episode. As such it marked the beginning of serial binge watching. That the series was designed to be, or benefitted from being, consumed in an addictive frenzy was illustrated by the ratings jump of 25 percent in the third season after the DVD release of the first two seasons, which supposedly encouraged bingeing the entire season.[21]

Barthes had spoken of the reader being implicated in the perpetuation of the codes, particularly the enigmatic code, and of having an interest "in not knowing the truth" (Barthes 1974, 162) in order to prolong the pleasure of the text. He had equally discussed the difference between playing with the text, in an extended or repeated viewing or reading, and consuming it, "insisting that we must create, not consume, aesthetic meaning" (Lesage 1977). The addictive television text, though densely layered in a way that adds to its pleasure, is primarily constructed for consumption, with its viewer gleaning just enough to get to the next episode. Equally telling is that by the end of the season the viewer often finds the narrative struggle to be an empty one, as when Jack kills the ultimate terrorist, Drazen, the last of a terrorist cell that had been pursued all season, in a fairly standard shootout. (The more contemporary series *Arrow* follows the same pattern with the ultimate but pedestrian confrontation in the 2015–16 season between its superhero protagonist and the powerful super-villain Damien Darhk, who—once shorn of his magic—is bested in a street brawl.) Barthes speaks of narrative "noise" (Barthes 1974, 143), which indeed characterizes *24*.

We will now look at the following Barthesian categories and see how they apply to the series and further the addictive elements: the way what the series says on its surface, its denotation, implies a meaning, connotation, that promotes persistent fear that keeps the audience in a state of agitation; the use of time to suggest a perpetual present that eliminates any historical past and instead promotes constant flow; the devaluation of the referential and character codes and their subsumption under the enigma codes, which promote a frenzied forward thrust at the expense of more developed character traits or more dense references to the world of espionage or global events; and finally the lack of closure of the narrative, which, far from connoting openness, in its final moments refuses stasis and reflection and instead fosters anxiety and suggests perpetual movement as the "antidote" to reflection.

24 is an intense "signifying system," or as Barthes says in *S/Z*, signaling system; that is, it operates very viscerally at the level of denotation, in the ways it employs the enigma devices to both retard the narrative and to repeat it. (*Arrow*, one of *24*'s disciples, which ends its fourth season similar to the way it ended its first, with a madman trying to cleanse the world by destroying it, has its characters acknowledge this repetition of the narrative device to make it seem less like simply blatant repetition.) The series contains elements of mystery, with moles often hidden in the bowels of Bauer's counterterrorist unit, the CTU, but much more operates on the level of thriller, amping up and continually accelerating the tension. Barthes talks about the difference between "threat," "a closed structure requiring an end" and "danger," which may be "open" and "infinite" (Culler 1976, 204). Like the "War on Terror" itself, *24* is constructed on a series of threats, or immediate provocations of anxiety, while also prompting a generalized feeling of danger, which does not cease and which acts commercially to promote more intense viewing.

Episode 8 of season 1, the one-third point in the first season, contains as its dramatic centerpiece an attempt to assassinate the African American Senator Palmer while he is speaking at a rally on the eve of becoming the first black candidate for president from a major party (anticipating Obama's successful run four years later). Agent Bauer's wife, Teri, and daughter, Kim, have been kidnapped by the assassins, who will kill them if Bauer refuses to participate in their plans. This episode reaches its zenith when Palmer takes the stage and Bauer stands by idly watching the assassin drawing a bead on him. Rather than simply focusing on this moment, the show then cuts to the captured Teri, who has overheard that she and Kim are expendable. She tells Kim she loves her as a guard passes ominously outside in a way that, rather than being an easing of anxiety and a moment of intimacy, simply ratchets up the tension in this secondary story before the show cuts back to Jack, who in a moment of further tension is told the assassination will be over in five minutes.

Jack then foils the assassination by clandestinely grabbing for a Secret Service agent's gun in a way that alerts those guarding Palmer that he is in danger, and thus the primary threat of the episode is averted. But we immediately cut away from this scene as Gains, the terrorist who was commanding Jack, then orders Kim and Teri's death, suspecting Jack has betrayed him. Guns are then pointed at the women's heads in another moment of high tension, but at the last minute Gains decides he still needs them alive and has them led to him.

In the last shot of the episode, Jack, now suspected of attempting Palmer's assassination, is led off by government agents. The foiling of the assassination then led not to a relaxation of anxiety but to events responsible for an increase in tension.

24 uses the enigma devices (snares, equivocation, jamming) to continually suspend the narrative, but more importantly—and differently from what Barthes analyzes—it employs those devices in a way that is unceasing to continually rev up the viewer, commanding the addicted viewer it produces to never lower their vigilance. Much has been written about the connotation of the series, as, for example, promoting torture when later on Bauer actively participates in various ways in inflicting pain to extract information, rationalized by the argument that he needs the information immediately. The series also has been taken to task for its racial branding of terrorists as the global elite's other: swarthy "Serbians" in the first season, with their East European accents, Arabs in the second season; and in later seasons Africans. But, if, as Barthes declared, ideology not stated but implicitly affirmed has much more force (Calvet 1990, 132), then it is in its overriding message that *24* acts most effectively as an ideological tool.

The series is a signifying system whose connotation, whose signified, is fear. Be afraid, be very afraid, because you are never out of danger in a perpetual war—that is the statement that the signifiers are working overtime to produce. In their book *Guerres et Capital* Alliez and Lazzarrato (2016) argue that capital's never-ceasing interior accumulation of property is itself an unceasing civil war against women, workers, the impoverished, and immigrants and is of a piece with exterior wars where the capitalist state brandishes force directly (17). What is most striking about this formulation is its description of an unceasing quality and its uniting of interior and exterior. In its turning of the home front into a battlefield, *24* illustrates and validates this proposition. The enigma codes here act to produce a text whose argument is that the frenzy of the chase justifies its existence. This correlates exactly with the commercial imperative of sustaining an audience through its twenty-four episodes.

Other aspects of the text ratify this presentiment, particularly the use of the mechanics and devices of time to signify a perpetual present where there is never time to question or draw conclusions, that is, to study the past or construct a less frightful and more thoughtful future. Jack Bauer's opening narration, which provides the series recap, begins: "*Right now, terrorists are planning to assassinate a presidential candidate.*" The show's creator, Joel Surnow, referred to *24* as "a race against the clock," and the clock, the present moment, is emphasized continually in a way that is exterior to the content of the series. The show's logo, appearing in the opening shot, is simply the clock reading 24. The title *24* does not explain or comment on or ask a question about the subject of the series, as many titles do. It simply reaffirms the gimmicks of "real time," where each show takes place over the course of an hour, with the ticking, pulsating clock opening and closing each act. Episodes have no titles but are simply named by the time period that bounds them; the title of episode 8 of season 1 is "7:00 a.m.–8:00 a.m."

Real time, oddly, includes time out for commercials which may cover character's mundane actions, such as when the CTU's Tony Almeida sends a car to pick up fellow agent Nina Myers from the field. This inclusion in a way ratifies and naturalizes the entry of merchandising into the hyperspectacle of capitalist life under fire and relates to George Bush's urging shortly after the event occurred to stop mourning 9/11 and instead "keep shopping."[22] The title also necessitated changing the series' format at the time so the show would run twenty-four instead of the standard twenty-two weeks. Because of the intensity of the series, its presentness, Fox attempted as much as possible to run the series continuously over twenty-four weeks rather than, as was usual, divide the season into two halves with the midway point signaled by the Christmas break.[23]

The show prides itself on not using slow motion, a device to slow down time, or flashbacks, which suggest that the past may be impinging on the present. (An interesting modification is *Arrow*'s season 4 use of flashbacks of Oliver Queen's return to the island that created him as Arrow. Here flashbacks run with a scene length much shorter than the present and are constructed as short bursts of action always ending with a cliffhanger, turning the past into a more frantic reflection of the present.) Time is also often referred to in the dialogue: in Bauer's admonition to Nina, "We're fighting the clock here"; in his extension of time to torture a witness, "Give me more time with him"; and in his condensation of time as a threat to another suspect, "You've had enough time" (Peacock 2007).

The other part of the show's presentness is the concentration on at least four major strands of the story and the emphasis, visually through the four-window split screen at the beginning and end of each episode, on amplifying the enigmatic codes by increasing the tension in each of the major strands. These strands break down roughly as the CTU itself, the villains, Jack Bauer, and Bauer's family (his wife and daughter). All are either in danger or under threat most of the time. In many ways, the show assumes a form similar to D. W. Griffith's *Intolerance* (1916), with its parallel telling of four stories of intolerance from four different periods of history in an attempt to understand intolerance throughout history in a stasis that is achieved only with intolerance narrowly being thwarted in the final, contemporary episode. Though *24* lifts the device, it drains that film of its meaning. In the series, distances are spatial, not temporal, and as we saw in episode 8 and as we shall see at the end of the season, stasis is never actually achieved. There is no final time for reflection, only again a continual present. The split screen also recalls the capitalist stock exchanges of New York, Tokyo, Frankfurt, and London, which if added together themselves constitute another twenty-four, the perpetual time of the market. Marx reminds us that under capitalism any kernel of the present may be a sedimented view of the whole history of development in the past (Alliez and Lazzarato 2016). As an echo of Fukiyama's "end of history," *24* trumpets the triumph of capital, which reaffirms that there is no past, only a capitalist present, but one that is far from reassuring. The present, with globalism's contradictions in full play, is fearful, and *24* argues through its signifying system that it is better to enjoy the adrenaline rush of danger than waste time contemplating why the threat exists.[24]

The show also operates by devaluing the character and referential codes in favor of an overvaluation of the action and enigma codes. The semes that build both characters and character relations are wafer thin, and the show spends little time in their construction. Thus, when Nina returns to the CTU and is visibly shaken, Tony grabs her hand, the mark of a relationship that he hopes will deepen, but she seems oblivious as they continue to talk about Jack and danger. Relationships go on around—and as an adjunct to—fear. Likewise, Jack is told at the assassination site that if he intervenes the terrorists will still assassinate Palmer and kill his family anyway. He has no reaction to this dilemma;

he just moves relentlessly forward. Finally, the immediate mole at the CTU is revealed to be Jamey, who by appearance is coded as a Latina, but whose name refuses that ethnicity. "Jamey" is judged to be a traitor by Tony and Nina, and this permits all kinds of intrusion into her life. Nina sadistically describes her as "squirming" over their discovery of a lie she has told concerning the where-abouts of Jack. Tony then rousts her by peering over the top of the ladies-room toilet to catch her on the phone. Finally, she is cuffed to a desk and roughly thrown by Tony into a chair. The part of the semic code that is her heritage is hinted at but suppressed in the dialogue, and once she is identified as a traitor, mental suffering, sexual harassment, and physical torture—performed by the duo of a Caucasian man and woman—are condoned and subsumed under the imperative to find out what she knows in order to save the life of the white patriarch, Jack.

As for the referential codes, those that refer to the outside world, they are seldom invoked beyond a simple connotation of terror with a similarly simple rationale. The show in its sanctioning of torture was so antagonistic that at one point in its run military representatives met with the producers to ask them to tone down the graphic scenes of torture since they were thought to be damaging the reputation of American troops abroad.[25] In addition, in the era of Serial TV simple referential codes have been augmented by intertextual references "to the culture at large to flatter the viewers who catch the reference" (Polan 2007, 280), which is again a kind of hypercoding pioneered in the era of branding that has magnified since Barthes's time.

Given these considerations, it seems almost ludicrous to maintain, as Steven Johnson (2006, 1370–73) does, that while "The content of the show may be about revenge killings and terrorist attacks . . . the collateral learning involves something altogether different, and more nourishing. It's about relationships." Instead, the lack of context and character development, and the concentration on the now, privileges the forward progress of a narrative which is entirely about instilling fear while glamorizing a world of perpetual terror by presenting it as an endorphin rush.

The symbolic codes, which for Barthes operate simultaneously with the action and enigma codes, often work through an emphasis on antithesis, on opposites, and may include an excessive element that disrupts the narrative

(Lesage 1977). The main antitheses in *24* as a whole and in season 1 episode 8 is family/country and terrorist / law enforcer. Jack's conflict in the episode is how to save his family and thwart the assassination, that is, stop the terrorists. This seeming pitting of family against country is of course not a real opposition, since the bourgeois family order is, though currently under attack by the selling imperative of mobile media, still the basis of the capitalist contractual system that Barthes claims underlies classical narrative. So, in one sense, there is no conflict between the bourgeois family and a state terror system that promotes it, but in another sense, the show's focusing on the persistent danger that Kim and Teri are in suggests unwittingly that the violence inherent in that family system projected out into the world through the state has come home to roost.

The other symbolic opposition of terrorist / law enforcer is one that many contemporary series struggle with. The question of *The Walking Dead* is all about how much of yourself you can lose battling the "zombies" before you have lost your soul, and indeed with the US having destroyed Iraq and Libya and participating in the destruction of Syria and now Yemen, this is a formidable question. The *24* variant has Jack moving further outside the law in his use of torture techniques in the course of the series; that is, increasingly he looks like a terrorist himself. In episode 8, he is much more victimized. It is his protégé, Tony Almeida, in dealing with the traitor Jamey, who plays the part of the intimidating lawman whose actions mark him as crossing over the legal line, including sexual harassment or worse in his rousting her from the woman's bathroom. The symbolic codes constantly suggest that the lines between these supposed opposites are permeable, and that is why, as opposed to Balzac's classic text in which the codes were equals, here the action and enigma codes simply overwhelm any questions that the symbolic raises. As they must if the war of "opposites"—which look more and more alike—is to continue.

One of the most startling plot devices on *24* is its habit of killing off lead characters. In one latter season almost the entire CTU staff had been "disappeared" except for series perennial Chloe O'Brian. This device premiered and was most startlingly engineered in season 1, with the death of Jack's wife, revealed in the last scene of the final episode of that season. Barthes pointed out

Unrelenting pressure at the season's end of *24*.

that the action and enigma codes "must function until the end" (Barthes 1974, 189), the point when the final mystery is resolved, when stasis is achieved. This series heralds a new era, that of the hyperindustrial code, where stasis is never achieved. In the final episode, Jack defeats and kills Drazen and all his men, the third terrorist cell in the season. Nina Myers is revealed as a second, more deadly mole within the CTU and is arrested. Jack returns to the CTU to reunite with his wife Teri, and in the last scene finds her dead, a victim of Nina, and the season ends with Jack holding her in his arms, crying in anguish, in the show's most startling death. There is no reprieve from what Jack calls in the summary narrative "the longest day of my life." It ends not in stasis, but in one of the season's highest moments of tension. That is, the ending is not an ending but culminates rather in the additional device of the startling death of a series character to keep the War on Terror open, to signal that indeed it does not end and that fear, anxiety, and tension in the post-9/11 world replace any stasis.[26] But also and at the same time, it keeps open the promise for the audience of an addictive rush that will continue into the next season.

Autism and addiction, the psychological conditions par excellence of hyperindustrial capital, each in their own way devaluing human relationships, are promoted in the serial television form. Autism is, in its contemporary media presentation, the emptied-out sign of the utopian dream of a high-functioning worker shorn of interpersonal conflicts. Addiction, through the hyperactivation of the codes of narration, produces a viewing mechanism that seals this new worker into a hyperactive process. This process, rather than a moment of relaxation, becomes instead a constant prodding to be ever vigilant in promoting a form of relating that is antithetical to relationships but that is now necessary in a world where the only true values are those of the imperatives of a now more openly warlike capitalist accumulation.

SERIALITY AND POLITICAL ECONOMY

Flexibility and Dominance in the New Television

> We've concluded the consumer is king. Remaining a slave to
> fixed consumption would be a huge mistake and at Disney
> we're refusing to do that.
>
> Robert Iger, Disney CEO

> "Pray, sir," said Candide to the Abbé, "how many theatrical
> pieces have you in France?"
>
> "Five or six thousand," replied the other.
>
> "Indeed! That is a great number," said Candide. "But how many
> are any good?"
>
> "About fifteen or sixteen."
>
> "Oh! That is a great number," said Martin [the Cynic].
>
> Voltaire, *Candide*

CONTEMPORARY TELEVISION IS CELEBRATED for now (finally) being attuned
to a viewer or consumer who it attempts to serve by supposedly overwhelming
them with choices not only of what but also of when to watch. As one technology writer put it at the turn of this century, "Whatever show you want, when-
ever you want, on whatever screen you want" (Lotz 2014, 217). Since 2011,
television-series production has increased 71 percent in the US, with Netflix
alone now claiming it will offer seven hundred original series in 2018 after
increasing its original programming to one thousand hours in 2017.[1] There
is so much "choice" that a device is now being popularized that enables *speed
watching* where it is possible to view a fifty-two-minute episode in thirty-nine
minutes with the image sped up slightly but with sound at normal speed.[2]

However, this cornucopia of viewing opportunities is set against a background of increasing centralization and conglomeration and a neoliberal ethos in which everything is for sale, including Fordist-era "free TV." Thus 2015's FCC rejection of the Comcast-Time Warner cable merger yielded to 2016's Charter-Time Warner merger, giving the two companies control of cable access to a majority of major US markets with the almost immediate result that Charter-Time Warner cable rates rose immediately and data speeds slowed.[3] Meanwhile the miracle of OTT (over the top) television watching, where viewers cut their cable cord and stream from a variety of sources, is beginning to look simply like the process of convincing TV watchers to pay in new and different ways for what was in the old days free TV.

Series themselves are more than ever created with smaller but more upwardly mobile consumer groups in mind, accompanied by algorithms that align specific demographic units with their matching tastes in a sleight of hand that is termed "personalization" (a process intimately bound up, it is now emerging, with data mining [Wu 2016]). Industry insiders are often hermetically sealed from the continuing global economic crisis in the wake of the financial collapse of 2008 and its attendant widening of the income gap. They speak of a "poverty problem," which they see as the question of whether impoverished viewers rather than subscribing to Hulu, Netflix, or Amazon may instead "opt" for a third daily meal while consuming free older catalogs of TV shows and movies in an environment where "40 percent of American households [are] 'essentially bereft of discretionary spending power'" (Moffett 2011).

Meanwhile, the streaming services and particularly Netflix, the most successful among them, have begun to look and program like the television networks of old. Netflix inundates its subscribers with new series. However, the repetitive and knock-off quality of its average series, rather than suggesting the utopia of a new golden age of television, instead harks back to the "vast wasteland" of network TV and to cable's nine hundred channels with nothing to watch. Even Amanda Lotz, among the most exuberant cheerleaders for the "new television," concedes that viewers may "win some victories but so long as most of the country has only one choice for broadband service [the route of access to the American home], the spoils will be minimal" (Lotz 2014, 3826).

Nevertheless, and in spite of these commercial constraints, the art of the serial form of storytelling continues to advance as showrunners persist in using the form to explore social and class tensions of the past and the present and to chart in a sublimated way, through complex narrative patterns, the inequalities and injustices that they are only too well aware of from dealing with the corporate ethos of their own industry.

This chapter first outlines the shift from network to cable to online-streaming services and the new dominance of the serial form in series production in all three television arenas. The emphasis here is on how traditional patterns of power and production have continued to control and influence these shifts, with the most prominent cable stations largely owned by the networks and with the streaming services employing far more network patterns of production and narration than is acknowledged. This section concludes with an examination of the similarities and differences in episodes of series on network (*The Office*), cable / pay-per-view (*The Larry Sanders Show*), and streaming services (*Orange Is the New Black*). The chapter then highlights how the dramatic serial form is consistently at odds with commercial imperatives and may challenge those imperatives on network, cable, and streaming television, focusing on the specific case of *Fringe* and its troubled history with the Fox network.

Network, Cable, and Streaming Seriality: Decentered Centralization and Stultifying Variety

The total dominance of television's network era lasted approximately thirty years, from 1950 to 1980, and coincided with the Fordist era of factory production, which saw for the most part profits and wages rise together. Leisure was mass-produced, and its television component was free, though rigidly controlled with essentially three programming options, ABC, CBS, and NBC. The monopoly practices developed in the network era and extended into the period of cable dominance were adaptations of the earlier classical era of cinema, which was essentially controlled by eight studios. With the arrival of cable stations in the early 1980s—at the dawn of the neoliberal era and in the moment when deregulation prompted both decentered production and more concentrated ownership—the networks, though ostensibly losing their power as their ratings declined, moved, as the film studios were doing, from being single entities to being part of a conglomeration where in fact the power of a few large companies increased.[4]

The networks, as had the film studios, created a system where they controlled production through distribution, deciding which shows got on the air and when, at the same time acting like banks to the studios that produced the shows. Actual banks were often unwilling to lend to producers to finance series production since the majority of series were not profitable. Instead financing came through networks "leasing" the shows, which gave them the right of initial broadcast and subsequent broadcast in reruns on the network. It was then up to the production company (sometimes a film studio) to resell the show in syndication to other stations in the US, internationally, and later on cable, with five seasons or one hundred episodes being the acceptable standard for a show to be sold. By the time of syndication, the producing company could be as much as $44 million in debt due to the difference between the (increasing) costs of producing the show and the fee paid by the network (Lotz 2014, 2320).[5] The narrative form adopted for series in the network era, a form especially suited to syndication, was episodic television where each episode was a self-contained unit with minimal character change or evolution and minimal story continuity.

With the rise of cable, the networks argued emphatically that their power was to a great extent eroded. In 2014 the audience for the three original networks amounted to only 33 percent of television viewers, down from almost 70 percent in 1985–86, with cable boasting almost half of the audience (Peers 2003). Their argument was accepted, and they were allowed to engage in the monopolistic practices of owning more stations and of producing series themselves,[6] shifting power again away from studios and independent producers, who had gained a wider market to sell series, and back toward networks, who were now creating their own flagship series. Ironically, it was ABC, always the Johnny-come-lately network searching for a new approach, that, in its big-budget extravaganza productions, pioneered network seriality, partly as an attempt to keep up with the popularity of the form as it had already developed in cable. The 2004 series *Lost* and *Desperate Housewives* (2004–12) brought seriality to network television by adopting earlier serial formats as a model. *Lost* with its *Island of Lost Souls* (1932) aspects was partially modelled on Hollywood Saturday afternoon B serials, and *Desperate Housewives* was modeled on the successful serial pattern of daytime soaps.[7]

Cable, which at first seemed to have broken the power of the networks, in fact did nothing of the sort as (a) the networks expanded into cable, and (b) in this era the four networks (the big three plus Fox) became part of vertically integrated media conglomerates that included the networks themselves, their cable stations, production houses, and in the latest ownership wrinkle, cable companies as well. Thus the cable-delivery-system Comcast bought NBC and then was barely thwarted from merging with Time Warner, the other leading cable system and the leading producer of series. The Big 5 companies control 70 percent of cable stations (News Corporation: Fox with FX; Disney: ABC with ESPN and Disney channels; National Amusements: CBS and Viacom with Nickelodeon, Comedy Central, and MTV; Comcast: NBC with Syfy and USA; and Time Warner: TBS, TNT, CW network, HBO)[8] and reach 80 percent of prime-time viewers. Christopher Anderson argues that from the viewpoint of ownership, "the American television industry hasn't changed all that much since the days when three networks dominated the industry. Power is still concentrated in very few hands" (Anderson 2005, 77). By 2003, twenty of the top twenty-five cable channels were owned by the five companies listed above (Peers 2003).[9] In addition, with the recent buying of the Fox cable stations by Disney, concentration will increase as the Big 5 becomes the Big 4.

There was, though, a change in revenue streams, which also prompted the rise of Serial TV, with 2013 being the watershed year when, for the first time in television, subscriptions to cable and streaming providers generated more revenue (53 percent) than advertising (47 percent) (Lotz 2014, 3894). Together these were part of a total revenue stream of $142 billion in profits.[10] Serial series then evolved into an effective branding mechanism that enhanced cable profits by increasing the value of advertising and the number of subscriptions.

However, the atmosphere in which these series were generated was one where again monopolistic practices dating from the classical cinema studio era still reigned. In producing their own series, broadcasting them on their own networks, and then syndicating them to their own and other cable stations, the networks are practicing a form of vertical integration reminiscent of the monopolistic practices of classical era Hollywood majors who shot their own films, distributed them, and exhibited them in their own theaters.[11] The network conglomerates also blackmailed cable companies into accepting their less-popular cable stations in exchange for free access to the network stations in a return to what in the studio era was called blind booking, where exhibitors were forced to accept less-popular films sight unseen in return for gaining access to the studio blockbusters (Peers 2003).[12] The networks have also continued a long-running practice of packaging weaker new entries with stronger ones in their "upfront" or prebroadcast sale to advertisers that is analogous to the studio era's monopolistic practice of block booking, making exhibitors buy less-desired films in order to get access to the studio's top-of-the-line product (Lotz 2014, 4155).

Rather than diminishing the power of the networks, conglomerates, during the twenty-year reign of cable that ran from roughly the 1990s to the first decade of the new millennium, in some ways consolidated network broadcasting dominance and increased monopolistic practices. High-definition TV innovation suffered as the networks became more interested in expanding revenue by multiplexing their channels; that is, showing their old series on network-knock-off, cable-like channels, rather than creating new channels (Lotz 2014, 2101). In addition, the networks were often able to demand a share of syndication profits from producers since it was now more difficult for an outside producer to lease a show to the network because the networks were producing their own shows (2364).

Conglomerates, to lock out independents, now also participated in cable coproductions, such as Fox and Sony Pictures Television co-creating *The Shield* (2002–8), a moneymaker for both studios. The raw, gritty look of that show, an attraction to its cable viewers, was used to justify cutting production costs of the average studio-produced series from $1.8–2.2 million per episode down to $1.3 million, partly by shooting each episode in seven rather than the usual nine days (Lotz 2014, 5511). Conglomerates equally used the synergy in their long tentacles to hold advertisers at bay. When Mattel threatened to cut off advertising because Viacom/CBS refused to run in prime time *Barbie in the Nutcracker*, a Christmas special the toymaker had produced, the network famously diffused the situation by threatening to blacklist Mattel from all the conglomerate's channels, including MTV, VH1, and BET (Peers 2003). The conglomerates also engaged in practices that short-circuited artists' rights in their in-house sale of product, as was revealed when David Duchovny won a lawsuit against Fox in which he claimed that in selling episodes of the actor's series *The X-Files* (1993–2002, 2016, 2018) below market value to its cable station FX the company had diminished his revenues (Lotz 2014, 2382).

CABLE PLENITUDE: OLD SHOWS IN OLD BOTTLES

By the end of the unchallenged-network era, in roughly 1980, this mode of transmission was so dominant that the year before when asked in a survey if they preferred TV or "daddy," 44 percent of four-to-six-year-olds answered "TV" (Nelson 1979). In the combined network-cable era that dominance increased with, by the mid-2000s, 90 percent of American homes wired for cable, satellite, or computer transmission (Lotz 2014, 1396).

The rise of cable has contributed greatly to the rise of television seriality, and both have been intimately tied to the commercial process of branding of cable stations, since each station often seeks a small but targeted and affluent audience, so much so that these audiences are sometimes referred to as "gated informational communities" (Lotz 2014, 1049). To attract these "communities," who are after all paying for cable television, "textual elements"—characters, story lines, special effects—took precedence over the networks attempts at seizing audiences by controlling distribution (Polan 2007, 277). Particularly important in HBO's creating of its brand of "quality television" to distinguish itself from network TV was a blurring of the boundaries between stand-alone episodes and "plots that remained unresolved over a series of episodes," or "cumulative narration" (278), i.e., Serial TV. HBO, a premium channel that required viewers to pay fees above the basic cable fee, also disdained that other network staple, advertising, claiming that it did not even accept product placement, another more subliminal form of advertising that locates itself within the narrative framework (Lotz 2014, 5331).

A modified version of branding, of producing "quality television," was then adopted by the network-owned cable channels, with the prestige of the series producing three commercial effects or sources of profit. First, with a prestigious series, the channel itself gets better known, something called in the business the "halo effect," and then can negotiate a higher carrier fee from the cable operator. With the success of *Mad Men* (2008–11), AMC doubled its fee from 20 cents per cable subscriber to 40 cents (Owen 2011). Second, on the standard Big 5 cable channels once a series brand establishes the channel, as *Queer Eye for the Straight Guy* (2003–7) did for Bravo, *The Shield* for FX, and *Mad Men* for AMC (Lotz 2014, 4603), advertising dollars increase not only for the particular series but, with the halo effect, potentially for other series on the channel that are part of the brand. Third, once the serial format was ratified by critics and audiences, the cable series itself may be syndicated either to other cable channels, as *The Shield* was sold to Spike, or to the networks, as the CW, owned jointly by CBS and Time Warner, ran AMC's *The Walking Dead*.

Branding, partially through the use of seriality, can also be employed to expand a channel's audience, as Bonnie Hammer of NBC's Syfy claims that the channel's move to more prestigious series coincident with *Battlestar Galactica* (2004–9) was an attempt to move away from the "fanboy world of dark and horrific science fiction" to "the world of the fantastical" (Owen 2011)—code for retaining the bloodthirsty younger audience of series like *Van Helsing* (2016–) while adding an older audience with series like *12 Monkeys* (2015–18). Branding also distinguishes one channel from another as they compete for similar audiences. Thus, NBC's Hammer viewed that network's USA channel as competing for a similar younger-male audience as Fox's FX, but with its shows (*White Collar* [2009–14], *Burn Notice* [2007–13], *Psych* [2006–14]) stressing a more "aspirational," "blue skies" approach with characters that are "flawed but . . . not dysfunctional" as opposed to Fox's FX dramas such as *The Shield*, with its near-fascist cop, and comedies such as *Its Always Sunny in Philadelphia* (2005–), with its amoral, entitled grouping of characters reminiscent of *Seinfeld* (1990–98) but with a nastier outlook (Owen 2011). This battle also carries into cable the network battle between the more standard, upbeat major three networks and the more cynical, "edgier," one-time upstart, Fox.

Similar branding wars affect premium or pay channels, with Starz, which on average costs 15 percent less to subscribe to than HBO, positioning itself as a kind of knock-off version of that channel, with its shows less concerned with "serious character development" and more blatantly featuring sex and violence in a more naked and less refined state. Thus *Spartacus* (2010–13) was a low-end version of HBO's *Rome* (2005–7), and the Michael Bay–produced pirate fantasy *Black Sails* (2014–17) is a more straightforward sex-and-violence version of *Game of Thrones*. Nevertheless, despite the heavy commercial overlay involved in branding, different channels make different choices. The often more politically involved and critical HBO series—most striking case in point, *Deadwood* (2004–6), a satire of Reagan-Bush era neoliberalism in the guise of a Western[13]—are stunningly opposite its main competitor Showtime's simply exploitative *Californication* (2007–14), its "morally complex" vigilante-serial-killer series *Dexter* (2006–13), and its espionage series *Homeland*, which as it progressed has become more and more politically reactionary.

The discussion of prestige and quality television however also conceals the standard nature of cable fare and its branded channels. These high-quality serial series, with the same episodes being repeated several times a week on the channels, conceal the fact that the vast majority of programming consists of old movies and network reruns. FX, for example, "makes more money off reruns of *Two and a Half Men* (2003–15) than its original programs" (Lotz 2014, 5606). The prestigious series themselves are much shorter than network series, often between ten and thirteen episodes for a season rather than twenty-two, and the cable channels produce far fewer series than do the networks.[14] Cable channels are also advertising platforms, or billboards, or shills, for their parent companies, with CBS seeing a 23 percent increase in its female audience for *Survivor* after running a "documentary" on the series on MTV (5630).

Contrary to the view of cable as a fertile ground for series experimentation is the fact that most cable viewers watch very few channels. Thus, in 2013 the average home received 189 channels but watched only seventeen (Lotz 2014, 1515). As the cable companies have demanded higher transmission fees, more and more, and especially younger, viewers, are unhooking from cable bundles that present mediocrity as abundance.

The Streaming Era: Let 1000 Serial Series Bloom, Though 999 of Them We've Seen Before

> Power is moving away from those who own and manage the
> media to a new and demanding generation of consumers—
> consumers who are better educated, unwilling to be led, and
> who know that in a competitive world they can get what they
> want, when they want it.
>
> —Fox's Rupert Murdoch

"Don't believe the hype," Public Enemy warned on their album *It Takes a Nation
of Millions to Hold Us Back*, and it is very difficult not to be overwhelmed by the
industry and scholarly celebration of the "post-network era" (Lotz 2014), an
era when free choice reigns and power is now concentrated in the hands of the
consumer. "Television is no longer a linear trickle of programming dictated by
network executives, but has swelled into a wide ocean of content that viewers
can dip into at will" (Lotz 2014, 3095). This is an era where "time shifting"
and twenty-four-hour availability has freed the viewer from the shackles and
"control" of the "staid domestic norm" (548) of network prime time to instead
emphasize "convenience" (1589) as streaming service customers can "choose
among programs produced in any decade, by amateurs and professionals, and
[choose] to watch this programming on demand on . . . 'living room' sets,
computer screens, or portable devices" (828).[15]

This liberatory jargon of course originates with the industry itself, with
Netflix's CEO and cofounder Reed Hastings declaring "linear television is
dead."[16] That service now accounts for 25 percent of North American internet
traffic,[17] and it had in the last quarter of 2016 signed 5.1 million customers
internationally while that year opening in 130 new countries.[18] A headline in
the *Financial Times* proclaimed the company was "on track to hit 100 million
customers after record growth,"[19] which it then claimed to have accomplished
in April 2017.[20] Netflix is the largest streaming service in the world, except for a
Chinese service which exceeds it and with which Netflix has now partnered.[21]

Much of this drive has been fueled by Serial TV series and Netflix's pioneering of binge watching with its release of all episodes of a single season at
one time. The service—now sometimes referred to as a network, suggesting
its continuation rather than abrupt break with the old order—produced one

thousand hours of programming in 2017, an increase of 40 percent from its six hundred hours in 2016, with much of that production being its thirty Serial TV series.

There are caveats, though, to this brave new age. As was pointed out in chapter 2, time-shifting, a boon to the consumer, is often necessary for the harried worker—the actual, not mythical, consumer—now working two to three jobs, for whom prime time's three-hour block of leisure has long since disappeared. Also, the "wide ocean of content viewers can dip into at will" Lotz celebrates is contingent on the fact that "they are willing and able to pay directly for content and services that enable such flexible, non-linear use" (Lotz 2014, 3095). So, these workers, forced out of prime time, now must pay for the privilege of being able to recoup on the run a few moments of a leisure time that used to come to them for free. This is neoliberal or "entrepreneurial" entertainment, where everything is for sale all the time. In addition, what is convenient for the consumer is cost cutting for distributors like Netflix, which no longer have to pay the expense of shipping and mailing DVDs as in the era of hard copies of content.[22]

There are a whole new set of players in the postnetwork era (Facebook, Amazon, Netflix, Google—known collectively as FANG, an acronym that suggests the level of ruthlessness in this new digital world) and new manufactures of hardware (Apple). However, in hardware the network-era manufactures (Sony, Samsung, Panasonic) are still prevalent, and in television programming the new players serve as purveyors of the content of the Big 5. When manufacturing their own content they adapt many of the industry practices to the (only slightly modified) postnetwork era. As opposed to the argument that "the very existence of media conglomerates" are being radically shaped "by technology and changing consumer habits" (Lotz 2014, 1299), Janet Wasko (1994) concludes that Hollywood studios (and, we could add, the combination of studios and networks), as part of well-heeled transnational conglomerate organizations, "will continue to be the dominant force in guiding whatever models prevail."

Netflix itself is first of all a purveyor of Big 5 content, having built its initial reputation on absorbing studio and independent films and making them easier to rent than video chains like Blockbuster, first through the mail and then digitally. This "abundance" is similar to the cable model of unlimited film reruns. Through complex licensing agreements, the network also leases old and contemporary Big 5 television series, again in the model of cable's syndicating of network-series content. The upstart company also works in synergy with the established conglomerates in promoting their current product by giving its members access to entire series back catalogs to the extent that *Variety*, in the wake of a boost in audience for the final season of *Breaking Bad* (2008–13), asked if perhaps the studios should be paying Netflix rather than the other way around (Lotz 2014, 3465).

Netflix has been praised for its quality series, but as it moves into mass production the company is adopting more of a standard network-and-cable model of producing a few quality, and many more mediocre, series; the twist being that each series is meant for a particular boutique audience rather than a mass audience. There is a heavily derivative quality to the series' content, which is drawn from studio blockbusters past and present as well as network and cable series. Thus *The Expanse* (2015–) is warmed-over *Battlestar Galactica* with much less at stake than the fate of the galaxy and shorn of the 9/11 references. The 2016 hit *Stranger Things*, with its children's investigation of alien creatures, recalls *E.T. the Extra-Terrestrial* (1982), *The Goonies* (1985), and more recently with the focus on 1980s technology, *Super 8* (2011). Elsewhere *Sense8* (2015–17), with its multiple characters in a utopian futurist setting, is *Cloud Atlas* (2012) remade for streaming, and *Frontier* (2016–), with fur traders in a bloody and savage wilderness, is *The Revenant* (2015), complete with its lead character in series publicity in Leonardo DiCaprio pose. Finally there is *Girlboss* (2017)—"She's saucy, sassy"—and so was Zooey Deschanel six years earlier when the Netflix show's prototype, *New Girl* (2011–), first appeared.

Critically praised Netflix series, such as *The Crown* (2016–), draw comparison to the HBO model of quality television. But they also remind us that that term is one which was constructed along joint industry-scholarly lines and may represent a place where cultural elites "have intensified the legitimation of television . . . preserving their own privileged status in return" (Cardwell 2007, 29–30). All this occurs in an era in which "meaningfulness itself becomes a marketing strategy to be trotted out at the right moment . . . a mere tactic among many others . . . where morality and meaning only matter so far as they remain saleable" (Polan 2007, 274).

Netflix operates also like a standard network in sometimes co-creating and other times leasing series from either independents or from media conglomerate producers—series it claims as its own. Thus *House of Cards*, the first series to have released an entire season at once, capitalized on the new profitability of steaming TV by adopting a financial mode analogous to the entry of hedge funds into independent cinema before the 2008 financial crash. The streaming service leased the show from the studio Media Rights Capital, which is backed by, among others, AT&T and Goldman Sachs (currently starring in its own Washington power play as its members are once again prominent in a presidential cabinet, which casts doubt on the seriousness of the show's critique). After four seasons Media Rights is able to syndicate the series (Lotz 2014, 2356) and thus is as prominent in its profitability as the streaming service. Netflix's other most highly touted series, *Orange Is the New Black*, is produced by Lionsgate, a standard producer of network and studio fare.

In the Netflix era—whose players also include Amazon, the Big 5–sponsored Hulu, and the networks themselves, who are creating their own streaming services and releasing their own back catalog of programs—data on subscriptions and viewer algorithms have replaced ratings, with an attendant slippage in transparency. Netflix tracks series viewers methodically but will not reveal those figures, instead concentrating solely on its overall subscribers. This gives the impression that the network's series are all successes and are all equal just by being bunched together on the website. Thus two of the worst-ever reviewed series, Netflix's French entry *Marseille* (2016) ("In refined language, this would be called an industrial accident. More colloquially, this is cowshit") and the network's epic adventure series *Marco Polo* (2014–) (a "Khan job" with Netflix's algorithms compared to the "villainous Mongrel" of the series),[23] were both renewed, supposedly because they had accomplished their tasks of, respectively, signing up French viewers and attracting Asian viewers. Thus, we have a ratings system, but one that is no longer transparent and that does not seem to respond to criticism.

In the network era, programming was done by slavishly following one successful series with others like it so that the field then became overrun with similar series until another hit was discovered and a new cycle began. This was the basis of the earliest dramatic-series programming at Warner Bros., the first studio to swing into industrial series production, flooding the airwaves with young, hip range-riders in Westerns (*Maverick* [1957–62], *Cheyenne* [1955–63]) and young, hip detectives in sexy locales (*77 Sunset Strip* [1958–64], *Hawaiian Eye* [1959–63]).[24] The equivalent in the Netflix era is the algorithm that selects films and series for viewers to watch based on previous selections and that, in the industry's public-relations parlance, claims to ensure more customer satisfaction than studio and network promotion (Lotz 2014, 2989). This however is a very low bar. Compared to the satisfaction of discovering a stimulating new series, the algorithms that select series of a similar type instead manufacture an aura of sameness, with series that are similar to but most often lesser than the series the viewer has initially discovered on his or her own. Indeed, the overwhelming flooding of series in all kinds of niches presents more than ever the question of how to discriminate between them, and the algorithm is in actuality often no better than network era promotion; it just induces a more personalized sameness rather than the network's mass lethargy.

In terms of production norms, it is crucial to point out that the goal of industrializing (mechanizing) serial production is both extremely attainable and possibly sought-after, so much so that a form that came into being for its, as Mittell says, "complexity" and thoroughness in involving viewers in a continuing story world can become rote. In this new twist the serial element, instead of expanding the narrative, becomes a trait that limits complexity and routinizes the storyworld. Let's take two examples, *Longmire* (2012–) and *Jessica Jones* (2015–). Both series, coproduced by Netflix, are kinds of detective dramas, though the latter is also a Marvel superhero series. Both begin with an interesting interplay between the episodic and serial forms, but both then move into "pure seriality," dropping the case-of-the-week element of the series. *Longmire* originated on the cable channel A&E and in its first three seasons featured a running narrative involving the sheriff's interaction with his careerist deputy and the deputy's cutthroat businessman father as well as individual stories often involving tribal life on the nearby reservation. Once Netflix took over the series in season 4, it moved to being more strongly centered on Longmire's entrapment by and subsequent pursuit of first the now-dead deputy's father and then two additional archenemies, an oilman and the Native American owner of a casino. The tribal dynamics, which had stressed the exploitation but also resistance of those on the "res" became instead a subplot about a tribal avenger. The condensing of complicated multifaceted stories into one or two more intensely pursued stories involving fewer characters was a way of streamlining writing and production by simplifying through manufacturing an industrializing seriality that reduced to an intense streamable and bingeable few relationships what was once a more complicated multiverse.

Jessica Jones, based on the little-known Marvel comic, stars *Don't Trust the B in Apartment 23*'s (2012–14) Krysten Rytter as a protopunk detective in Manhattan's Hell's Kitchen and—unlike Marvel/Netflix's prior effort *Daredevil* (2015), set in the same part of the city—uses New York location shooting, enhanced by Rytter's own quasi street toughness, which gives this series a bit of a lived-in New York feel. Netflix and Marvel signed a deal to develop five binge-worthy series, and to do so they have fabricated a kind of industrial model, judging from the similarities between their first series *Daredevil* and *Jessica Jones*. Both begin in a more complicated world with a strong episodic element; in *Jessica Jones*, that element is Jessica's individual detective cases. Both then jettison this model and simply focus on the battle between the superhero and a single opponent. The plotting gets thinner as the thirteen-episode grind wears the characters down, so that *Daredevil* flounders by asking Vincent D'Onofrio, as the rotund mob lord Kingpin, to do too much. Frankly he's not Orson Welles, and it shows. In *Jessica Jones*, the midpoint of the series takes a very strange turn, with Jessica in one episode submitting to the villain tormentor and then in a later episode reversing the tables and in a single location tormenting him in a repetition that grinds the episodes to a halt but made them easier and quicker to produce.

Thus seriality, a mode and form that had carried a political and social thrust and that by its engaging nature fought television's bland commercial routine, has now in the Marvel/Netflix formula become routinized. If audiences accept this model, we will soon have intimate and simplistic seriality that might, rather than being representative of what is sometimes called the new golden age, instead remind older TV viewers of Warner's aforementioned compulsive repetition of Westerns and private eyes at the dawn of the television dramatic series in the late 1950s.[25] In contemporary streaming, television seriality, rather than being a mark of creativity, may beget saturation.

The Series Is the Thing in which to Catch the Routinization of the New Kingmakers

Though the changes in contemporary television have wrought significant creative changes in television form (explored in the next section), there is, in line with the expansion of the Big 5 and its modes of production into cable and streaming, also a sameness about this new seriality. It is necessary to temper the hype—"It is little wonder that subscriber-based services such as HBO and Netflix have been able to innovate so extensively in recent years in comparison with the muddled advertiser-supported space" (Lotz 2014, 5028)—with a more realistic accounting of how the brave new world in many ways looks a lot like the cowardly old one. We will focus on a single episode of each of three series representing the network (*The Office*), cable (*The Larry Sanders Show*), and streaming (*Orange Is the New Black*) modes of production with each built around a stock sitcom situation: take-your-kids-to-work day.[26]

Before discussing the nature of the theme and how each series treats it, let's look at how each acts to brand its network or channel. All three series refuse the traditional sitcom three-camera format and are shot on film without a laugh track, which sets up a more sophisticated audience interaction since the audience is not commanded to laugh at each moment and also allows for devices such as voice overs, flashbacks and fantasy sequences (Lotz 2014, 2458), all three employed especially in *Orange*.

The Office, with its satirical take on corporate office politics, on NBC in the early 2000s, was a successful attempt by a network to co-opt the cable ethos. The series pushed the limits of network television and dealt obliquely with more outré subject matter in line with the network's *Seinfeld* in a continuation of presenting NBC as "Must See TV," meaning its schedule was an attempt to cajole a younger, hipper, urban demographic. The take-your-kids-to-work episode hints at office pornography (as the loner Kevin worries one kid will look at what's on his computer) and, with a subplot focusing on the African American accountant Stanley's daughter, ventures into interracial underage relationships (as Michael, the office manager, inappropriately calls the teen-ager a "stone cold fox" and the girl replies, "I'm in eighth grade," while later the girl asks for the intern Ryan's number and Stanley counters, "I don't want to see you sniffing around her anymore").

Larry Sanders was an HBO series in the mid-'90s characterized by its strong satirical thrust aimed at the television industry, sometimes bawdy language, and more frank discussion or exposure of entertainment-industry power rela-tions based around the sanctimoniousness of the television star. Its reflexivity also, with actual talk show guests playing themselves, was part of this package, which was meant to illustrate the channel's motto, first used during the run of this show: "It's Not TV, It's HBO." The portrayal of the industry and Garry Shandling as the talk show host himself as venal, petty, and manipulative was an enhancement of Shandling's persona developed on Showtime in an earlier series, *It's Garry Shandling's Show* (1986–90) which harkened back to *The Jack Benny Program* (1950–65) with its folksy, at-home portrayal of a celebrity. The satirical thrust of *Larry Sanders* served to distinguish HBO from its pay-cable-rival Showtime as being more serious and socially astute (which it is).

Finally, *Orange* presents itself as left of the dial of HBO and—with its multicharacter, racially mixed cast that includes the Shakespeare-quoting Crazy Eyes, the steadfast older Caribbean woman Claudette, and the trans-gender hairdresser Burset—expands the range of African American women on television. The outré factor also includes its hour-long run time, doubling the length of the average sitcom, and mixing the TV sitcom and the prison drama. (It's both HBO's *Oz* [1997–2003] with its prison setting and flashbacks and *Sex and the City* [1998–2004] with a more standard sitcom focus on the white middle-class lead Piper.) Its theme, "You've Got Time," with its lyric "Remember all their faces, Remember all their voices," suggests American indie filmmaking, a staple of Netflix's catalog.

The groundbreaking aspect of each series is an integral part of its brand-ing, but each also employs standard sitcom formats and tropes, with all three utilizing a plot that is so common it was later on the noninnovative TBS series *Are We There Yet?* (2010–12) simply referred to as "The Take Your Kids to Work Day Episode."[27] The *Are We There Yet?* logline indicates how trite and standardized the story has become: "When Lindsey accompanies Suzanne to

Michael and Dwight "Teach Your Children" in *The Office*.

work, she uncovers a secret from her mother's past, leading to a misunderstanding." The point of the story, even in the TBS version, is often to expose the workplace as less than perfect, but then in the standard sitcom to squelch that truth-telling by a palliative or moral that stresses that nothing and no one is perfect.

The Office presents the most standard version of the story,[28] with Pam, the office secretary, in the opening anxious over whether she will be able to impress one of the visiting children, followed by the children as unknowing truth tellers laying bare, for example, that the paper-supply business the characters are in will soon go out of business because of Office Depot eliminating the middle salesperson, and finally with Michael's own unhappy childhood exposed and then covered up as he and his fascist-hillbilly aid Dwight perform a very condescending version of "Teach Your Children" that goes entirely over the kids' heads.

The *Larry Sanders* variation on the story has the show's producer, Artie, taking his UCLA class onto the set of the show to see "what a producer actually does, not that bullshit they teach you in college." "Young people are a delight," Artie says. "Hope for the future," Larry blithely intones, but Artie concludes in an apt summary of entertainment-business rivalry, "And eventually they will try to steal our jobs." The most careerist student, Kevin, flatters Larry in asking him how he "keeps the monologue so damn fresh every night," which exposes Larry's vanity as he suddenly perks up, offers him a soda and access to his office, and replies, "The core of any monologue is delivery," an answer that focuses not on the writers or the show as a collective but only on him. What the students, though, are eventually exposed to is the near psychopathy of the performers in the business. First, they hear Larry complaining that an exercise machine his girlfriend Maxine has gotten from his on-air sidekick Hank, called the Hankercizer, has her "so banged up she couldn't have sex." Then they watch Hank break down in the office when he finds Maxine is doing an exposé of the machine he is hawking. Finally, after being told by Artie that "today is a typical day at the Larry Sanders Show," they are confronted with Hank yelling "Shiiiiiiiiiiit" as he finds the new product he is sponsoring, cell phones, may cause brain tumors. This denouement crosses the two stories—of the Hankercizer and the student visit—in a way we will see repeated in *Orange*.

The women's prison drama seems to be the most radical of the three yet also employs its own version of the story with "delinquent" teens coming to the prison so that the inmates can warn them to go straight. Lotz quotes *Oz*'s showrunner, Tom Fontana, as extolling the virtues of the cable pay-per-view and streaming era: "When you don't have to bring people back from a commercial, you don't have to manufacture an 'out.' You can make your episode at a length and with a rhythm that's true to the story you want to tell" (Lotz 2014, 4430). Yet this most typical sitcom plot unfolds in a fairly conventional manner following standard sitcom story structure. The first half of the show forecasts the coming of the teens as a hardened guard says, only somewhat cynically, "It's for the children," as Pam does in the opening of *The Office*. The teens arrive at the midpoint and are encroached on by five inmates, one of whom says, "I'm going to make them shit their delinquent panties." They seem at first unaffected by the office/show/prison, especially the most hardened, Dina, a paraplegic, or "roller," with her own gang. In a more typical climax, the roller is talked to by Piper, who tells her why prison is horrible, then, in the conclusion of the story, she is scared out of her wits as Pennsatucky, a hillbilly transformed into a faith healer in this episode, knocks her out of her chair and mounts her, claiming to cure her, in a way that again as on *Larry Sanders* crosses two disparate plot strands in its conclusion.

As an aside, the similar plots do expose the fact that all aspects of American life, at least as depicted in Hollywood, are essentially part of a spectacle.

Thus in the three series the office and the prison are treated much like the late-night television show. In *The Office* Michael worries that he is too "raw" for the kids—he's "not TV but HBO"—and when the teens show up at the prison in *Orange* they are introduced as "today's special guests."

Finally, there is a moment in traditional sitcom structure, called conventionally the climax, where each character "learns a (moral) lesson." Each show approaches that moment in a different way with, oddly, *Orange* most slavishly following the older tradition. Post *Seinfeld*, which shunned and mocked the lesson and indeed the whole concept of character change, *The Office* acknowledges its NBC forebear and opens a deep cleavage by exposing Michael in a tape he plays of himself as a child appearing on a local kids show as an always inauthentic, lonely person. On the show he embarrasses the puppet host by explaining that his goal is to be "married with a hundred kids so I can have a hundred friends and no one can say no to being my friend." The kids then find out he is not married, and one of them intones the actually awful lesson they learn about adult disappointment: "You didn't get to be what you wanted to be." The show then covers up this moment by, in more typical sitcom fashion, having Michael working on his goal of having a family by joining a dating site.

Larry Sanders foregoes the lesson for a simple reveal where the students experience Hank's egotistical conduct on the set. Later, behind closed doors we see that in essence Hank does not care at all if his Hankercizer causes physical harm to its users and instead is only concerned that he will be named in a lawsuit. Larry equally does not worry about the physical harm the machine has caused to Maxine, only about how soon she can return to having sex with him. The HBO series most severely rejects the lesson, or rather, the lesson it teaches is about the venality of the industry.

In *Orange*, after the other (African American) inmates fail to "scare straight" the roller, it is up to the white upper-middle-class lead, Piper, to tell her why she does not want to end up in prison. The true terror in prison Piper explains is "coming face to face with who you really are. . . . The truth catches up with you in here, Dina, and it's the truth that's going to make you her bitch." Not only is this a more typical sitcom type moral but it is delivered by the privileged Caucasian character through whom the series is often focalized, a

Piper's lecture in *Orange Is the New Black*'s version of take-your-daughter-to-work day.

character who seems to be just passing through, almost as if she were modeled on the young boy in *The Wonder Years* who is above all the misfortunes that happen to him since we know he will grow up to use this material as a writer.

The episode's narration in a different way presents a cautionary tale to its audience; the teens are warned to not enter cell block B, and we discover that there the drug addict Trish has overdosed and then been hanged in a closet by a guard to disguise his own peddling of drugs to the inmates. In flashbacks the episode has shown Trish outside the walls trying to go straight and not making it, with her arrest a result of a misguided attempt to pay back what she has stolen. This is a harsh and innovative way of teaching a lesson about prison, yet not the lesson, but the episode itself is softened and regularized by a contrasting series of flashbacks that explain how Piper met her boyfriend Larry, played by Jason Biggs (*American Pie* [1999]) as a kind of '80s teen-film straggler now in early adulthood. In the flashback Piper is told by her friend at her wedding that she has settled for a comfortable lover who "knows when to order Chinese." Later, when Piper, after being bit by a dog, meets Larry house-sitting her now-married friend's place, he bandages her, invites her to stay, and tells her he is about to order Chinese. *Orange* is a groundbreaking series, as are the other two mentioned here, but one that also employs and is often restrained by its links to the still dominant, in terms of narrative tropes and story construction, network mode of production.[29]

Seriality to the Rescue: How the Form Challenged and Remade the Profit Motive

Television itself is often seen as either a continually advancing form in a new golden age (with that term itself being really just another form of branding of the product as a whole), as in the present, or as a "vast wasteland," its critical sobriquet in the network era, where nothing of quality emerges to challenge the status quo. It may be more accurate to see the history of television and of the television series as a perpetual—in the words of the Italian cultural theorist Antonio Gramsci (2012)—"site of struggle," a battleground of ideas and meanings that results in a constantly shifting array of openings and closings. The reason for this contention is the constant battle between the profit motive and creativity, as Gilles Lipovetsky and Jean Serroy (2013) point out in *The Aestheticization of the World*, in which they characterize the contemporary era as that of "Artistic Capitalism":

> On the one side investors, managers and marketing people turned toward efficiency and economic profitability. On the other, creators in quest of autonomy and the love of artistic ambition. Questions of creative liberty beat against the processes of rationalization and control exercised by the companies on narration, scenarios, scripts, design and casting; toward assuring the greatest commercial success and the greatest profits. The [media] businesses must attract the talent and stimulate innovation, but at the same time, to the end of diminishing risk, they attempt to put the brakes on audacious creations, to reproduce some formulas which "work" the easiest. Financial and organizational logic can thus come to contradict the creativity that they must elsewhere imperatively favor: it's one of the contradictions of the system which forces the business of artistic capitalism to employ some degrees of strong creativity, different according to their mode of organization and according to the [specific] moments [of their production]. (48)

The present television era is one in which the creative agents, often for commercial reasons, have been allowed to reassert themselves and have had a strong hand in remaking the medium by short-circuiting both the episodic era of network television and the cost-cutting mediocrity of Reality TV.[30]

The networks' "safe bet" was "the episodic series that features a small group of recurring characters involved in plots that are resolved by the end of the episode" with narratives that relied on "a high degree of redundancy and repetition" (Anderson 2005, 79). In a 2005 article Christopher Anderson noted that "Young adults, the demographic group most desired by advertisers, have not shown an affinity for hour-long dramas" (67). But in the next decade all this would change as the Serial TV form became a driver of young-adult demographics in the industry. A recent survey showed nineteen-to-twenty-five-year-olds spending almost 40 percent of their TV time streaming, a significant portion of that content one assumes being serial series.[31]

This remaking of television form that challenged the industry, illustrated below in the serial odyssey of J. J. Abrams's *Fringe*, made television a haven and the replacement for what used to be middle-brow, more thoughtful films—termed "adult" in the industry. Situated between blockbusters and low-budget exploitation films, these films, which also included the American independents, tended to focus on examinations of relationships and often to at least in some way address social problems. The "Amerindie" ethos, for example, came to television with the Sundance Network's *Rectify* (2013–16), a slow-moving examination of the effects of the prison system on a wrongly accused prisoner freed after nineteen years, with the series concentrating on the prejudice of small-town Georgia and the mental devastation of the years of solitary confinement and sexual abuse rather than on the mystery of who committed the crime.

The serial series form has also been in general more accommodating to incorporating a geopolitical dimension in its storytelling, and US seriality has sometimes absorbed the more directly critical attitudes of foreign series it has rewritten. Thus FX's *The Bridge* was described by its original Danish and Swedish creators as in line with Swedish noir writers Maj Sjöwall and Per Walhöö, whose work was "a scalpel opening the belly of an impoverished ideology and exposing the reputed morality of a pseudo-welfare society."[32] The US version of the series performed, especially in the second season, a similar operation on US-Mexican unequal border relations, though Fox then canceled its two-year run.

The form has also redistributed power within the industry to writers, and especially to the head writer, now called the showrunner. This new attachment to the serial narrative is in some ways a cost-cutting device, since a powerful script and the presence of an "independent" ethos can sometimes excuse or reify a lower shooting budget and an unknown cast.[33] Nevertheless, the elevation of writers to auteur status in television has increased their power within the industry and enabled them to win some battles with network executives. Frank Spotnitz, one of the key writers on *The X-Files*, relates that Hulu, desperate for story ideas when the network was first moving into original production, asked to produce whatever series idea he might have. He responded with an old adaptation of a series about a fascist America, based on Philip K. Dick's *The Man in the High Castle* (2015–), which he felt in the network era would never have gotten on the air and which is now in its fourth season on the streaming service.

The serial series also wrested power in television away from the dominance of Reality TV, a form that had come to prominence because of its cheap production values at a time when one-hour dramas were "the most costly program to produce" (Anderson 2005, 66). In the 1980s, costs had soared over $1 million an episode, largely driven by " 'above the line' costs such as talent, direction, scriptwriting, music composition, computer animation, and location costs" (Raphael 1997). As opposed to narrative-series production, Reality TV employed handheld cameras, natural lighting, and location shooting and featured shoestring production budgets with minimal above-the-line costs— mostly for the show's host—so low that deficit financing was not required. Consequently the producers profited from the initial licensing run to the networks (Lotz 2014, 4598), and the networks and cable channels profited by paying a lower licensing fee.

The form was distinctly antilabor, coming to prominence partly in response to a 1988 writer's strike that crippled production for twenty-two weeks and delayed the opening of the fall season (Raphael 1997). In the "below the line" costs for technicians, engineers, and extras, producers shed union jobs, with Fox's reality trendsetter *America's Most Wanted* (1988–2012) using different freelance crews for each segment in an attempt to undercut union power (Raphael 1997). The above-the-line costs, which on scripted series were higher because of the power of the actors and writers guilds, on these shows were negligible.

Reality TV, while claiming to permit citizen participation and promising to turn individuals into stars, equally was a part of a kind of mass surveillance in the neoliberal era—the executive producer of *America's Most Wanted* described the show's provoking of callers to inform on their fellows as "the birth of a new era of citizen involvement" (Raphael 1997). Likewise, French viewers in 2016 turned away in droves from an adaptation of *The Apprentice* (2004–) that billed itself as about "the positive values of enterprise" but which French critics claimed viewers saw as actually about "arrogance, contempt, violence." The lack of ratings were seen as a French "rejection of the concept."[34]

The cost-cutting format, with its miniscule budget, had so dominated television that even in 2010 a glance around the prime-time TV schedule in Los Angeles revealed more than half of all programming on the twenty-six most accessible cable channels to be this form. Network serial series began to wrest this domination away by using the audience appeal of Reality TV. Thus ABC's *Lost* in 2004 was a narrativizing of CBS's *Survivor* (2000–), with the action of both taking place on a deserted island, and Fox's *Glee*, with its unknown high schoolers on the way to stardom, broadcast its pilot immediately following the season finale of *American Idol* (2002–16) (Lotz 2014, 2934).

The unforeseen triumph of the more fulfilling and in many cases more committed values of serial television changed the face of an industry where the profit motive alone was promoting the lowest common denominator. This was an extraordinary victory for creative artists who transformed in less than a decade the then-moribund form of television drama, which Christopher Anderson declared looked increasingly like "an extravagance that survives from a distant era of television" (Anderson 2005, 77), into a new dominant.

GLOBAL, LOCAL, "GLOCAL," AND DISTRIBUTION AS DOMINANCE IN US SERIAL EXPORTATION

As we have seen, seriality in most series is not a pure form but rather a fascinating combination of the episodic and the serial, the finished and the continuing, perhaps in fact geared toward two different audiences, playing as it does on the dialectical tensions between "the ultimate mobility of the metropole of the globalized city and lack of mobility of the periphery" as Christopher Guilluy terms it in a book subtitled *How One Has Sacrificed the Popular Classes* (Guilluy 2014, 116). In general, those outside the globalized cities are workers or small shop owners left behind by globalization, where for its "upper classes . . . hypermobility is a fact" (18). The episodic elements of serial television (recurring characters, strong presence of genre, stories that end within the episode), that is, the familiar values of network-era-stay-at-home television in the serial form, are mixed with, as Jason Mittell notes, complex and constantly shifting storytelling, hypergeneric melding, and repetition within change. The form appeals to both the hypermobile globalized classes—for whom travel and constant change, though within an increasingly homogenized world, is a way of life—and, to a lesser extent, to the immobile working- and lower-middle classes, for whom travel, post the 2008 crisis, in the time of the staycation, is no longer possible. (In 2013 60 percent of French workers did not depart for *vacances*, while only 30 percent of corporate executives did not [Guilluy 2014, 117].) As Guilluy points out in terms of the combination of the forms, "One has not brought about the universal in destroying the local and delocalizing it," but rather "the universal is the local less the walls" (119).

Serial series also appeal to much smaller, more particular groupings, a "collection of niche audiences" (Lotz 2014, 302), in a process Lipovetsky and Serroy term a "merchandising of difference" (Lipovetsky and Serroy 2013, 140) but one that can allow for more particularity. However, there is an area in which seriality is not positive or individual, and that is aggregate global distribution, where the form is being used as an American intervention to conquer, penetrate, and saturate foreign markets. Though foreign serial series may be adapted to American television, the flow outward from Hollywood films and television to foreign markets many times dwarfs any influence from outside. This has always been true on television, with, at the end of the unchallenged-network era in 1979, the US exporting three times as much programming, 150 hours, as its leading three competitors combined—enough programing to fill eighteen hours a day of the schedules of twenty-two foreign networks (Nelson 1979).[35]

The global success of serial television, binge watching, and streaming services has greatly increased this output. More than half of all Netflix customers now reside outside the US, with the service growing from a little over 3 million foreign subscribers in 2012 to over 68 million in 2018.[36] This surge was aided by massive opening campaigns in France, which in 2015 included the Netflix-produced *Marseille* with French acting-icon Gerard Depardieu, followed by openings in Italy and with well-publicized assaults on Spain and Portugal as well. HBO then followed suit in Italy with its series *The Young Pope* (2016–). Foreign media are unable to compete with the global reach of the streaming services as Netflix now claims to operate in 132 countries while in 2016 HBO broadcast the opening episode of season 6 of *Game of Thrones* to 194 countries.[37] In 2014 Netflix invested $200 million in the British television industry to co-opt its competitor from the inside. The French head of a rival commercial station noted that the company that European media competitors refer to as the "red devil from Los Gatos" (Netflix's California home) now employs nine hundred engineers in England, "more than any channel in France can mobilize."[38]

Thus at a moment when Western economic dominance is in rapid decline, when particularities supposedly "are glorified," the dominant image in aggregate that emerges is everywhere the same "individualist-technical-consumerist standard of beauty" (Lipovetsky and Serroy 2013, 419). These differences, which seem so magnified in the US, are projected across the globe only as local "flava" subsumed under a dominant narrative and technical pattern. Witness how Netflix's *Narcos* (2015–), with its mixed Latin American and Anglo cast and writers, still fits largely American patterns of storytelling of a gangster's rise and fall.[39] In addition, the fact that foreign scholars stream American series that seem to be detached from their original mode of distribution makes them appear as though they are free from commercial constraints. The series seem to appear out of nowhere, and foreign scholarship tends to treat them almost as purely aesthetic objects, encouraged in this treatment by the objects themselves effacing their mode of production.[40] As Jeremy Tunstall (1977) in *The Media Are American* phrased it, "A non-American way out of the media box is difficult to discover because it is an American-built box. The only way out is to construct a new box, and this—with the possible exception of the Chinese—no nation seems keen to do."

This onslaught translates as a loss to global film and television production, as seen in the case of France and Canal Plus. There, the pay channel, in return for the right to broadcast French films ten months after they open in theaters, must invest 12.5 percent of the revenues from its subscriptions into both French and global film and television production. The service though is fast losing subscribers to Netflix and to Amazon, which in 2016 challenged Canal Plus at Cannes by becoming the leading presenter of auteur films (from Woody Allen's *Café Society* to Jim Jarmusch's *Paterson*) and literally usurped its coveted booth on the Croisette, formerly termed the Canal Plus patio.[41] The French company lost over four hundred thousand subscribers and 3.8 percent of its revenue in 2017,[42] presumably to the American services, and this translates as less money to finance French and global production. This is also a net loss for film and television production since Canal Plus and Britain's Channel Four are leaders in socially conscious global television and film financing. Thus Hollywood, having been unable to encroach on the French subsidy system in an earlier attack during the Clinton administration in the 1990s when it attempted to cancel under the GATT agreement the French subsidy tradition called the "cultural exception," has now been able to accomplish digitally what it could not accomplish through direct negotiation. (Netflix is quartered in Amsterdam, the equivalent of Delaware in the US, where they pay much less in corporate taxes than other countries on the continent and so benefit from the European market while contributing little to it except "Europudding" productions like *Marseille*.)

Seriality's Assault on Network Conformity: J. J. Abrams's War of Position

Gramsci (2012), as regards political movements but also as regards culture, talked about the difference between a war of position, where progressive forces gather their strength and slowly consolidate, and a war of maneuver, an out-in-the-open attempt to seize power. For over a decade networks have warred with writers over the issue of seriality, continuing to rein in storytellers who they felt might potentially lose viewers with plots and arcs that were too complex and involved. As we've seen with the new mechanization of seriality, this is no less true in the present era of streaming service "freedom" than in the older network regime. Serial TV, where the story dictates where the series will go, rather than advertisers trying to ensure audiences for selling products or streaming services or cable networks competing for subscribers, can be a dangerous anticommercial imperative in itself, regardless of the content of the seriality.

Two instances of these wars of position occurred in J. J. Abrams's series *Person of Interest* (2011–16) on CBS and *Fringe* on Fox while a third example of interference, most likely quite common in this continuing war, was the disciplining also by Fox of the horror series *Sleepy Hollow*. Below, I describe *Fringe*'s leap into ever more complicated and less commercial forms of seriality accompanied by corresponding punishments by its network. First, I would like to mark these two other series, whose accelerating seriality challenged their respective networks.

Abrams's desire to continually erode the established episodic style took a bizarre, contentious, and progressive turn in *Person of Interest*. The show's quasi-fascist premise, one that Steven Spielberg had criticized in his Philip K. Dick adaptation *Minority Report* (2002), was that a computer called the Machine has spewed out a social security number of someone about to be involved in a crime. A former intelligence-agency assassin, John Reese, was then charged by the Machine's creator, Harold Finch, with stopping the as-yet-uncommitted crime in a highly illegal vigilante-style thought-control plot that fit in well with CBS's plethora of procedural teams in the wake of *CSI*. The series followed the CBS line for the first two seasons but in season 3 began to develop a minor arc suggesting another more terrifying version of the Machine, which came to be called Samaritan, and which was then featured in ever more complicated and continuing season 4 and 5 arcs where the battle over the openly fascist thought control of Samaritan was countered by the now-more-humanitarian Machine.

In a sense Samaritan, in an allegory of production, was the CBS episodic machine itself, regularized, instrumentalized, and in its valuing of a questionable science (or ratings) over more human values (like those of the writers) itself moving toward fascism. Critics called this new turn in the series "dystopic and politically acidic" (Favard 2016, 60), gave the combined seasons 3 and 4 a 100 percent approval rating, and noted that one episode titled "If-Then-Else" might have been as close as genre television comes to perfect.[43] CBS's response to this serial acceleration was to remove the show from its fall schedule the following season and belatedly announce that they had canceled its run but would allow a final thirteen-episode season to be broadcast not in the regular season but starting in May, partly it might seem, as with *Fringe*, to appease Abrams, whom the network would still hope to be in business with in the future. CBS CEO Leslie Moonves then admitted that—besides presumed network dissatisfaction with the series' subversive contesting of the network's staple form and content—a major factor in the show's cancellation was that CBS did not own and produce the series and so did not directly profit from it, as it did with series such as its remake of *Hawaii Five-0* (2010–), which generated almost no critical interest.[44]

A third example, of many, of network contestation of seriality occurred in the second season of Fox's *Sleepy Hollow* (2013–17), developed by *Fringe's* Roberto Orci. Over the first two seasons the show had carefully constructed an overall series arc involving the coming of the apocalypse and the return to earth of the evil demon Moloch, who the time-travelling Ichabod Crane and the sheriff's deputy (later turned FBI agent), Abbie Mills, opposed. Abruptly, in the middle of season 2, Moloch is simply, and almost arbitrarily, done away with, and the entire arc ends with the series returning to a more scattered, episodic "monster-of-the-week" format. For a few episodes after the ending of the arc the two lead characters seem to wander, stunned, unable to figure out what their new mission might be. It's a bit like Scottie's wandering after Madeleine's sudden midpoint death in *Vertigo*. The vertigo here, though, was caused by Fox executives, who ordered an end to the serial plot, and the stunned feelings of the characters were an expression of the stunned feelings of the writers unable to deal with this dismantling of their work. The Fox Television Group co-chair claimed this decision to grind the show back to "pied pipers, wendigos and weeping ladies" was made because the show had become "overly serialized" and Fox wanted to "return the fun to it." Fun, for Fox executives, presumably being the increasing revenue they were (perhaps wrongly) anticipating by making the show look more like everything else on television.[45] (The show, in the wake of this change, was canceled after four seasons.)

FRINGE'S PARALLEL UNIVERSES: COMMERCE AND CREATIVITY
One of the most stellar examples to date of the war being waged by writers against commercial dictates by employing the tropes of Serial TV is *Fringe*.

Abrams's series was initially described by Roberto Orci, one of its co-creators along with Abrams, as a "new kind of storytelling," combining the extremely popular at the time procedural series (six out of ten of the then highest-rated series),[46] that is, criminal-investigation content, with an "extremely serialized and very culty" show (like Abrams's *Lost*) that consisted of the parallel-universe content.[47] The first season hewed more closely to the procedural framework, though it had an overriding arch that connected all the individual cases, which it referred to as "The Pattern." The second season announced itself as about travel between parallel universes while continuing to integrate the "monster of the week," a phrase borrowed from its acknowledged predecessor, *The X-Files*, into a now more developing "totality" (Favard 2016, 62). The third season, though—and especially its first eight episodes—featured parallel plots between the two universes, which were resolved at the end of that cycle and constituted the high point of the series and a rejection of the episodic procedural framework.

Just after this creative leap, at the midpoint of the third season, Fox moved the show from its coveted Thursday-night time slot to the following night at nine, commonly referred to in the industry as the "Friday night death slot." The show struggled through a fourth season, in which the compromise with the network was that it could have not a series-long but rather a season-long arc that had to be wrapped up at the end of the season, a compromise that was anathema to its overall impact. Finally, Fox, even after this compromise, canceled the show but brought it back for a shortened, cable-like run of thirteen episodes. Abrams and company chose to use the last season in the Friday slot to "take more creative freedoms,"[48] with a frenzy of seriality that began by "blowing the show up" by projecting the Fringe team twenty-four years into the future in a highly involved arc in which they battled the fascist menace of the Observers (white, bald businessmen in drab-gray suits, sort of like commuters returning from Wall Street on the Long Island Railroad),[49] who had been a persistent but minor element in the show previously.

The series tracked the activities of a group of investigators of the paranormal, the Fringe unit, and it began by stressing its direct relationship to that earlier pioneering serial series, *The X-Files*, with its similar musical theme and its opening credit sequence, which lists types of paranormal activity, as well as its female-male detective team in a direct line with the former series. However, post *Lost*, the serial element, even in the first season, is much stronger. *The X-Files*, alternated between more constant self-contained monster-of-the-week episodes and serial episodes that explored the government conspiracy involving aliens and the mystery surrounding the abduction of the lead character Mulder's sister, referred to by Chris Carter, the show's creator, as the "mythology." The two types of episodes hardly ever crisscrossed, though the mythology episodes began with what looked like a monster-of-the-week element.[50] From the first season, *Fringe* increased the serial or mythology element by having the monster-of-the-week occurrences be connected to something that Broyles, the FBI head of the Fringe unit, called "The Pattern." That is, the villains the agents Olivia and Peter battle are seen as related in a way that we and they as yet do not understand, so there is from the beginning a combination of the two types of story.

The showrunners have referred to specific kernels of the overall series arc planted in the individual episodes as "mythalones," with the most famous being season 2's white tulip, a continuing symbol of attempts by Walter, Peter's father, at atonement for his transgression in crossing dimensions, which precipitated the season-3 war between the two dimensions (Favard 2016, 59) and contributed to "an increased density in the fictional world" (57). "The Ghost Network" (S1E3), for example, introduces another mythalone, amber, a mysterious frozen coating-like substance that seals its victims, here as an element of the monster-of-the-week plot. Later it figures prominently in a serial plot as the device that seals the leak between worlds in season 3 and the substance that allows the Fringe team to survive and be thawed out in the future in season 5.

In the *X-Files* there was often a note of ambiguity about the explanation for the phenomenon the agents observed, but this ambiguity between the supernatural and the scientific—with the series refusing to resolve the distinction—remained a factor mostly in the single episodes. In *Fringe* the ambiguity adds to the overall effect of "The Pattern," deepening the serial content. Olivia, Peter, and Walter solve the mystery of the telepathic communication of the members of the Ghost Network but have no idea where they come from and what overall mission they are trying to accomplish. Only the Fringe team leader, Broyles, seems to understand The Pattern, which in a final scene he discusses guardedly with the head of the big-pharma company Massive Dynamic, Nina Sharp, as he shares the device they have uncovered in a way that suggests an ongoing *X-Files*-like business-government conspiracy and deepens the mystery. (The fact that the company and its female head turn in the series from fount of corporate evil to cheery science fair project with a loving den mother most likely has to do with the Fox network, which in an earlier and less restrictive pre-9/11 age, tolerated Carter's government evil but in the neoliberal surveillance age was not brooking criticism of corporate technology.) In effect then, there were no stand-alone episodes, even in the first season, or rather, each supposedly stand-alone element cumulatively built the serial content in a way that did not happen in the *X-Files* with its clear distinction between the mythology and monster-of-the-week episodes.

The Pattern is revealed in season two to be the effects of an invasion by a parallel earth, which itself is being destroyed. The first eight episodes of season 3 are the high point of the series, as the two worlds collide, with Olivia trapped in the parallel world and her Earth 2 double, the character series fans referred to as "FauxOlivia," seducing Peter in our world. Episode 8, "Entrada," begins with a complicated summary of what has transpired in the two worlds. The previous episodes in this sub-arc had both a stand-alone quality and an episodic element, with the teams in each world investigating different crimes in alternating weeks. Episode 8, though, is pure seriality, about Peter's discovery on Earth 1 that the woman he has slept with is not Olivia but her Earth 2 facsimile, and on Earth 2 Olivia caught by the fascist "Walternate"—Walter's doppelganger and head of defense in that world—and about to be lobotomized by the sadistic lab technician who on Earth 1 was the lead scientist at Massive Dynamic.[51] Instead of the action taking place primarily in one world, the episode constantly alternates between the two, using a series of markers to distinguish them. In Earth 2 the Twin Towers are still standing, a dirigible hovers over the city, and Newark Penn Station has been renamed "Springsteen Station" (in honor of New Jersey's famous rocker). There are narrative leaps between the two worlds, as when the evil Walternate proclaims FauxOlivia as "on the other side focused on the task at hand" and we cut to her in bed with Peter after having seduced him. With the help of Earth 2's Broyles, whom Earth 1's Olivia convinces that the parallel Earths can coexist without destroying each other, she makes it back to her world as FauxOlivia returns to hers, ending the eight-part sequence while pointing ahead to the remaining season-long arc about Peter's building a machine that can restore both worlds. In the hospital after her return, Olivia tells Peter "you were the only thing that got me through; you saved my life," and he kisses her while we know this personal arc will continue as he is obsessed but silent about having betrayed her.

For the fifth and final, shorter-run season, the producers chose to "blow up" the show and restart, projecting the characters into a future where the Observers have invaded earth, turning it into a technicized, nonhuman world. The season requires a complicated summary at the opening since it features the familiar Fringe team but now in a different world. It begins with Walter intoning, "If you are watching this you know very well that the Observers have invaded." In this final season the crime-and-monster-of-the-week format is abandoned completely, and the team begins by thawing themselves out and then must recover and effectuate Walter's plan from the past to thwart the invaders. Episode 3, "The Recordist," begins with the lab technician Astrid thawing Walter's videotape, frozen in season 1's amber, and then attempting to restore the tape as the team watches, recalling the videotapes of the Dharma Project discovered in the hatch in Abrams's earlier series *Lost*.

This final frenzy of seriality, though, oddly, in also being constructed within the constraints of weekly television, prompts some retreats into earlier forms. In "The Recordist" the team finds a group of survivors and their leader, Edmund, who have chosen not to resist but simply to document the invasion. The team needs to find copper to build their machine, and in the end Edmund sacrifices himself and moves away from his status as only a recorder in order to restore himself in the eyes of his son River, who sees him as a coward. The construction of the episode within the overall serial arc reverts to the television form of the anthology, a remnant from the '50s golden age of television, as the episode centers on the relationship of a nonseries character, Edmund, and his son. A subplot involves Olivia afraid she will not be a good mother, with her accepting she can be and moving toward a highly conservative element in the series conclusion, the establishment of the white nuclear family—Peter, Olivia, and baby—as the epicenter of a restored humanity, with Walter, the remnant of both '60s and '70s social revolution encompassing CIA mind experiments and hippie liberation, now dead and removed from this sterilized world.

Through its evolution, though, *Fringe* fought the good fight for a highly creative expansion of seriality that continually moved toward a grasping of not just a more complex mode of storytelling but one that continually strove to halt the breaking of narrative into commercial parcels and instead to construct a totality in an attempt to grasp a narrative world, the reflection of the parallel universe of our world as a whole, and to substitute this totality for bite-sized, pre-digestible, commodified nuggets.

II

SERIAL SPECIFICITY

SERIAL AESTHETICS

Philosophical, Artistic, and Media Histories of Seriality /
Hegel and Richard Kimble on the Trail of the
One-Armed Man

SERIAL TV DID NOT spring full-blown from the minds of its creators but rather draws on a long aesthetic history in multiple art forms and media. In order to contextualize contemporary television evolution, this chapter presents initially some philosophical underpinnings of the form and then the instantiation of those tenets in a variety of art, music, and literary instances as well as in the media history of comics, radio, film, and television.

There are two strongly differentiated, competing philosophical concepts of seriality that nevertheless often operate in tandem. The first is the Nietzschean view of the ever-repeating eternal return, which Dickens seemed to embrace in his description of the process in *The Pickwick Papers*: "We shall keep perpetually going on beginning again, regularly" (Hayward 1997, 1). This emphasis on repetition also includes the Sartrian view of serial events as emblematic of capitalist mundanity, where human and, in the realm of art, aesthetic relations are fashioned with the precision, control, and repetition that defines the factory process. The positive valuation of this mode of seriality stresses the nonhierarchical character of this structuring system as "conjunction" rather than "subordination," a "stringing together" of "disparate" elements "in a principal not of unity but of connection."[1] It is this mode that often conditions, especially as it has expressed itself in Minimalism, the use of seriality in art (from Monet's wheat stacks and Rouen Cathedral to Warhol's postmodern Campbell's Soup Cans and Marilyns) and music (Steve Reich / Philip Glass). This repeating quality is noted by Rust Cohle in the HBO serial *True Detective*: "Someone once told me, 'Time is a flat circle.' Everything we've done or will do, we're gonna do over and over and over again."

However there is an alternate view if not of seriality itself at least of its use: that it is as a device to instead of bifurcating unite by expressing through its multiple and sometimes repeating elements at least an aspect of the (capitalist) totality. As we have seen, seriality is employed cleverly within a capitalist mode of production to create the demand, "the desire to find out 'what happens next,'" that it then feeds (Hayward 1997, 3). Nevertheless, it is this view of seriality as totality that Sartre (1984) describes as evolving from the disparate, merely fragmented group to the collectively aware "group-in-fusion." Before Sartre, Hegel had described this process as a historical essence, and Marx, inverting Hegel, had historicized it as the totality of capitalist relations that also included the proletariat, the means of the destruction of the bourgeois order. It is this view also that predominates in the serial literature of the nineteenth century, described at the time as "social cement" (Hayward 1997, 5) encompassing Dickens but more pointedly Balzac's Human Comedy and Zola's Rougon-Macquart series of twenty novels.[2]

Zola's was the most ambitious use of seriality up to that time, attempting to map the totality of the corruption of Napoleon III's Second Empire through a continuing examination of its parts, from its rise in crushing a people's rebellion in 1851 (*The Fortune of the Rougons*) to its humiliating defeat in the German invasion in 1870 (*The Debacle*). This use of seriality was the stated aim of David Simon in mapping the socio-politico-economic deterioration of Baltimore in *The Wire*. The impulse also less consciously but perhaps even more effectively lies behind David Lynch's mapping of the sexual abuse at the core of bourgeois life in *Twin Peaks*, Jane Campion's charting of the fury of masculine power and its feminist alternative and subduing of that power in *Top of the Lake*—both of which have now returned in second editions—and Lars Von Trier's account of the destructive nature of capitalist instrumental (scientific) reason and its contestation by natural and feminine forces in *The Kingdom*.

This chapter explores this form, called one of, if not the, "dominant mode[s] of narrative presentation in Western culture" (Hagedorn 1988),[3] as its twin poles are defined in philosophy and express themselves in nineteenth and twentieth century art, music, and literature. We then discuss the form in twentieth and twenty-first century media, including comic strips, radio, and cinema. We finally trace it through its evolving history on television, concluding with an examination of *The Fugitive*, an early example of a series containing elements of the serial form that strained the episodic mode and were employed in expressing the totality of capitalist legal relations and their contradictions.

Nietzsche's Schizoid Seriality versus Hegel's Dialectical Totality

There is certainly in contemporary serial narratives a powerful element of continual repetition of narrative devices such as cliffhangers and multiple characters and story lines, and of recurrent plot motifs such as the sudden death of lead characters. In addition, the continued story itself plays out recurrent stories that can seem to recirculate in continuous patterns. Jessica Jones, for example, is in one episode captured and tortured by the villain Kilgrave and then in a later episode captures and tortures him. All this encourages bingeing, watching episode after episode, in a way that suggests Freud's description of a repetition compulsion.

Philosophically this aspect of contemporary television seriality traces back to Nietzsche and the concept of eternal return, a prospect that time does not evolve or advance but just circulates, as "endless duration," "eternal present," or "timelessness"—"The impermanence of everything actual which constantly acts and comes-to-be but never is" (Mical 1998). Nietzsche describes his first awareness of this conception of time as "convulsive," as inducing a paralyzing vertigo where this "labyrinth of recurrence" summoned up for him the need to accept "existence without signification" (Mical 1998). This persistent repetition "includes all the things we regret and despise" and goes against "what we find meaningful" (Hatab 2015). Yet there is for him in accepting this world without origins—one with neither beginning nor end, or where the end is foreseen in the beginning (Hatab 2015)—a kind of power, or an ultimate affirmation of living life by facing the void:

> What, if some day or night a demon were to steal after you into your loneliest loneliness and say to you: "This life as you now live it and have lived it, you will have to live once more and innumerable times more." . . . Would you not throw yourself down and gnash your teeth

and curse the demon who spoke thus? Or have you once experienced a tremendous moment when you would have answered him: "You are a god and never have I heard anything more divine." (Nietzsche 1974, 341)

Is this recognition not intimately bound up with taming the fear of death, where each repetition is a kind of death, and is it not possible that the pleasure of seriality as Walter Benjamin (2006) suggests, has to do with the continual prolonging of death (Hayward 1997, 18), or in this case the end of the serial, which nevertheless must come eventually but which then may be avoided again in binge watching by moving to the next serial? Nietzsche drew his conclusion from the Stoic doctrine of *ekpyrosis*, where the world ends as it begins, in a total (apocalyptic) fire (Mical 1998). In much the same way, many serials end by suggesting their beginnings—most dramatically in Jack's eye opening as he survives the crash in the first shot of *Lost* and closing as he watches the others flee the island in the last shot.

Eternal return is certainly a basis for the structuring of serials and sometimes as a philosophical principle, as expressed in *True Detective*. However, the principle as it is ofttimes commercially interpreted is, as one Nietzschean scholar interested in stressing the life-affirming aspects of the philosopher's denial pointed out, simply a way of mystifying an underlying pessimism that, in its denial of even Nietzsche's heroic facing of the void, simply "naturalizes and essentializes late-capitalism" as the way life is and always will be (Johnston 2014). It is also a principle that may rationalize perpetual wheel-spinning for the purpose of addictive viewing in serial construction.

Sartre's concept of seriality on the other hand, as outlined in *Critique of Dialectical Reason*, is two-pronged, both binding and liberatory. Seriality, as Sartre's "stupid forward movement of everyday life," as Benjamin's (2006) "homogenous empty time," or Adorno's "afterlife of the production of the assembly line" (Cash 2015, 7), Sartre describes as "the form collective life takes where no group formation is emergent as that collective's negation [which would allow it to challenge the status quo]. Individuals function as elements in a series . . . constitute[d] . . . in their interchangeability: each of them is effectively produced by the social ensemble as united with his neighbors, in so far as he is strictly identical with them" (Sartre 1984, 256). The serial relationship in this instance is "an infinite regression," akin perhaps to Nietzsche's perpetual repetition, where each is alienated from themselves and thus from others (3). This "plurality of isolations," "lived as a negative structure because of the impossibility of uniting with others" (256), however can be transcended when each individual in a group—Sartre's example is the group waiting for a bus—realizes that what they have in common with the others is their own distance and isolation from them. In that moment "otherness is converted into identity" (260), and the group is perceived as a common unity (374). However, this realization may be only momentary, and it is easy for "the group to disperse back into seriality" (Jameson 2004, xxx).

Sartre's explication of both a binding and a liberatory seriality may also describe the constant battle between art and commerce in the commercial-television arena. There are many moments when television seriality struggles to express something beyond repetition and to attempt to map a totality, but these moments are often interrupted and reframed again as compulsive repetition, just as Sartre's crowd disperses. The first season of *Arrow* presented the superhero as a kind of masked avenger of Occupy Wall Street, pursuing the town's 1 percent, but that was quickly thwarted and he was instead by season 2 reimagined as a simple vigilante pursuing crime on the streets in the poor neighborhood of Starling City. The second season, although it had an overall arc, refused a liberatory movement and fell back into costume-hero repetition. Similarly the first season of *Hell on Wheels* (2011–16) set out to consciously map the moment of Eastern capital's domination of the West through the building of the transcontinental railroad while questioning the effect that domination had on both the indigenous population and nature, focusing on a rebel foreman with a criminal past. Season 2 rejected that critical thrust and adopted a procapitalist stance about the inevitability, sad or otherwise, of the enterprise, while converting the fugitive to a Southern aristocrat as the series moved back to a seriality that supported and was a product of capitalist mundanity.

In contrast, the concept of totality, as developed by Hegel, Marx, Lukács, and Adorno, is a direction in seriality that grasps narrative as moving beyond repetition and perpetual return toward an understanding of some aspect of capitalist relations as a whole. In this way a serial series may fulfill the function that Steve Neale (1980) discusses for genres under a capitalist mode of production, that is, illuminating (the contradictions of) aspects of bourgeois life. For example, the crime film mediates the often-strained relationship between the individual and the law.[4] There is, however, always a narrative serial totality, whether contestatory or not, a whole that is deeper and more revealing than the sum of its parts. The writers of *Fringe* for example claimed they had mapped out the entire series before beginning to write it.[5] However, while this whole may express the totality, it may also simply, in a far more pedestrian way, be the end-point rationale for the series' continual repetition, that is, the eternal return of its serial alienation.

Against the breakup of knowledge into fragments in the eighteenth century covering different aspects of society in both the social and natural sciences and in the wake of Napoleon's carrying the French Revolution to his Prussia in the beginning of the nineteenth century, Hegel, in *Epistemology of Spirit*, theorized that thought could not be scattered into "momentary, incomplete or isolated parts of a process." For Hegel, what was true was the whole, which included each of the categories that constituted it,[6] but was itself a relation superior to its elements. Marx, in extracting the "rational kernel" from Hegel's "mystical shell," grounded thought not, as Hegel had done, in the whole history of humanity but in each historical epoch. For Marx, thought was not an expression of human consciousness guided by an Absolute Spirit but an expression of consciousness conditioned by the specific material relations of production of each age so that coming to self-consciousness was not effected by a mystical force but was instead the self-consciousness of "real man [and woman] as he [and she] lives in the real world of objects by which he [and she] is conditioned" (Marx 1977, 120).

Marx's goal was to understand how consciousness was patterned in bourgeois society through complex self-developing totalities and how it was conditioned in bourgeois thought itself, which studied phenomena in isolation—an isolation that developed in part from the division and specialization of labor (Shortall 2005). The crucial determination for Marx was whether this process of isolation was a means of understanding the whole or whether it remained abstract knowledge in autonomous fragments, that is, somewhat akin to seriality as addictive eternal return or as revelatory totality. For Marx, and against the socialists of the time, private property was not the core of the problem with bourgeois society but was a symptom of its maladjustment. Marx's core category was labor, exploited and hardened into capitalist profit in a way that then stood outside itself—and outside those who labored—"as an alien power" (Shortall 2005). Capital, and the particular form of wealth called private property, was nothing more than ossified labor: an accumulation of alienated labor stolen by the capitalists in an exploitative process in which the worker is underpaid and undervalued. All wealth in its creation then is not private but social. The plurality of totalities that followed from this proposition in all the capitalist spheres of production—including the aesthetic—though in some sense autonomous, still referred back to this basic truth.

Modern bourgeois society then could be known through an examination of the "functional interlocking and unified action of the separate spheres" (Grumley 1986), just as linking serial series with an overall critical ambition (see Lynch, Campion, Von Trier above) might equally be used to define various aspects of the separate spheres of contemporary capitalism and might be seen over and against those serial series that remain simply in the addictive realm of the eternal return.

A primary way of knowing the totality was through its contradictions, its dialectical movement, with contradictions either resolving toward a higher unity or—under late-capitalism, in Adorno's understanding of the negative dialectic—often not resolving at all. The clash of contradictions might be a way of alternately understanding serial movement that would stand in contrast to the eternal return. Thus the death of Trish, the addict in the episode of *Orange Is the New Black*, referred to in the last chapter, convinces Red, the Russian inmate who heads the kitchen where Trish worked, that the inmates themselves must act to get rid of the guard who supplied Trish with the drugs on which she overdosed since the prison officials will not act. She is then compelled to institute a plan to get the guard fired, which has a prominent place in the rest of the episodes for that season. The death, rather than an eternal return—that is, just another serial plot device for addicting the viewer—might be seen as spurring the inmates to take action, to contest the totality of prison relations and move to a more liberatory expression.

The Totality versus the Eternal Return: Zola and Monet Meet Warhol and Philip Glass in an Aesthetic Tag Team

In general in art and music over the last century, seriality and repetition, in works organized around Nietzsche's concept of eternal return, have taken up the mantle of Foucault's Nietzschean concept of the end of origins, rejecting the idea of beginnings (and endings). Works such as Donald Judd's boxes furnish "multiples without originals" (Rottman 2014, 19) while Joseph Beuys's "multiples" seem to replicate democratically mass-produced industrialized objects and challenge the "singularity, unity and uniqueness of the art object."[7] This Minimalist movement in art developed in a parallel dimension in music where Steve Reich and Philip Glass in the mid-1960s, following Andy Warhol's repetitive Marilyn Monroe silk screens, created compositions that seemed to simply repeat but instead were subtly means of expression within repetition through "gradual changes of certain individual notes or entire figures."[8]

However, in this extended history there were counter movements that within a repetitive framework sought to illuminate aspects of the whole with repetitions building to an understanding of some aspect of a totality. Monet, who is credited with perhaps beginning these serial and minimalist movements, in his grandest series, the Rouen Cathedrals, had as a goal grasping the totality of the expression of light and the changes in color wrought on a fixed object over an entire day. John Adams in his *Doctor Atomic* Symphony uses the devices of repetition to present the awe and horror of the atomic bomb. Finally, in literature at the dawn of the Nietzschean age, Émile Zola in his Rougon-Macquart series of twenty novels with repeating characters—even more so than Dickens—attempts to map the political, social, and economic life of France's Second Empire in a way that is critical of every aspect of that life.

Monet established the moment of seriality in art when in 1877 he exhibited eleven paintings of the Paris train station the Gare Saint-Lazare, a moment that less than a century later became the "dominant paradigm" of the art movement called Minimalism, where multiple paintings or sculptural objects were assembled in sets or series in "a nonhierarchical juxtaposition of equivalent representations." The tropes of minimalism in the art world consisted of serial repetition, an extreme reduction of form, and assembly processes that were similar to "industrial fabrication" (Rottman 2014, 4), not in fact dissimilar to the attributes of contemporary Serial TV. The titles of the Minimalist works specifically called attention to this repetition, such as Roni Horn's *The Experience of Identical Things* (1986–88), later retitled *Things That Happen Again* (1987–90). Rosalind Krauss explains that the effect of this "uniformity, invariability and repetition" is a "flattening of hierarchy" and a calling into question of the premises of art-world production so that the original, which had wielded authority over mere copies, is negated by the "seriality of mechanical reproduction" where "each consecutive serial element mutely affirms the order of the series itself" (Krauss 1986, 18).

But for a moment let's return to the "origin" of seriality in art with Monet, who prior to painting the loosely serial Gare Saint-Lazare series, in 1886 painted the Needle Rock series on the Belle-Ile-en-Mer. The series was not about the rock formation itself but about the way light near the rocks struck the sea. Monet proclaimed that "to paint the sea one has to see her every hour," and so he redid or did another painting "every four hours" (Dombrowski 2015), with the rock formation remaining stable while the light and its reflection on the sea currents changed. It was on this island that Monet met the critic and republican Gustave Geffroy, who introduced him to the work of the socialist Auguste Blanqui, who in the wake of the defeat of the Paris Commune in 1871 proposed his own cyclical-return theory in which events happened simultaneously in opposition to the bourgeois ideology of perpetual progress (Dombrowski 2015) but also in despairing repudiation of the possibility of revolutionary advancement.[9]

While Monet's embracing of a repetitious subject for the purpose of studying momentary patterns of light was, as Andre Dombrowski (2015) claims, "a way to actualize history itself in painting not just embed metaphors of it," there is an opposite current that claims that what Monet received from Geffroy at a time that was "awash in notions of 'wholeness' and 'universality'" was a challenge to depict in painting not "ephemeral reality" but "its underlying essence, its perennial truth" (Athanassoglou-Kallmyer 2015), which he chose to accomplish through repetition where the subject does not change. The idea of gesturing toward a totality through seriality can be most clearly seen in the Rouen Cathedral works. These thirty-one canvasses, painted from 1892 to

1893, may have seemed to be simply a repetitive series, especially since Monet only presented twenty of them for exhibition in 1895. However, in contrast to the Haystack series of 1889 to 1891 and the earlier Needle Rock series, here he set out to more methodically map the play of light over an unchanging object, the cathedral and its tower, altering slightly only the point of view. What the paintings as a whole map is the play of light during the course of a day: blues in the morning, ochre and gold in the midday and afternoon sun, and browns and grays later in the day and on cloudy days. The totality here is not evidenced in the object, but in the play of light itself. The cumulative effect of seeing the paintings arranged morning to night is a kind of culmination of Impressionism's goal of depicting the moment played out over time:[10] a totality expressed by and through seriality.[11]

Monet's project of mapping a totality counters in art a splintering of the work into only its parts, and in that way it accomplishes something similar to what many serial series accomplish in television narrative. Not dissimilar in goal, for example, is David E. Kelly's mapping in *Goliath* (2016–) of the power of contemporary corporate-military institutions through that series' multiple iterations of the viciousness of the law firm in collusion with the arms manufacturer in its many attempts to derail a lawsuit alleging criminal weapons testing.

There is a remarkable congruity between Minimalism in the art world and the development of Serial-Minimalism in music. That moment begins with Arnold Schoenberg's twelve-tone method, which uses a systematic approach to ordering the tones of the chromatic scale to structure compositions with a recurring series of ordered elements. Karlheinz Stockhausen takes up Schoenberg's approach, defining the principle of seriality in a musical composition as a method where "every situation must occur once and only once" but within a formation that seems to be forever repeating.[12] The approach, which is a reaction against classical tonality, stresses coincidence in its distributing of the fixed tones within a dispersion over time, and it has antecedents, for example, in Liszt's *Faust* Symphony.

Stockhausen's dictum to use all the components of a given number of elements with equal importance replaced the classical tonal hierarchy with a "spiritual and democratic attitude toward the world"[13] and had its direct echo, as we have seen, in the art world's repeating series of forms. As employed in the US in the 1960s by Philip Glass and Steve Reich among others, Minimal music was a use of the Nietzschean eternal return by applying repetition not only to the composition but to the material itself. Thus, Reich's 1967 *Piano Phase* has, for over eighteen minutes, two pianos facing each other repeating with slight variations similar phrases then altering which piano is playing and which is silent. Again, the factory process is also quoted, with Reich's piece first performed but later recorded using a tape loop, suggesting that the human piano players could be replaced by an automatic player piano. Glass's eight-minute piece of the same year, *Strung Out*—originally for violin and later played on the xylophone[14]—which seems to have just a constantly repeated melody, in effect continually shifts the melody to lower registers which, in the title's pun (which also suggests a drug experience), taxes the violinist attempting to play while reading a score "strung out" along a wall. A key to the experience of both pieces is detecting subtle change within what first appears to be mechanized repetition (Shelley 2013). These works also suggest the assembly line and factory modes of production, with which "television production has much in common" (Bell 2016, 27).

However, as in art, there is a counter movement, a movement toward employing the techniques of repetition for expressing a totality. The opera composer John Adams, ten years younger than Glass and Reich, in his *Doctor Atomic* Symphony, a condensation of his opera based around Robert Oppenheimer and the creation of the atomic bomb, constructs the piece based on a series of repetitions. These move in gradually repeated phrases during the composition's forty-five minutes from an in-medias-res opening romantic flourish suggesting the full power and awful destruction of the bomb to a contemplation and regret over its creation, mapping this crucial moment in capitalism's new ability to destroy the world. Here again, as in the best serial series, repetition is employed to map a totality.

It must also be noted that seriality and gradual variation over time is an element in the shaping of the musical themes of various serial series. Thus the *Fringe* theme is deliberately an alteration of the repeating, eerie theme of *The X-Files*. There is a minor theme in the expansion of the *Fringe* theme played over the closing credits that has been appropriated almost note for note to suggest the tension of the Cold War in *The Americans*. Here musical seriality, variation within similarity, plays out in a confluence of related serial genres.

ZOLA'S SERIAL TOTALITY

Literary seriality, essentially pioneered by Dickens, grew, as did seriality on television, out of the possibility of new modes of production in the wake of the nineteenth century. These consisted of the following: new consumer goods through mass industrialization; a transportation system allowing for a dispersal of goods, including now-proliferating newspapers and magazines; and the "manufacturing" of new, more literate audiences clamoring for these serial representations (Hayward 1997, 28). Dickens, "the first capitalist of literature," helped fashion the entertainment industry by transforming in 1836 what had been a series of sporting stories into a picaresque novel, *The Pickwick Papers*. Dickens patterned a formula of increasingly more socially explosive and socially critical content in the wake of the horrors of industrialization but "under a platform of conservative 'family values'" (38), which would not only become the serial dominant for the next fifty years in its establishing the tropes of the mass-entertainment industry but would also prevail in the next century in Hollywood. The moral perspective would later be challenged in the serial realm by Zola's (2016) "naturalism," claiming to be morally neutral and blatantly antibourgeois.

Dicken's novels were "part-issued" three or four chapters at a time with forced pauses and cliffhangers between editions and thus more able to be consumed by "increasingly rushed readers" (Hayward 1997, 39), the equivalent of serial television's increasingly under-pressure consumers. The serialized form itself through its "richness of detail and expansion of the text over time suggested, at the height and in the center of the industrial revolution, a world of [capitalist] plenitude" (4) just as the serial television series suggests and often validates the abundance of capitalism's expansion into a virtual world. The novels also served the function of "organizing random, apparently senseless social relations and economic facts into narrative trajectories" (41) just as serial series like *Fringe* map the new and terrifying expansion into parallel online worlds. They also marked a new prominence and freedom for their writers as Dickens became wealthy and his novels celebrated by literary critics.

Zola, who created the first consciously serialized-from-the-start novelistic series, proclaimed his gratitude for "the realistic possibilities which the reign of money offers to an author," this freedom from the former world of aristocratic patronage, in which the power of the market might be turned against its creators. "It is necessary," he wrote, "to recognize the dignity, the power and the justice of money" (Bordieu 1992, 156). Zola's description perhaps forecasts the new power in the current serial form of the showrunner, at long last an acknowledgement of the crucial role of the writer in Hollywood.

Over the course of Dickens's almost thirty-year serialized career, his books grew in critical status so that by 1864, the time of his last complete novel, *Our Mutual Friend*, an essay by a prominent critic titled "Novels with a Purpose" declared him to be "a genius" whose "power over the community . . . [is] beyond that of any author" (Hayward 1997, 37), anticipating the contemporary anointing of television showrunners such as David Chase (*Sopranos*), David Milch (*Deadwood*), and David Simon (*The Wire*) as not only the equivalent of cinematic "auteurs," itself a term derived from the word "author," but as in line with Dickens, Zola, and Balzac. However, the form could still be explosive. Zola's initial flurry in 1867 into novelistic writing after a journalistic career, *Thérèse Raquin*—an early version of the plot of murderous adultery as a way out of the disaffected lives of the lower classes and, increasingly, desperate middle classes taken up in James M. Cain's *The Postman Always Rings Twice*, and on the screen in Visconti's *Ossessione* (1943) and Billy Wilder's *Double Indemnity* (1944)—was deemed by the French press "*la literature putride*."[15]

Zola's seriality, following on from Dickens, was a conscious effort to map a totality. Balzac had been the chronicler of the period of the Restoration, a corrupt moment of a return of monarchical privilege in reaction to the French Revolution, but his series of novels were only named collectively the Human Comedy after he began writing them. Zola, like serial showrunners, had from the start the ambition of mapping every aspect of life under the equally corrupt twenty-year Second Empire of Napoleon III. The series begins with the usurping of a democracy in 1851 detailed in *The Fortune of the Rougons*, in which the family of characters benefits from the coup. It then traces the "greed, graft, stock jobbing (*Money* [*L'Argent*]) and conspicuous consumption (*The Ladies' Paradise* [*La Bonheur de Dames*])"[16] of a rapidly expanding industrial bourgeoisie, particularly in the wholescale rebuilding of Paris (*The Kill*) and the railroads (*The Human Beast*) managed by a government that amounted to a kleptocracy (*His Eminence Rougon*) and left a class of workers in ruin (*Germinal*). The series concludes with the ignominious and cowardly defeat in 1870 of a phony monarch presiding over a country its financiers had pillaged and left in debt (*The Downfall* [*Le Debacle*]). Along with the detailing of a particular socioeconomic milieu through following multiple characters in various strands of a single family, each novel also, on the more overtly psychological level, tracks some aspect of what Zola thought of as genetic or inherited deficiency and which we would call addiction, here viewed not as destiny but as an outgrowth of the neuroses springing from the rise of a new wealthy owner and upper-middle class and the consequent oppression of workers.[17]

The plot of each novel is self-contained, and the series does not follow a particular chronological order in tracing three generations of the Rougon-Macquart family, though it does begin with the 1851 coup d'etat and end in 1871 after the defeat of France by Bismarck's Prussia. A final, summing-up novel, *Doctor Pascal*, lays out the ultimate fate of many of the serial characters. The totality then is assembled loosely and cumulatively. Zola's chapters are also self-contained and build to a climax, with each representing a unit of the overall narrative, much like an individual episode of a serial series, with each novel perhaps being the equivalent of a season-long arc. (This is the way that *The Wire* and *Un Village Français* [2009–17], with each season mapping a different moment in the Nazi occupation of a French Village, are structured.) Thus the opening scene of *The Kill* (*La Curée*), the second novel in the series, introduces the storyworld of a wealthy class at leisure, its members all returning at once in a carriage traffic jam from the Bois de Boulogne with Maxime, the son of the developer Saccard, professing his admiration for his father's new wife, Renée, who for the first time notices her stepson as a potential suitor.

The subject of *La Curée* is the expansion of Paris under Baron Haussmann in an era of massive public works (where "Paris was disappearing under a cloud of plaster" [Zola 2016, 7436]) that led to the construction of broad boulevards and the founding of perhaps the first modern city. However, Zola's focus in the novel is not on the heroic monumentality of the project but the petty thievery involved in its execution.[18] The lead character in the novel, Aristide Rougon, is set up by his brother Eugene, a minister in Napoleon's government, as an official in the city-planning commission. He uses his insider knowledge of where Haussmann's boulevards will be built to buy up a series of working people's houses, evict them, and sell them to the city at a profit. (The Haussmann project of "urban renewal" had to do, as does ours, with massive cleaning of the poor and workers from their enclaves in the center of the city.) Eugene forces his brother to change his name so their connection will remain a secret, and he chooses the name "Saccard," which sounds like the French word *saccage*, a sacking or looting. The book focuses on avarice and the frenzy of speculation that grips Saccard and those participating in this public swindle who, though they were making a profit in boom times, still managed to outspend or outspeculate what they were making:

> Saccard was a worthy offspring of the Hotel de Ville [City Hall]. He had undergone the rapidity of transformation, the frenzy for enjoyment, the blindness to expense that was shaking Paris. He now again resembled the Municipality in finding himself face to face with a formidable deficit which it was necessary secretly to make good; for he would not hear speak of prudence, of economy, of a calm and respectable existence. (Zola 2016, 8277)

The title of the book, *La Curée*, is a French expression indicating the scraps, the spoils of the hunt, left to be devoured by the hunting dogs. Saccard, an arriviste, a new bourgeois, makes his fortune by foraging off the scraps that the more established, though not less corrupt, older bourgeois discard until the point where he decides, as he goes more in debt, with the dogs leaping at his feet, to go for broke—disdaining "to glean and pick up the gold which men like Toutin-Laroche and the Baron Gouraud let drop behind them. He plunged his arms into the sack to the elbows" (Zola 2016, 7502).

The book then details how frenzied investment dictated city planning at a time when "the new streets were speculated in as one speculates in stocks and shares" (Zola 2016, 7432) so that profit, not public welfare, guided the construction of the modern metropolis in a way that resulted in the haphazard construction of, for example, modern Naples, a city in ruin whose detailing in Francesco Rosi's *Hands over the City* (1963) opens with a building collapsing.

Speculation is perhaps the single word used most in the novel, and in Saccard's case it also involves or subsumes his private life. In order to get title to his wife's inheritance, a family estate which she will not sell, he sets in motion a plan to throw his son, her stepson, Maxime, at her and then blackmails her with the knowledge that she has engaged in quasi incest in order to have her cede her property to him. He withdraws his affection from her while favoring his lovers about town with gifts (scattering "banknotes on certain mantelpieces") to enhance his reputation ("as a signboard to his speculations" [7668]), all the while noting that he and his son frequent the same brothels, that is, training Maxime as a wanton seducer. He refers to his personal deception in financial terms as an "expropriation" (9411). The moment of the "expropriation," when Renée realizes father and son are working together to deceive her,[19] is described through her eyes as a rape. She refers to herself as "the maggot-eaten fruit of those two men" and feels that "Saccard had unhooked her bodice, and Maxime had let down her skirt. Then between them they had at last torn off her shift. . . . They had stripped her naked" (10360), with the "her" in this case signifying Renee herself on the personal level and the feminized city of Paris victimized by these men on the political level.[20]

Zola used the serialized novel not simply as a repetition of similar actions—though he does repeat characters throughout, with Saccard again appearing in the depiction of the Crédit Mobilier swindle in L'Argent—but to map the totality of existence under the Second Empire. Each novel functions to define one aspect of that totality. The series as a whole is related not so much through the progression of the characters but through its place in defining both a social milieu or economic sector and a neurosis, here Saccard's avarice, which accompanies life in this corrupt world of an ever-expanding capitalism.

Transmedial Seriality: Mapping the Totality through Repetition in Comics, Radio, Film, and TV

The history of seriality begins perhaps with Shahrazad, who in One Thousand and One Nights must narrate one story each evening in order for the sultan to keep her alive. Melodramatic plots and recurring characters figure as well in the Bible, Greek myths, medieval recountings of the Arthurian legend, the commedia dell'arte, and Shakespeare (García 2016, 4). Serialized fiction has its origin, pre-Zola, in Eugene Sue's *Les Mystères de Paris*, which appeared in 147 installments beginning in 1842. There is a significant leap, though, in the development of seriality in the twentieth century involving comic strips, radio, film, and television soap operas that culminates in the twenty-first century in the serial television series, which has now become the dominant form, at least critically, of this century's dominant medium. We can see this dominance in the fact that every winner of the Emmy for Outstanding Dramatic Series since 2000 was a serial series: *The West Wing* (2000–2004); *The Sopranos* (2004, 2007); *24* (2005); *Lost* (2006); *Mad Men* (2008–11); *Homeland* (2012); *Breaking Bad* (2013–14); *Game of Thrones* (2015, 2016, 2018); and *The Handmaid's Tale* (2017).

It is impossible to separate the growth of seriality from its appearance in increasingly powerful capitalist media, so that the form in the twentieth century and continuing today appears across various platforms as a way of promoting itself and other media. Soap operas, as Jennifer Hayward says, "arouse a need that can only be satisfied by—more soap" (Hayward 1997, 155). A similar "need" is satisfied by network and serial series, just as comics, radio, and film serials worked to promote each other in last century's transmediality—with that line now culminating in the Marvel Studios continuing film saga.[21] Frank Kelleter (2017) claims that serial media, as a capitalist "structural utopia" embody and sustain the capitalist myth that "there will be no end to the return to our stories," so that the disruptions of the system are experienced in a familiar way in serial narrative ups and downs. Thus the form itself reproduces "a sense of infinite futurity," without which capitalist market cultures would be seen as continually collapsing "at every crisis point" (Kelleter 2017, 104).

The twentieth-century forms of comics, radio and film seriality have also been seen as reproducing in mass entertainment the segmenting techniques of the Fordist assembly line in developing—in Gramsci's phrase—"a new type of man suited to the new type of work and productive process" where "animality" is replaced with "more complex and rigid norms and habits of order, exactitude and precision" (Gramsci 1971, 286). This production process worked in concert with the scientific management of workers called Taylorism, where time "took on the character of an enclosed space" that could be divided, filled up, and expanded by labor saving machines and by segmenting workers and turning them into a cog in those machines (Mumford 1934, 17). Thus the truncated panels of comics, the compacted story lines of radio serials, and the continual and steady flow within disruption of film serials reproduced the factory flow while also, as in streamed serial series today, speaking to a new workforce on the go, so that comic strips streamlined Dickens and Zola's novels and "delivered the pleasures and satisfactions of narrative in three minutes a day" (Hayward 1997, 94) in a "frame by frame construction enabling sudden cuts from one time or space to another" (101). This form also furthered mass production in serial development by moving from one-off gag comics to continued stories, since these were easier to write than a new joke and gag line every day (127), in much the way we have discussed Netflix industrializing seriality by simplifying through intensifying story lines.

But there is another side to the twentieth-century serial boom, and that is that it was taking place largely in the 1930s and early 1940s—in a period that Michael Denning (1998) has termed the Cultural Front, or the Laboring of American Culture—as working-class and second-generation immigrant artists moved full force into the culture industry and helped democratize it. There is also within capitalist production, as the Italian Autonomists have pointed out, a tendency for socialist forms of work to dominate,[22] as cartoonists working side by side within the newspaper syndicates in this era created "highly imaginative narrative and artistic experimentation with comic-strip themes and techniques" (Hayward 1997, 94) in what was called the golden age of adventure comics. One can then point to a competing pull within the history of seriality to map the contradictions of the system in developing the complexity of serial storytelling. Thus the moments of exploring totalities in contemporary serial television could be seen as a culmination of this competing tendency toward exposing, rather than simply validating through blind and addictive repetition, the incongruities and inequalities of the capitalist mode of production.

Comics: From One Golden Age to the Next

The adventure comic of the 1930s followed in a sense from Dickens and Zola's illustrated serial texts of the previous century and broke away from the comic strips of the teens, which were often one-frame situation cartoons. The form, parallel to narrative and serial cinema,[23] developed in place of gag strips, introducing a kind of comic realism intermixing romance and adventure plots with the hero righting social wrongs and dialogue involving harder-edged, recognizable (often working-class or ordinary) figures who sometimes spoke in working-class slang (Hayward 1997, 105). *Terry and the Pirates*, for example, employed backlit, shadowy effects; close-ups (often of weapons); and a modified four-panel use of Hollywood analytical editing. A sequence would begin with an establishing shot of the action as a whole giving way to a medium shot with character dialogue, a medium close-up of more crucial dialogue, and finally a close-up of important action or a key bit of dialogue (100).

Each four-panel daily strip often had a cliffhanger or dramatic ending, similar to the endings of the movie serials. In addition, the strip's creator, Milt Caniff, used parallel stories or parallel actions within the same story, which D. W. Griffith had pioneered in the cinema.[24] The strips also employed cinema types, such as Marlene Dietrich in *Shanghai Express* (1932) as *Terry*'s Dragon Lady (Marschall 1981, 216), to easily characterize a gallery of characters but then later to deepen characterization. The villainous Dragon Lady, based on a female Japanese pirate captain, was made more ambiguous by the admiration of and quasi romance with the strip's adult lead, Pat Ryan, making her even more like the Dietrich film persona. She later became the Chinese leader of the naval resistance in World War II. Caniff in his establishing shots used a panoramic view, suggesting a "scientific mapping of the social totality" (Hayward 1997, 119) that approximated the detachment of a Balzac or Zola and perhaps also the desire to expand the range of comic-book art.

These advances are then further layered in the second golden age of comics, that of the beginning days of the Marvel Comics Group in the early 1960s. Again there was an advance in realism, as Marvel distinguished itself from its primary competitor in the superhero realm, DC, by a new kind of vulnerability in its superheroes who were now often located in actual landscapes or working-class neighborhoods. Thus, Peter Parker's neurotically passive and quiet high school student living in Queens, who over the course of the *Spider-man* comic strip becomes more confident, was an advance on Clark Kent's eternal mousiness in Metropolis. Characters aged (somewhat); changed; had momentous events happen to them, such as "The Wedding of Sue and Reed" in

The Fantastic Four; and appeared, in terms of relational seriality, in each other's comics. The standard four-panel format was also adapted to CinemaScope and to the dawning alternative cosmologies of the 1960s as Jack Kirby's now enshrined comic art for *The Fantastic Four* allowed for full-page canvasses of the villain Dr. Doom's infernal machines and the Silver Surfer's strobe-light galaxy to be intermixed with the standard multipanel page. The changes in these two eras suggest a gradual increase in not only the techniques of expressing the social totality but a willingness to utilize these techniques for that purpose.

RADIO: ORSON WELLES'S SERIAL SHADOW

Radio drama began in the 1920s, came of age in the 1930s, and essentially disappeared with the rise of television in the 1950s. The weekly radio shows were referred to as serials, and they featured sustained settings and ongoing characters but without the open-ended quality of the comic strips or film serials. Sartre had noted that radio "produces me as an inert member of a series" (Sartre 1984, 274) through "a common voice" that constitutes a listener whose "passive, indirect action derives from his very impotence" (276). But he also noted that radio's production of subjectivity was "the social result of a political praxis" and that it was possible to question that practice and to "refute the nonsense offered" (274).

In this light, Orson Welles stressed the resistant element of the medium, defining it as "a popular democratic machine for disseminating information and entertainment" (Denning 1998, 383). In 1937 and 1938, at the moment of the height of the Mercury Theatre productions—including the Negro *Macbeth*, the Popular Front musical *The Cradle Will Rock*, and his antifascist *Julius Caesar*[25]—Welles brought his company to the air in an expansion of the power of radio to illustrate literary texts. This experiment would culminate in his 1938 *War of the Worlds* broadcast, where he used the documentary techniques he had learned while working as the voice of *The March of Time* news series to present the horror genre in a way that was believed by many to be real.

Prior to that though, Welles was the voice of Lamont Cranston, hero of *The Shadow*, in a serial drama that also advanced that form. The character has a long intermedial history, appearing in comic books, comic strips, television serials, and films, with its most famous iteration that of the radio show, which opened with the line "Who knows what evil lurks in the hearts of men? The Shadow knows," accompanied by crackling laughter.[26] The Shadow first appeared on radio in 1930 not as fully developed character but as a narrator of the *Detective Story Hour*. By the time that Welles was enlisted to play the character in 1937, radio drama had matured, with character interaction through dialogue replacing clumsy and continual narration, engineers designing sound effects that would "create pictures in the minds of the listener" (Morris 2017, 71), and radio news broadcasts themselves being integrated into the fictional world to enhance the story.[27] Welles's own improvisation, a result of not knowing what would happen next since his contract allowed him to simply show up and read the scripts, also made the dialogue livelier.

A 1938 broadcast, "The Society of the Living Dead,"[28] opens with Margo Lane, the Shadow's female protégé—a character created especially for the radio series—listening to a radio broadcast about a gang who uses confiscated passports, a complex subplot that in the end explains how a kidnap victim's death is faked. The narrative is then split, with Margo going to interview the victim's daughter, and Lamont as the Shadow approaching her suspect fiancé. The Shadow seemed to have the power of invisibility, but the power was actually that of being able to "cloud men's minds," a perfect vehicle for Welles's powerful voice to intone suggestions. The last scene, in an underground vault with the villainous fiancé and the victim, Adams, revealed to be still alive, opens with the sound of wind whistling through the cavern. The dialogue then expertly sets the scene: "There's Adams on the floor in the corner." It paints a powerful aural picture of the situation of Adams's desperation: "Give me a drink, all I've had for days is the moisture on stones." Finally, it depicts Adams's and the Shadow's predicament as the villain floods the vault—"The water is rising all around us, up to our waist now. Even though I have the power of invisibility I cannot walk through stone walls"—and their relief as in the end they are saved by the police.

Welles and the show's eschewing of the omniscient masculine narrator for more democratic dialogue was a major advance for radio and in the serial technique of the show. Narrators could often be constraining, in early soaps, for example, confining "the soap heroine by acting as master of ceremonies of the narrative itself" (Hayward 1997, 142). The drama also introduced female agency with Margo Lane, played in the show by the Mercury Theatre's Agnes Moorehead in an early attempt at bringing elements of that theater to radio. Welles himself later recalled the character in a 1946 radio commentary where he accused a Southern policeman who had beaten and blinded a black man, Isaac Woodward, suggesting that the seeds of fascism were being planted in America. In the Shadow's authoritative voice, he brands the cop as someone "who brought the justice of Dachau and . . . [Auschwitz] . . . to Aiken, South Carolina. Who am I, a masked avenger from the comic books? No sir, merely an inquisitive citizen from America" (Denning 1998, 400). Welles's intervention helped democratize the radio serial form and push it away from simple repetition to a people's form more capable of representing a totality.

FILM: SHAZAM AND WONDER IN THE CINEMATIC SERIAL

There is no more formulaic production than the cinema serial that began in the silent era—the most famous entry being the American *Perils of Pauline* (1914), with the heroine being tied to the railway tracks in the veritable definition of a cliffhanger. This early iteration of the form included the French epics of Louis Feuillade (*Fantomas* [1913], *Les Vampires* [1915–16], and *Judex* [1916]), tracking gangs often menacing Paris in serials that were beloved by the Surrealists. Cinematic seriality reached its production apogee in the Hollywood of the 1930s and 1940s, where three studios, Universal, Columbia, and Republic, churned out productions of twelve-to-fifteen episode Western, crime-fiction, espionage, and science-fiction serials.

The Republic studio's master plot, as exemplified in *Adventures of Captain Marvel*, commenced with a thirty-minute opening to set the stage, with the 1941 serial beginning as a jungle epic in "Siam," where a scientific team discovers a tomb that contains the ultimate alchemy machine, which transmutes stones to gold. Each team member is given one of the lenses of the machine so that it cannot be recouped. Meanwhile the only member of the team to refuse what he calls grave robbing, Billy—described by the native guide as "the wisest one among us"—receives the secret of transforming himself into Captain Marvel by saying the word "shazam" (an amalgam of first letters of the names of Greek sages) in order to protect the tomb's secret from the master villain named the Scorpion, who is out to reassemble the machine.

Captain Marvel in a Popular Front cinematic serial.

The following episodes have a similar structure, with the masked Scorpion, who is one of the scientists, and his men each week, in shorter, twenty-minute episodes, out to steal the lens from one of the other scientists in an episode that always ends with one of the characters in deadly peril. The next episode would begin just before the peril erupted and open with solving the dilemma. Sometimes the solution was ingenious, as when Billy and the female assistant Betty are about to be machine-gunned while reaching for one of the lenses: it is revealed the villain's henchmen are also in the room, and it is they who step into the line of fire. Other times the solution was more pedestrian, as in another episode where Captain Marvel is on a conveyor belt that ends in a guillotine, and he is simply revealed to be too strong for the blade to affect him. In this structure, the concluding episode is longer and involves the revealing of the identity of the masked villain (in this case the Scorpion is one of the two remaining scientists) and his vanquishing (here by being annihilated by the machine itself in his lust for gold). In this case, it also involves the vanishing of the hero, Captain Marvel, whose mission is accomplished. This mode of narration has been termed "incessant" by the Frankfurt School's Siegfried Kracauer (1995) and as alternating "between familiarization and spectacular disclosure" between "continuity (through formulaic storytelling and stock figures) and . . . change (through its frantic pace and special effects)."

Nevertheless, there is even in this most-routinized form a series of elements that question the mode of production, that of a bottom-line profit motive, that produced it. Billy, the youngest member of the team is referred to as the wisest, the one who is not obsessed with gold, as is the Scorpion, or with power and fame, as are the other scientists. Billy and Betty, the democratizing forces, are constantly imperiled by the greed of the master villain (capitalist), who is finally impaled by his own greed as the serial returns to Siam, site of the original grave robbing. The serial moves through a series of fits and starts that heighten the condemnation of the avarice of the villain to the ultimate vanquishing of the capitalist threat to democracy and to the world at large. Here, the repetitious movement of incessant cliffhangers does operate to reinforce the menace of greed and is resolved in its elimination. Thus, even this most-routinized serial form may struggle toward the truth of a totality.

Television: From Daytime Soaps to *Doctor Who* to *Dexter*

This brief history of television seriality will concentrate on the development of seriality as a means of mapping the social totality, then it will illustrate how an early example of Serial TV, *The Fugitive*, forecast the development of the form while synthesizing currents active in early television.

In terms of the centrality of soap operas to the development of the contemporary serial form, it is interesting to note that the first prime time television serial was perhaps the early TV network DuMont's 1946 soap opera *Faraway Hill*. Soap opera itself began in radio in the 1930s perhaps with *Painted Dreams* (1930–43), created by actress Irma Phillips, which followed the life of a bold Irish American woman and her daughter. When the genre arrived on television beginning in 1951 with *Search for Tomorrow*, the cast, now visible, needed to be expanded, and this prompted the extension of multiple characters and plot lines (Hayward 1997, 138), a distinguishing feature of the genre and one that has greatly influenced contemporary seriality.

Jennifer Hayward's description of the structure of daytime soaps is undeniably similar to that of contemporary serial television and argues strongly for a direct link. She cites as narrative codes: "resistance to closure, producing attenuation of events instead of the temporal compression of most other narrative forms; . . . distinct 'acts,' . . . ending on a note of indeterminacy;

cutting, within each act, from one to another of three or four scenes involving distinct characters and storylines; and construction of an interior world and of a complex network of character interrelations" (Hayward 1997, 149). Her description sounds a lot like the plotting of *Lost*. She notes an interweaving of "multiple *and equally weighted* plot strands" (152) but here in a form of "women's fiction" whose themes together constituted an attempt to map the position of women under capitalism: "family interrelations, romantic triangles, money and its relationship to power, and social issues" (143). Soaps also have endured, and their popularity has grown both before the Serial TV era, when they functioned as a future model, and during, when they have incorporated aspects of serial plotting into their ongoing stories.

The longest-running prime time television serial is perhaps the BBC's *Doctor Who*, which began in 1963 and is still running today, matching the longevity of many of the American soap operas. In the US in 1964, the serial-soap formula appeared successfully in prime time in the form of ABC's *Peyton Place* (1964–69), which was to serve as a model for David Lynch's most important later satirical serial *Twin Peaks*. In the mid-1970s Norman Lear syndicated the soap satire *Mary Hartman, Mary Hartman* (1976–77), and ABC followed with its own satire, *Soap* (1977–81). In the late 1970s the form briefly became a near network dominant with the oil-family drama *Dynasty* (1981–89, 2017–), *Knots Landing* (1979–93), and *Dallas* (1978–91, 2012–14). *Dallas* contained a highly serialized third season that ended in a cliffhanging final episode, resolved in a hoax, whose audience disappointment briefly ended the format.

However, in 1981—the same year as *Dynasty* premiered—the format received new life with the creation of *Hill Street Blues*, a series most famous for its morning precinct roll call and which featured continuous character arcs within a storyworld that concerned contemporary urban issues. This development was followed by the hospital drama *St. Elsewhere* (1982–88), which also featured characters whose memories did not end with the ending of the show in a continuous format that attempted also to discuss the vagaries and inequalities of the health-care system. The next wave of partially serialized series consisted of detective dramas with character arcs that attempted to map the moment of the US infiltration by drugs during the Reagan and Bush presidencies. These were prominently represented by *Miami Vice* (1984–90), which flaunted, validated, and critiqued the craze for cocaine present in Miami (and Hollywood) at that time; *Crime Story* (1986–88), a more serious example of the genre that considered the Iran-Contra relationship between South American drugs and US-government agencies; and Stephen J. Cannell's *Wiseguy* (1987–90), about an undercover cop whose multiweek arcs evolved from an opening more typical of a mafia chronicle to its grandest arc, featuring Kevin Spacey as Mel Profitt, a decadent, incestuous, upper-class drug dealer whose tentacles spread across Latin America and into the US.[29]

The most serious advancement of the form took place in 1990 and 1991 with *Twin Peaks*, which combined two previous serial forms, the television soap opera and the detective of radio, film, and television. This continuing multicharacter saga, whose purpose was to expose the seamy underside of American society in both its socioeconomic and psychological dimensions, traces the primal crime of the murder and rape of a teenage girl in its ultimate moment to her entrepreneurial father, in an intermixing of prostitution, incest, and real-estate development. The next two most serious advancements of the form included the sometimes neglected Danish medical drama *The Kingdom* by Lars Von Trier, with its multiple developing story lines centering on the destruction of nature, in the form of a child murdered long ago, by the rationalist, profit-led, masculine brotherhood of a powerful hospital. This more-politicized version of the form reached its peak with *The X-Files*, where over the course of the series the concentration on horror in individual episodes gave way to a blend of science fiction and conspiracy theory in the "mythology" or serialized episodes. The series gave voice to and seemed to define the fear generated by the growing presence of the "deep state," that hidden element of the government sensed to be infiltrating its own populace as it had manipulated prior events in the world at large.

What followed hard upon in firmly establishing the form were the cable dramas *The Sopranos* and *The Wire*, with the latter now consciously imitating the forms of Balzac and Zola in an attempt to map the totality of life in the wake of the neoliberal era of shrinking government spending in Baltimore. Seriality then spread to network television with *Lost* and *Desperate Housewives* and reached a kind of cable apogee perhaps with *Deadwood*, a series that attempted to metaphorically describe the effects of the Wild West–style deregulation of the Reagan-Bush years by localizing the metaphor in a lawless border town that with its rewriting of all laws to conform to commerce seemed to be the endgame of the neoliberal era.

The serial form, which did employ stand-alone plots, nevertheless featured a novelistic approach in "series that favor backstory and utilize the entire season [or the entire series] as the main narrative unit" (García 2016, 9). The form became so dominant that by the middle of the first decade of the new millennium even series that formerly would have been entirely episodic such as CBS's *The Mentalist* (2008–15) felt the need to feature at least an *X-Files–*throwback "mythology" of a serial killer, Red John, who had murdered the lead character's wife and daughter and for whom he occasionally searched. Serial TV became so well established even on network television that, post *Lost*, a series such as *Revenge* (2011–15) that had its own "deranged temporality" was criticized for being predictable, that is, for being only a repetitious eternal return: "What was once surprising has now become merely a formula, a soggy *déjà vu*" (12).

TV Seriality and the Totality in Embryo: *The Fugitive* and Capitalist Law versus Justice

One of the most trenchant examples of the prehistory of contemporary seriality was *The Fugitive*, a show that though it seemed to operate within an episodic format actually was in many ways serially constructed, containing a dominant, almost overpowering series-narrative arc as a feature of a show that attempted cumulatively, in an additive fashion involving its serial construction, to map the totality of the American justice system of the 1960s. The series was extremely popular (its concluding episode had the highest rating of any show broadcast up to that point, watched by almost half of all Americans with a television, and in its second season had the fifth-highest ratings of any show that season) and garnered exceptional critical platitudes (with *TV Guide* naming it best dramatic series of the '60s, James Ursini labeling it "the most self consciously noir series and undoubtedly the most successful one" [1996, 286], and J. Peder Zane terming it "the most daring and subversive network series ever broadcast" [Zane 2007, 1]). Its popular and critical success was undoubtedly connected to the fact that its serial nature was inextricably bound up with its examination of the gap between the law and American justice.

The series' premise necessitated a series-long arc: A man, Richard Kimble, sentenced to be executed for the murder of his wife, but wrongly convicted, must try to find the one-armed man he saw fleeing the crime scene while more preponderantly eluding the policeman, Lieutenant Gerard, from whose custody Kimble escaped and who is obsessed with recapturing him. Single episodes might be classed as falling into a "semi-anthology" mode in the dramatic vein of such golden age of television series as *Playhouse 90* (1956–61). This format consisted of "a small set of continuing characters whom viewers readily recognize coupled with changing weekly dramatic scenarios featuring well-known television actors" (Pierson 2011, 466). However, there was equally an overriding continuity in the hunt for Kimble by Gerard, who appeared in almost one-quarter of the episodes. Kimble's persistent outwitting of Gerard and his escape as well as a consistent developing of Kimble's status as fugitive and his relationship to Gerard and to the one-armed man, elements that were in a sense the "mythology" of the series, at times overshadowed the guest-star anthology elements.

Season 1's episodes 4 and 5, "Never Wave Goodbye," a continued story forecasting the series' two-part finale, had Kimble for the first time trying to fake his death, but Gerard proving that this avenue of escape would be unlikely as he pursues him even in the fog of a stormy sea by commandeering a lifeboat against the will of a Coast Guard captain who pronounces Kimble dead and turns back. The one-armed man is first introduced in episode 14, "The Girl from Little Egypt," as Kimble in the hospital flashes back to his spying the man leaving his house the night of the murder. The character first appears in the flesh in episode 19, "Search in a Windy City." Season 1 concludes with "The End Game," an episode almost totally focused on Gerard's attempt to catch Kimble in a manhunt, which does not even introduce the week's anthology characters, two bickering old men, until the midpoint. In "Never Wave Goodbye," Kimble also returns to save Gerard, which he will repeat many times in subsequent episodes—including stopping him from being beaten in a migrant camp ("Ill Wind") and executed by a gang of moonshiners ("Corner in Hell"). In addition, Kimble will rescue both Gerard's wife, blinded in a bus crash in the two-part "Landscape with Running Figures" as well as his son, saving him from a crazed hunter in "Nemesis."

Against the episodic dictate that the characters remain timeless, the lead characters aged, with each repeatedly tracking each season of the show as a year, and with Gerard in the final episode admitting, "I've lost a lot of things these past four years." The show concludes with a two-part finale that sheds the anthology format entirely and focuses on Gerard capturing Kimble (end of part one) and Kimble's final confrontation with the one-armed man (end of part two). This was the first dramatic series to feature a concluding episode (Pierson 2011, 159), a choice opposed at the time by the network (ABC) and the production house (QM [Quinn Martin] Productions), which feared it would interfere with selling the series in syndication. However, Roy Huggins, the series creator and a creative consultant, won out in an early assertion of the showrunner's prerogative.[30] The conclusion initiated the serial trope of recalling the beginning of the series in the final episode, with Gerard and Kimble on a train (the series had begun with a train wreck that facilitated Kimble's escape), now speeding in the opposite direction, back to Kimble's fictional hometown of Stafford, Indiana. *The Fugitive* concluded with Gerard this time saving Kimble in his ultimate confrontation with the one-armed man—and thus acknowledging Kimble's innocence—by shooting the actual murderer off a water tower.[31]

The serial element is in fact embedded in the lead character's personality and also cumulatively impacts the anthology aspect of the series, that is, the character of the weekly guest actors. Kimble is a pediatric surgeon and does effect middle-class mannerisms, speech, and thought, but his position as fugitive, as outsider, "toiling at many jobs," dominates the other aspects of his character, linking him with other working-class and marginal figures and also linking him to Huggins's own experience watching blacklisted Hollywood leftists being hunted out of jobs at the height of the McCarthy period.[32] Huggins described the appeal of the show, which one ABC executive labeled "a slap in the face of the American judicial system" and "the most repulsive concept in history": "Kimble is pursued and in the eyes of the law he is guilty. But no American of any persuasion will find him so. The idea of natural law is too deeply embedded in the American spirit for anyone to question Kimble's right, after all recourse to law has been exhausted, to preserve his own life" (quoted in Broe 2009, 110). The flight itself and Kimble's continued marginal (and in many social circles in the show immediately despised) position as a "fugitive" determines the way his particular personality is expressed in the series. In a very Marxian fashion, for Kimble and his fellow creatures on the run, "it is not the conscience of men that determines their being; it is rather their social being which determines their consciousness" (Marx 1977). It is the overriding force of the serial premise, which defines Kimble's character as primarily and foremost in flight from the law, that manifests in the series in his moods as pensive/caring/terse and which creates a dynamic character within the semi-anthology-series format, which had previously been "plagued by weak continuing characters that were tangential to the guest characters" (Pearson 2017, 474).

Kimble's innocence was not proved until the end of the series but was demonstrated each week not by the "facts" (Gerard was associated with the clinical, rationalist manhunt) but by his actions and kindness toward others, even toward the cop who is pursuing him, often at the risk of his own imprisonment, which "proved" to another character he could not be guilty of murder. Sympathy for Kimble is also generated through the deployment of a host of film-noir techniques, a form that often aligned the audience with a fugitive, borrowed from Huggins's expertise in that form in 1940s and early-1950s cinema. These included second person narration, in the booming baritone voice of William Conrad doing his best Orson Welles—who in the pilot episode intones, "In a low-rent hotel. In a side door. You're safe for now"; subjective sequences, such as the two extended dream sequences in "Nightmare at Northoak" where Kimble is finally trapped at the end of a dark alley by Gerard who fires on him; and "choker close-ups," as when we watch the fear etched on the face of Kimble as he tries to escape a murderous marshal in "Nicest Fella You'd Ever Want to Meet." In that sequence the hitchhiking Kimble sits tensely at a gas station on the edge of town as the driver nonchalantly waits for his change to give to his children. The sequence ends with the marshal pulling in front of the car and saying to Kimble, "You've just made a bad mistake, mister."

The critique of the criminal justice system is also seen in the noir association of Gerard with the lawman of the 1950s police procedural, here viewed not as community protector but as coldhearted obsessive, blind to any notion of justice. Gerard's inability to cease the chase is labeled pejoratively by a fellow police lieutenant in "End Game" a "killer instinct." He is seen as nearly suicidal as he pilots the lifeboat alone before it capsizes in a storm when it appears Kimble is dead in "Never Wave Goodbye." Gerard's name is a homonym for Javert, the villainous police officer who hounds the fugitive Jean Valjean in *Les Miserables*, perhaps the most despised character in French literature.

Quinn Martin's previous most successful show had been *The Untouchables* (1959–1963), and Huggins's show reverses the polarity, viewing the obsessive-ness of Elliot Ness in pursuing Frank Nitti as not heroic but instead the prod-uct of a diseased, small-minded bureaucrat. Gerard's depiction in this series is the inversion of the dogged Joe Friday in the McCarthyite *Dragnet* (1951–59), with *The Fugitive* questioning and satirizing the motives behind the American paranoia prompted by that witch-hunt.[33] In "Never Wave Goodbye" a former Norwegian quisling (played by Robert Duvall) who had betrayed his family to the Nazi SS ultimately refuses to betray Kimble and the woman he loves to Gerard, a parallel which indirectly associates Gerard with the Gestapo.

The serial aspect and critique of the justice system also governed the anthology aspect of the series. The secondary protagonist, who in the semi-anthology format becomes the primary protagonist for the individual episode, prototypically involved someone who Kimble encountered and helped to chal-lenge authority in their own lives. In the process, they realize their kinship with Kimble, intuitively grasping his innocence and then defying the law themselves by helping him to escape. In the pilot, "Fear in a Desert City," which established this trope, Monica, a wife separated from an abusive husband, a local power figure in Phoenix, after Kimble protects her, helps him escape. In the epilogue, standing over her husband's grave once she is finally free of him, she tells Kim-ble's pursuer, Lieutenant Girard, "He's innocent." "The law says guilty," Girard replies coldly. But the last word belongs to Monica, "The law isn't perfect. Wherever he is, he knows I believe him. I always will." The anthology aspect of the series then often involves Kimble converting (radicalizing?) one member of the populace each week as they are called upon to "harbor" a fugitive.[34]

"Nightmare at Northoak" brings together many of these strands in its quoting of a Bertolt Brecht / Fritz Lang film, *Hangmen also Die!* (1942), about the Czech execution of the Nazi butcher Heydrich. Kimble is knocked unconscious after saving a busload of schoolchildren and wakes up in the home of the town sheriff with the townspeople proclaiming him a hero. The sheriff's wife, Wilma, daughter of a judge who had told her that people must always "stick to the letter of the law," discovers Kimble's identity and turns him in to her husband, who notifies Gerard. At dinner in the sheriff's home, Gerard awaits Kimble's extradition and coldly relates near misses in his capturing of the fugitive. Larry, the woman's son—whom Kimble saved and who allowed his photo to be taken, which alerted Gerard—runs screaming from the table. Wilma asks what will happen to Kimble. Gerard, while complimenting her on the meal, mechanically explains that "a new date will be set for his execution" and then echoes the words of her father—"what's right is right."

Later the townspeople file past the jailed Kimble, shaking his hand and thanking him, with Wilma the last to approach him. After she grabs his hand, Kimble discovers the key to the jail, which allows him to escape. In the epilogue, Gerard accuses the sheriff of giving the fugitive the key and says, "You'll be arrested." His wife comes forward and claims she delivered the key. There is a hesitation, and slowly each of the townspeople claim they are guilty. Gerard furiously leaves the office, unable to arrest them all, while the sheriff puts his arm around his wife, validating her decision. Here the entire town is converted to belief in Kimble's innocence and challenges the law just as in the Brecht/Lang film when the Nazis threaten to execute hostages until the killers of Heydrich reveal themselves, everyone in the town claims to be the assassin and are thus saved execution.

The series challenged and attempted to define as unjust and rigid not only the American justice system but in many cases authority in general. In "Fear in a Desert City" one of the plainclothes cops who take Kimble for a ride in a squad car, in a visual sequence that echoes a similar false arrest sequence in Hitchcock's *The Wrong Man* (1956), explains as his reason for the humiliation, "I was born here, I'll die here, I like to keep Tucson clean as its air—I don't like strangers." The authoritarian legal figure is defined in this instance not as upholder of a universal law but as petty enforcer of a rigid and parochial conformism. In the same episode the abusive husband and businessman Ed Welles (Brian Keith), who the police trust implicitly in his distrust of Kimble

Richard Kimble being passed the "key" to his freedom in a collective resistance in *The Fugitive*.

and who eventually becomes crazed and fires on them, is a potential candidate for governor in the state. In "Nicest Fella You'd Ever Want to Meet" the sadistic small-town Arizona marshal colludes with the town mayor to whitewash an investigation into a murder the marshal has committed in return for hiring the mayor's son as his replacement.

The show also is critical at times of the citizenry who support this apparatus. The woman in the marshal's town, who Kimble risks his neck to help by telling her the marshal has killed her brother, unlike the citizens of Northoak, still believes Kimble to be guilty. When he remains behind to examine her wounded future fiancé and tells her that the injured man will be all right, she replies, "What difference could it make to a man like you?"

The series was also stridently anti–capital punishment since in its premise an innocent man had to flee to keep from being unjustly executed. In "Nightmare at Northoak" Kimble tells Gerard, apropos the actual murderer, "Your nightmare is that when I'm dead you'll find him." The series was originally to be set in Wisconsin, but Kimble's home state was changed to Indiana because it still had the death penalty when the series began in 1963, though by the time the series ended, and perhaps influenced by its intervention, Indiana had abolished the death penalty.

The series also took a condemnatory view against informing, a loaded term for the blacklistees of the previous era and for Huggins himself. In "Never Wave Goodbye" the Norwegian sailboat maker (Duvall)—who throughout the episode has appeared surly while casting lecherous looks at his sister, Karen—redeems himself and makes up for his history as a Nazi informant by first confirming but then later denying to Gerard and the Coast Guard captain that he knows where Kimble and Karen have gone. Even the mobsters in the corrupt gambling city of "A Clean and Quiet Town" have their honor, as the town's gang leader sets Kimble free because, "I don't turn over even a yellow dog to the police."

The intersection of the serial and anthology aspects with the mapping of the criminal justice totality took a unique turn in "Nicest Fella You'd Ever Want to Meet." There the anthology character, Joe Bob Sims (guest star Pat Hingle) was, underneath his smiling veneer, a cruel sadist who rather than believing Kimble wants to annihilate him. The teaser at the opening, an extract from the episode, shows Kimble beating the marshal, and the episode then slowly explains and justifies Kimble's behavior. In the opening the marshal's voice intones to a group of boys he has in thrall, as the camera pans across his trophy-laden wall, "The [wild]cat was going to go down on me and I'd be a dead man." He claims to be part Native American but when one of the boys responds, "My father says you have as much Apache blood in you as the Easter Bunny," he blanches. He is in line for being called up to join the state Attorney General's office and has a pet project of establishing an Apache park. He arrests Kimble for hitchhiking, and when Kimble's cellmate, Haley, is visited by his sister, Thelma, Joe Bob lecherously calls her into his office and closes the door, angering the (perhaps incestuous) brother. Later at the Apache Ranch, while Kimble and Haley are put to work, Joe Bob proclaims "We don't run a chain gang around here," though the strenuous work in the Arizona sun later causes an inmate arrested for drunkenness to collapse.

The marshal murders Thelma's brother by running him down in his squad car but not before revealing the sexual inadequacy that lies behind his sadism: "What am I going to do with you boy, running around with all the pretty girls in town making us old men jealous." A close-up of the marshal's face, gashed with blood after the murder is a deliberate crossing of the Norman Bates of

Psycho (1960) and the more abstract monstrous vengeance of *The Birds* (1963). Joe Bob threatens to call Gerard when he finds out who Kimble is and indeed is in the episode a kind of Gerard substitute so that Gerard's obsession here takes the short step to sadism.

A final scene has Joe Bob about to shoot a fallen Kimble. His deputy Floyd, faced with this replay of the marshal's murder of Haley and now aware that his boss is a murderer, is still about to leave the site and allow the murder of Kimble, which Joe Bob had claimed would be "my ticket to the state capitol." Floyd hesitates and finally shoots Joe Bob only when Kimble tells him Joe Bob has sold him out and will not give him the marshal's job. Thelma, also at the scene, does not believe Kimble but dismisses him—"Just go away and leave us alone"—in a way that shows that Joe Bob is not an aberration in this town but the marshal the town deserves. Kimble, the convicted murderer who is in truth the only innocent in the town, must leave stowed away in the back of a truck.

Here the seriality of Kimble's continuous plight is intimately bound up with the cumulative, week-by-week description of a justice system in defining a country that was still a McCarthyite America badly in need of the coming social revolution, which at the moment of the *Fugitive's* pursuit, had not yet dawned.

SERIAL TV AND NARRATOLOGY

Hybridity, Time Travel, and Complexity in the
Service of What Ends?

THIS CHAPTER ATTEMPTS TO define and illuminate the cluster of narrative tropes that combine to form Serial TV. These include an overriding story arc that generally encompasses at least a season but that may involve the entire series and which prompts a persistent and shifting reorganization of the episodic (ending) and the serial (developing) elements of the series; character as well as series arcs involving a multicharacter perspective; a particular attention to the construction of a densely layered storyworld, the setting that the characters inhabit, that strives either to illuminate or to fetishize some aspect of social reality. The show also features narrative breaks or caesuras, narrative leaps that include "blowing up" a series and restarting the storyworld as well as shocking series beginnings and endings and that on the character level feature deaths or startling appearances of new characters; a multiplication and expansion of time within the serial and episodic frameworks featuring flashbacks, -forward, and -sideways; an acceleration of genre hybridity in a hypergeneric fashion that may even feature each character summoning a different genre; and, an increased reflexivity on the part of the series toward other series, toward itself, toward television and the commercial reality that surrounds it, as well as toward its audience. This will also be the occasion to consider whether a final characteristic of seriality, increased audience participation, does indeed influence the direction of series or is instead merely an elevation of the addictive quality of the form in a deceptive engagement of an elusive agency that simply serves the networks and streaming services. These characteristics together describe a kind of hyperseriality developed in the hyperindustrial age.

The formal functions of seriality are best illuminated through the gains of the discipline of narratology, the study of stories and narrative. However, the field itself is, as Sarah Kozloff noted in an essay on television narrative in 1992 at the dawn of seriality, "inescapably and unapologetically 'formalist'" (Kozloff 1992, 68). The concentration here will be on extending the techniques of "making meaning" (Bordwell 1989) to show how those techniques are employed in contemporary seriality by showrunners and creators either to critique the society as a whole in mapping the totality of a social experience or, whether under the sway of the network or streaming service, to veer toward a simply repetitious eternal return. Thus, series are either moving toward an understanding of various social totalities or toward ever-deepening levels of addiction, or engaging both at the same time.

In that vein, two series that underwent startling transformations from their first to second seasons, *Arrow*, whose superhero protagonist moved from an Occupy-Wall-Street-type opponent of the 1 percent to wrecking vengeance on the underclass, and *Hell on Wheels*, which moved as a whole from a critique of industrial capitalism's drive for profit in building the transcontinental railroad to a representation of the project not as destructive but as foreordained and necessary, will also serve as a point of reference to show how a series may start out using these techniques in a progressive fashion but then employ them in a more regressive manner.

As an example of imbuing the narratological techniques with a more socio-economic perspective Sarah Kozloff (1992) points to the fact that if the text itself may be thought of as the narrator, as telling the story through the techniques of televisual discourse, the network, in the previous era, might be viewed as a supernarrator (personified by the CBS eye and the NBC peacock logos [94]) through its organization of its schedule to fit its branding. In the contemporary era the supernarrator might be personified by the burst of the dramatic musical phrase accompanied by the logo before each episode of a series on Netflix. In this discussion we will be interested in factoring in the way the supernarrator through program selection and program input makes itself felt in the process of narration of a text as well as the way the showrunner, sometimes as personification of the network and sometimes as opponent, also operates within the narrational system. The chapter will conclude with an examination of season 2 of *Justified*, which employed these serial techniques to define the socioeconomic reality of the desperate life of contemporary Appalachia.

The Narrative Tropes of Seriality:
How the Soup Comes to a Boil

SERIES AND SEASON ARCS

The defining characteristic of contemporary Serial TV is the increased or dominant presence of series and season arcs, the importance of which now may take precedence over the individual episode. In narratological terms this may be referred to as the metanarrative, or "metadiegesis," which may dominate the individual story, or "diegesis" (Favard 2016). In industry terms, we may speak of the serial versus episodic elements of the series, and in the creative language of television artists, originating with Chris Carter and *The X-Files*, we may see this as the "mythology" versus the "monster of the week." The mark of this heightened continuity is the necessity for the recapping intro that begins "Previously on . . . ," which was reflexively reinterpreted on one series in the teen language of its audience as "And that's what you missed on *Glee*."

The arcs are usually both an overall story arc (the effects of the planet-wide loss of 2 minutes 17 seconds in *Flashforward* [2009–10] or the question and ramifications of why the lights went out in *Revolution*) and individual character arcs (Jack Shephard's need in several senses to bury his father on *Lost*) that often intersect with the overall story arc (Jack's saving the island survivors as means of redemption). It should be noted that the series arc, which did define even network seriality for a period in the wake of *Lost*, has now on network, cable, and streaming services largely given way to the season arc, and this is somewhat being dictated and defined by the streaming-service release of all episodes of a season at the same time. Thus the Amazon series *Goliath*, writer David E. Kelley's (*Ally McBeal* [1997–2002], etc.) digital debut, has an overpowering single-season arc about an alcoholic lawyer's (Billy Bob Thornton) quest for justice against an arms manufacturer, which pits him against his former corporate law firm and which has a definitive ending with his winning the case and besting his former partner, so that the series characters begin again with a similar motif in the next season.

This pattern also encompasses the more rigid season seriality of Netflix/Marvel's *Daredevil* and *Jessica Jones*. Far from being in the forefront of a more open and persistent seriality, the streaming services in this instance are dictating a model for limiting the form, confining it within the season rather than opening it up to a series-long arc. This taming of seriality is also being accomplished by the networks and cable services to the point where ABC created a Sunday-night duo of series, *Once Upon a Time* (2011–) and *Revenge*, which featured sharply drawn, not season-long- but half-season arcs that conclude just before the Christmas-holiday hiatus. *Once* ends by then leaving a narrative "kernel" that will be developed in the next half-season arc,[1] and *Revenge* employed a self-referential twice-a-season bloodletting where key characters are extinguished.[2] The form, talked about as achieving a new narrative openness and thickness, is now in danger of a more patterned narrative foreclosure of its stories as the season arc has for the most part replaced the series arc,[3] both of which having originated in an "industrial context of narrative production" (Newman 2006, 25).

Nevertheless, it is not the amount of episodes but the degree of seriality that may be important in defining the progressive nature of the form. The BBC's *London Spy* (2016) lasted only five episodes, yet its combination of the gay world of *Weekend* (2011) with a John le Carré world of deception and corporate and government corruption—*Fifty Shades of MI5*—was able to map the ominousness of British surveillance and the near impossibility of exposing it while also providing in its conclusion a hope that the effort to contest it was still worthwhile. The (open-ended) closure in this serial operates in a very noncommercial way in a world in which closure itself "is becoming increasingly less economically desirable in the media landscape of high capitalism" (Smith 2013, 1) where serials and spin-offs are the order of the day.

The creation and sustaining of continuity is often discussed in terms of raising questions that create an enigma (Barthes 1974). These may be questions about the past, as in the most famous—"Who killed Laura Palmer?"— the driving enigma of *Twin Peaks* stated explicitly and elevated to a series trademark or the intense first-season arc in *Veronica Mars* (2004–7), which revolves around the question of who killed Veronica's friend Lilly Kane and whose reverberations encompass whether her sheriff father mishandled the investigation and why subsequently her mother left. These questions about the past impact the present, as Veronica, for example, must investigate her former boyfriend as potential murderer of his sister Lilly. There are also questions about the future, as all the characters in *Flashforward* move toward an event six months in the future that they have already glimpsed.

However, the characterization of the narrative as simply a question poser leads toward an eliciting and enumerating of its addictive qualities in a kind of Skinnerian model that stresses manipulation. In looking at the type of meaning the series makes, it might be better to revert to an earlier way of viewing series where the overriding question is posed as a theme rather than as a narrational-propulsion unit. Thus Kozloff sees the question in the early proto-television-feminist *Mary Tyler Moore Show* being "Will Mary Richards make it on her own?" (a question proposed in the show's opening theme) and in the working-class sitcom *Roseanne* (1988–97, 2018) as being "How are Roseanne and Dan to cope with the limitations of their life?" The answer *Roseanne* continually proposes is "through defiance and self-deprecating humor as armor for life's troubles" (Kozloff 1992, 76–77). This suggests an element of continuity even in the preserial era, where the continuing strand was thematic. To reinflect the Barthes-enigma approach with a sense of more than just how the series means, we might, for example, ask of *Twin Peaks*, "What light does the viciousness of Laura's death cast on the American middle-class inhabitants of the town?" or with *Veronica Mars* we might reframe the question as, "How does the death of one privileged member of the California coastal elite raise questions about the uneven nature of class relations in the town and the ruthlessness of its privileged elders?" This also contains a way of evaluating whether the serial concerns in the series fulfill their initial promise or betray that promise by reworking the theme, which, as has been stated, is what occurred with *Arrow* and *Hell on Wheels*.

REORIENTING THE EPISODE

The serial era, even in this most-commercial medium, has necessitated a change in the relationship between serial and episodic content even in series that were straightforwardly episodic and thus effected a change in the basic building block of television since the establishment of the series era in the mid- to late 1950s. Thus even the stick-figure *CSI* investigators have a minimal continuing arc associated with them—often involving office competency or office romance. The episodic format, especially in its police-procedural phase, rigidified in the 1990s with the syndication success of selling *Law and Order* (1990–2010) to cable (Newman 2006, 20),[4] which with its "recyclable characters and interchanging situations" jibed with network research showing that only about one-third of viewers watched a series regularly (Mittell 2010, 79–80) and thus discouraged experiments in seriality.

However with the success of, first, DVD series seasons and, second, new techniques developed by writers to refresh viewer's memories (Mittell 2010), Serial TV became instead a form that might compel sporadic viewers to return each week. The watershed season for network seriality was 2004–5 as *Lost* proved that viewers would be excited about an intricate series and *Desperate Housewives* returned the earlier soap-era serials to TV but in a more reflexive context that also emphasized a season enigma. Thus began an experimental period in network seriality (*Flashforward, Heroes* [2006–10]) sustained also by the form's success on cable but which currently has been tamed to the season arc, prompted by competition with the streaming services that now adhere rigidly to the more limited, single-season approach to seriality.

"Every serial establishes a rhythm of how much plot gets resolved in the individual episode versus how broadly the narrative disperses its information" (Smith 2013) so that fashioning markers that delineate the level of seriality of the series is now an accepted part of the work of the pilot episode. In general the serial form, even as it locates itself in the individual episode, struggles to express a totality, though this totality is registered dialectically through repetition of narrative events where finally the cumulative impact (Mittell 2015, 23) and not the repetition is stressed. Thus the mysterious events that created the monster-of-the-week scenarios in the first season of *Fringe* were seen not simply as *CSI-style* crimes of the week but instead built toward the season-1-ending revelation of a parallel world that itself was only the opening of the series arc involving the two earths.

Contemporary seriality works through enigmas, continually posed questions, but with the expectation that the questions will eventually be answered and resolved in a satisfying manner (Mittell 2010, 80). The satisfying manner in this interpretation is the truth about the particular totality, which is the series' subject and which presents its particular take on the storyworld. Thus, the answer to "Who killed Laura Palmer?" is not simply the solution to a murder mystery but also an indictment of an American bourgeoisie that is as intimately bound up in incest and corruption as was Freud's fin-de-siecle Vienna. The revelation of who committed the murder reaffirmed that this critical exposé had been the subject of the series of *Twin Peaks* from the beginning.

Thus, while there is a continual tension between "episodic closure and serial deferment" so that in the industrial context "episodic unity mitigates any textual instability caused by serialized aperture," that is, the weekly resolution allows the season's or series' enigma to continue, there is also now a greater emphasis on endings, either season or series, in which the concluding understanding of some aspect of the totality allows "a moment of rest and respite" (80) but also of clarity. With *Twin Peaks* this moment comes in the middle of the second season when the patriarchal real-estate developers Leland Palmer and Ben Horne are revealed in all their incestuous corruption. This revelation effectively ends the series, which then stumbles and sputters for the remainder of a season that existed artificially to satisfy the commercial dictates of the network.

In the process the episode is remade into a moment that though complete in itself also contributes to the overall defining of the totality, and is replete with series kernels that speak to previous moments and activate future moments, and which is much less satisfying if experienced piecemeal.[5] As Jennifer Hayward points out in discussing Dickens, comic strips, and soaps, "The serial slummer gains almost nothing. The text will appear to contain only a series of unconnected, irrelevant, and melodramatic exchanges between interchangeable characters against meaningless backdrops: narrative in a vacuum. Each serial episode means little in isolation from its long history and contextualizing narrative flow" (136).

CHARACTEROLOGY: DECENTERED, MULTIPERSPECTIVAL, AND OFTEN IN THE SERVICE OF THE TOTALITY

The claim has been made that the contemporary (golden?) serial era, or perhaps the one that has just come to a close and which is now been replaced by a more limited seriality, features "highly elaborated characters of greater accumulation and depth than any contemporary medium" (Pearson 2007, 56). With the focus on multiple characters and story lines, what was true of television previously has now amplified. Though the story lines themselves may be formulaic, the way these multiple story lines involving a host of characters combine with, parallel, contrast, or comment on each other adds layers of complexity in, as Sarah Kozloff (1992, 74) points out, a continuation and deepening of patterns developed in the episodic era. Thus births and deaths, for example, may be contrasted in a single episode (Newman 2006, 22) as often what is important is the meaning accumulated by "alternating between different storylines" (Tischleder 2017, 125).

This embracing of multiple characters and a (perhaps limited) decentering of the single-character protagonist has an antecedent in what Maria del Mar Azcona (2011) terms "the multi-protagonist film." She traces the history of the genre back to 1932's *Grand Hotel* and notes its most prescient instantiation in Robert Altman's *Nashville* (1975) and the genre's crystallization in Altman's *Short Cuts* (1993). The difference though is that in cinema, until recently under the influence of television, the multiprotagonist film remained simply a genre, whereas in the Serial TV era it is now a defining attribute of what is becoming the television dominant. Mar Azcona also points to significant films by Altman and John Sayles that construct a less-hierarchical character universe in an attempt to map a social totality. Sayles accomplishes this in delineating the corruption of the modern metropolis in *City of Hope* (1991), Altman in mapping British class relations in *Gosford Park* (2001), and George Clooney in characterizing American neocolonial relations in the Middle East in *Syriana* (2005). The majority of the multiprotagonist films, though, have simply expanded the number of characters without necessarily attempting a markedly social implantation of those characters, often dealing with individualized and purely psychologized families and relationships. The Serial TV model has borrowed from the cinema but in making multiple-character protagonists in a social setting its basis has advanced the predominance of that form.

Serial TV multiple story lines are a democratizing aspect of seriality in general, a form which historically "subverts the conventional narrative focus on a single hero and/or heroine" (Hayward 1997, 46). Multiple story lines are also a means of expressing different aspects of the totality and are conceived of as such. *Lost*—which envisioned itself as a series akin to global Hollywood films such as *Babel* (2006)—set not in the US but on a South Pacific island, was continually at pains both to retain the traditional white male/female hero/heroine in the forms of Jack and Kate while also decentering them. The series countered Jack's practical ingenuity and group leadership with the cured paraplegic Locke's mystical stoicism and rabid individualism; introduced the third element of Sawyer into the Jack and Kate relationship; and, most importantly, increased the importance of a host of characters and plotlines involving less-standard characters, such as the Iraqi Sayid, the Korean husband and wife Jin and Sun, the Puerto Rican lottery-winner Hugo, and the African American father, Michael, and son, Walt—though the last two, in more stereotypical fashion, were the first ones "kicked off" the island.

Hell on Wheels organized its characters around the project of the railroad in a questioning of that enterprise. The more-traditional lead character, the outsider and railroad foreman Bohannon, shared time with the self-serving railroad magnate Thomas Durant, whose capitalist, ruling-class world also included a corrupt senator benefiting from this building boondoggle; the ex-slave Elam, whose compatriots are actually building the railroad; the Native Americans who oppose this imposition on their land; and two sets of female characters, the camp prostitutes, led by Sara, trying to make a better life for themselves and the educated middle-class surveyor, Lily Bell, who, though her husband is dead, wants a stake in the enterprise. In a similar way, on *The Walking Dead*, the traditional authority of the lead character, the Southern sheriff, is often questioned by the multiple characters who make up the zombie-holocaust survivors and particularly at the end of season 5 by the evolving strong black woman, Michonne, who views his rigid re-creation of the Southern legal system as unnecessary and sadistic in the postapocalyptic (or post-global-warming) world. Thus, the multiple-character perspective has somewhat decentered the more traditional white, male, hetero lead character and has furthered a multiperspectival approach to defining the series totality that has because of the broadened point of view, which includes those outside the mainstream, heightened the criticism of the aspect of the social world with which the series is concerned.[6]

Hayward maintains that the serial form itself, because of its history of multiple perspectives, promotes the "gradual visibility of populations marginalized by race, class, gender, and sexual preference" (Hayward 1997, 26).

However, as practiced in television, the gradual inclusion of these minorities in the serial series may also prompt a disappearance of any sort of radical difference even in its more sedate TV version. Thus, for example, the Fox series *Sleepy Hollow* had an African American female lead whose sister was also a major secondary character. But, her blackness on the series is ignored, as is her sister's. She is simply written as any other character—adding a slight "flava" to the *Sleepy Hollow* brew, with whatever actual race and class tensions the character may suggest only appearing at a supralevel above the script in what the actress Nicole Beharie supplied of her own experience. These multiculti story lines have replaced what was in the case of African Americans in the episodic era blocks of black programming, which the networks had always been trying to eliminate without being accused of being racially biased. Fox famously was (rightfully) characterized as biased in its full-scale elimination of its black programming at the end of one season in the early 1990s in what was termed, after Nixon's Watergate-era firings of his staff, the "Saturday Night Massacre."

Finally, though character development is important, the serial era has seen that development much more centered on the exploration of the storyworld and the totality, as in the case of the characters in various aspects of the social life of a Baltimore whose institutions have been devastated by neoliberal policies in *The Wire*. Jason Mittell (2015) makes a useful distinction between centripetal series, where the emphasis on the character organization is sociological and outward toward an expanding storyworld (*The Wire*), and centrifugal, where the organization is psychological, with the multiple characters illustrating aspects of the single main character (*Breaking Bad*, whose title locates the series' subject as the downward trajectory of its lead, Walter White). However, even centripetal series that feature an individual character may be organized around illustrating a social totality, as *Breaking Bad* charts the increasingly diminished level of expectation of the American middle class. *You Are Wanted* (2017), a German series with an extremely strong centripetal focus on the intrusion by perhaps government/corporate hackers into the life of a Berlin building manager who appears to have it all, charts the character's descent into paranoia and his increasing helplessness. The series uses this intimate focus to illustrate the point that we are all already and constantly being "hacked" by corporate/government collusion and intrusion in an economy that increasingly functions through more desperate modes of centralization and programming. The "you" in the title is a social as much as an individual "you," meaning each of us.

THE SERIAL STORYWORLD: DENSITY VERSUS FETISHIZATION AND PROGRESSIVE VERSUS REGRESSIVE SOCIALITY

The concept of storyworld is a way within narratology of discussing more fully what Barthes referred to as the "referential" codes, which "refer" to the outside world, that is, the way the story, what is being told, approaches the world it seems to be representing in its construction of a parallel world "not unlike our lived reality" (Tischleder 2017, 125). This "thickening" of the storyworld in its social references is an essential element of the new seriality as serial series attempt to map specific social locales and milieus, for example, the advertising world of *Mad Men*, the New Jersey mob in *The Sopranos*, and small-town Texas as defined by its attachment to the adolescent world of high school football in *Friday Night Lights* (2006–11) (124).

David Herman (2002) describes this thickening in terms of both space and time. The episodic-era "sets," a practical way of shooting the series by having it inhabit similar spaces each week which also instill a sense of comfort, have been in the serial era expanded in a way that the living spaces of the series are imbued with an added layer of detail to thicken the expression of social reality. Thus, the transcontinental-railroad construction camp in *Hell on Wheels* was ablaze with mud and squalor, the underside of the empire-building enterprise. A scene in season 1 had the Cheyenne riding into the camp appalled with the filth and neglect in a way that recalled a similar scene in Terrence Malick's *The New World* (2005) where the Algonquin survey the equally appalling site of the decadence of the European settlers after a winter spent holed up in Jamestown.

However, the thickening of detail of the storyworld, sometimes expressed through a density of language featuring jargon or professional dialect in a way that began with the elaborate medical language in *St. Elsewhere*,[7] may simply serve an addictive rather than an illuminating end and may function as no more than writerly special effect. The Showtime series *Billions*, a struggle for power between an investment-house head (Damian Lewis) and a not crusading, but equally power-grubbing attorney (Paul Giamatti), employs Andrew Ross

Sorkin *New York Times* columnist and creator of the online investment-news service DealBook to "thicken" the financial-industry dialogue. However, since the series presents the corruption of the company head as dynamic while the attorney is simply self-seeking, the entire enterprise smacks of not revealing but fetishizing the complexity of a language where complexity itself is used to deceive and thus the series participates in the financial chicanery it nominally seeks to expose.

The second major point to be made about the storyworld and its relation to its real world referent is that the discourse around that referent may change, and as it does, in this commercial medium, this change will affect the story-world. Hence, for example, the first season of *Arrow* has the DC superhero behaving much more like a member of the Occupy Wall Street movement, which was prominent the year before the first season aired. Oliver Queen, scion of a wealthy tech company and in season 1 ominously called the "Hood," spent the season attempting to bring down the upper echelon of his native Starling ,City which included his own family and which his father, who died in his arms, had named as corrupt. The Hood was a kind of embodiment of the energy of the Occupy movement, attempting unsuccessfully to stop the devastation of the inner-city area called the Glades.

However, with the crushing of the Occupy Wall Street movement, most prominently with the police invasion in New York of Zuccotti Park, in the next season, Oliver, now with the more typical superhero vigilante name "Arrow," focused his attention instead on "fighting crime" in the Glades, which, rather than the place where Oliver's sister formed a cross-class alliance with a down-on-his-luck pickpocket in season 1, now becomes a criminal location to be feared. The Hood in season 1 laid waste to the town's elite, which is a rather radical position for a CW series, though he did express guilt at this carnage. In season 2, though, Arrow expressed no remorse for murdering the now "warlord"-controlled underclass population of the Glades, turned in its scenic decor from victimized ghetto to a dangerous terrorist-infested, third-world Baghdad, recalling the persistent presence of the US in Iraq.

Equally, season 1 of *Hell on Wheels*, conceived in a moment of the hope of change being effected in global warming in light of the approaching of the conference at Copenhagen, viewed the enterprise of railroad building as a

The Hood intimidating the local elite in season 1 of *Arrow*.

gigantic instance of speculation that devastated both nature and the Native American way of life. In light of contemporary capitalism's destruction of the environment, the series initially questioned, often through the eyes of the Cheyenne, the morality of such a venture. The lead character, Bohannon, was an outside-the-law former Confederate soldier seeking revenge against the (Eastern capitalist) Yankee imperial army that had killed his wife.

With the failure of Copenhagen and an oil-industry publicity offensive defining natural gas and fracking as "safe," season 2 effected an abrupt turn-around in a Trumpian neoliberal shift. Durant, the railroad owner who had earlier in the season expressed regret, later simply took the Cheyenne land in a way that fell in line with Exxon's "progress is inevitable and we're providing jobs" advertisements. Bohannon similarly was revoiced from film-noir outsider to Southern aristocrat, moving from being a foreman allied with his men to co-owner, now enlisted as company visionary in an enterprise he had formerly viewed as conceived by forces that had destroyed his way of life. In both cases, a change in the referential world may have directly contributed to changes in the presentation of the series' storyworld, which may "thicken" but may also turn regressive.

NARRATIVE CAESURA: THE BREAK AS SPECIAL EFFECT

Another major narratological feature of contemporary seriality is a kind of audacious use on several levels of caesura, or narrative break as a means of stunning the audience and also a kind of cost-cutting writerly special effect that on the level of narration takes the place of the much more expensive Hollywood-blockbuster visual special effects (Mittell 2015, 43). This kind of cost cutting through a script perhaps has its origin in the RKO of the post-war era, when the production head Dore Schary created a studio unit that produced low-budget but socially aware films on the model of the studio's major hit *Crossfire*, which dealt with anti-Semitism in the form of a fascist-like murderous army officer and where the "value added" was the low cost of the socially conscious aspect of the script (Broe 2009). That unit was snuffed out by HUAC and by Howard Hughes's purchase of the studio, [8] but the impulse has reemerged, shorn of its political rationale, in Serial TV, a current competitor on its own smaller scale to the big-budget studio special effects of the Hollywood extravaganza.

It must first be noted that serial narration has always abounded in narrative leaps that featured, for example, "sudden returns from the dead, doubles, longlost relatives, marginal or grotesque characters, fatal illness, dramatic accidents . . . , grim secrets, dramatic character transformations" (Hayward 1997, 4). The first major type of caesura pioneered in the hyperindustrial series is its willingness to reboot or "blow up" the series—to effect a major change not to the characters, who often remain constant, but to the storyworld, ripping the setting and its stability out from under the characters. Perhaps the most dramatic use of what is now a trope of the new hyperseriality was the suburban drug dealer Nancy's burning down of her *Desperate Housewives*–like milieu in her destroying the storyworld centering around the wealthy suburban community of Agrestic at the end of the third season of *Weeds*. Nancy and her family then take to the road, and each season thereafter involves the establishment of a new milieu, ranging from that of Mexican drug lords to a final return to suburbia, this time in Connecticut.

This reboot seemed to be a creative expression of showrunner Jenji Kohan's contempt for the now overexploited suburban milieu, but later reboots have had more commercial rationales. The abrupt dissolving of the high school glee club at the midpoint of the fifth and final season of *Glee* to concentrate exclusively on the careers of the original members of the club was an admission that the series was unable, after the original cast had for the most part graduated at the end of the third season, to accomplish anything more at the Lima, Ohio, high school level than rerun knock-offs of the already established characters. Here the reboot tacitly acknowledges that the series should have ended after its third season and was only extended beyond its organic life for commercial broadcast reasons. Likewise, the J. J. Abrams series *Alias* (2001–6) was notoriously rebooted in an episode that was broadcast after the Super Bowl in an attempt commanded by the network to attract more viewers by making the series' highly convoluted and global espionage plots more linear with neater resolutions in what Christopher Anderson characterized as a "betrayal" of viewers "who had invested thirty hours in the story" (Anderson 2005, 47).

A second type of caesura consists of shocking beginnings and endings for series and seasons, and this most spectacularly interacts with the third major type of break, the seemingly random and sudden deaths of characters—a caesura on the character level. The teaser, or opening sequence, of the *Sleepy Hollow* pilot exhibits this trend. The beginning of the episode goes out of its way to establish the relationship between the young deputy Abbie and her champion on the force, her elder, August Corbin, who is pushing her to apply to Quantico and the FBI. The mentor, who initially seemed to be a crucial series figure, is killed before the first commercial. He is the first victim of the series' foe, the headless horseman, though Corbin appears to Abbie later at crucial points in her decisions in the series. Likewise, as has been pointed out, the death of Jack Bauer's wife, Teri, at the end of season 1 of *24*, at the conclusion of a major subplot of the season that had been constructed around them reuniting, was equally shocking. Death on *24*, after the demise of Teri, became a continual spectacular effect. In the course of the series, approximately 40 percent of the characters were killed, with the device at first shocking, then becoming mundane with overuse, and finally achieving a kind of campy aspect with the series in decline. On the level of the season finale, *Revenge* developed a sweeps-period bloodletting where a major character often died in November or May at the end of the half-season arc in a way that disrupted the storyworld.[9] The trope became so standard that the question was not whether a major character would be killed but rather which major character.

Hyper- and Asynchronous Temporalities in the Service of Totality and Addiction

Just as major breaks in the narrative characterize this new hyperseriality and raise it a level from previous media's serial iterations, so too on the temporal level serial series may be characterized as generally expanding time through the use of flashbacks (analepses) and flash-forwards (prolepses) in a way that initially may be felt as a narrative break but that is often then integrated into the contemporary story or narrative frame. The level of integration often determines whether the device is simply engaged as a narrative special effect or whether time-shifts contribute to the definition of the totality by illuminating the present. The serial flashback pattern coalesced in the first season of *Lost* and was itself a continuation and heightening of the employment of the effect in the HBO prison-series *Oz*, where flashbacks were used to explain how the characters arrived in prison.[10] In the first season of *Lost* the flashback pattern consisted of a character experiencing a defect on the island, with a subsequent flashback showing how the defect had ruled their lives, accompanied by a return to the present, where in some small way they overcome or make some progress and move toward resolving the problem because of their interaction with other characters on the island. In the season-1 episode "Numbers" Hurley, who in flashback after winning the lottery believes he is under a curse that has contributed to the misfortune and death of those around him, in the present on the island is told that he is a valuable member of the island and not simply maladroit. The end of the third season of *Lost* involved a narrative trick in which a supposed flashback instead was explained as a flash-forward, and this then prompted persistent flash-forwards that later gave way to parallel universes inhabited by different sets of characters where two timelines were instantaneous (termed flash-sideways).

A backstory in a parallel milieu then became de rigeur on many serial series, with some commentators celebrating this development in which "the past becomes a world of its own" (Tischleder 2017, 123) but with sometimes mixed results. Season 1 of *Arrow*, for example, contained a backstory that sought to explain how Oliver Queen became the Hood by creating a *Lost*-type world on an island that was in its more blatant savagery a kind of mirror of the civilized savagery depicted among the upper-class leadership of

Starling City. Season 2, though, in light of previously stated changes in the series, used the island backstory simply as a prop to magnify the villainy of the island-character Slade (whose thirst for revenge is clumsily based on a misunderstanding about Oliver) who then appears as Arrow's main foe in the present. The season-3 backstory, where Oliver returns to the island after having escaped, seemed hardly to relate to the present at all, with the backstory challenge simply being to tell a separate adventure tale—one about Oliver and prisoners on the island where he repetitively returned after escaping in the previous season's flashbacks—in the most efficient and shortened way possible. Thus, the device passed over from character-enhancing addition to purely adrenaline-inducing addiction.[11]

In general, Serial TV, though, has employed the device to deepen character and storyworld and in a way that differs sharply from the way time-shifting is used in the contemporary episodic series, most notably *CSI*, where flashbacks at first illustrate correct or incorrect hypotheses about the crime and ultimately confirm the concluding scientific (forensic) discovery of the "correct" criminal in a way that simply forms part of the pseudoscientific law-enforcement apparatus that is simply the modern replacement of Joe Friday's voice of authority on *Dragnet*. The serial series with its deepening of character subjectivity through flashbacks is opposite *CSI*'s "objective" use of the technique as reaffirming what critics claim is a highly questionable and far from exact forensic science.[12]

One of the most effective uses of analepses is on the series *Once Upon a Time* which begins in its first season with a past that is also a different, fairy tale world from the New England contemporary present, followed in subsequent seasons by fairytale parallel worlds that are in time sometimes situated as parallel to the present (flash-sideways). The first-season flashbacks to the fairytale world functioned also as origin stories, and in episode 18, "The Stable Boy," the flashback to Regina, the evil queen, explained her animosity to Snow White, a trait that was central to the series, expressing itself in the present in her attempt to frame Mary Margaret (Snow White) for a murder. In this episode the backstory of Regina's love for a stable boy, Daniel, quashed by her mother who eventually kills him, dominates the contemporary plot. At the end point of the flashback story Regina, who had believed that "love is magic," adopts her mother's outlook that love is an illusion that "fades and then you're left with power; true power endures." She hardens and stiffens her voice and proclaims, "What I had with Daniel wasn't real, it was an infatuation." She embraces the child Snow, who unwittingly betrayed Regina to her mother, with an evil grin that replaces her search for love with a thirst for power and revenge that explains and deepens her actions in the present. In this instance, in the terms of the melodrama, the greedy lust for power is contrasted with a competing search for (heterosexual) love and also is viewed as a substitute for a fulfilling mother-daughter relationship.

SERIALITY AND GENRE HYBRIDITY: THE TOTALITY AS OVERLAPPING CAPITALIST SPHERES

The era of hyperseriality has also seen a hypercombination of genres, which goes beyond a previous pairing of two clashing genres in the same series. Hayward claims that this mixing is a historical feature of serials that "intertwine multiple subplots" that are "often derived from subgenres as different as romance, adventure, mystery, and crime, again to attract wide audiences" (Hayward 1997, 4). The prototypical example of the clash of genres at the beginning of the cable-serial era was *The Sopranos* with its mix of the gangster and domestic family drama, startlingly exhibited in the pilot where after the gang leader Tony has had a contentious interaction with a rival, a shadowy figure climbs into the second-story window of the family house, and we think this is a mob hit, but it is instead revealed to be his teenage daughter returned from a clandestine meeting with her boyfriend. That shocking mix of genres continued throughout the series and partially distinguished it. There is also, at a moment just prior to *The Sopranos*, *The X-Files*' combination of horror and the conspiratorial thriller, here used not merely for startling effect, but to suggest that there is something horrible and terrifying about government conspiracy with the noirish shadowy lighting that also predominates in the horror film shading over into and defining the clandestine murders and concealed sources in the world of a murky government "deep state" that Mulder and Scully are forced to inhabit. Thus, the combination of genres may also depict the way certain capitalist spheres, the provinces of those genres, interact and overlap.

While serial series began with jarring combinations of two or more master genres, they have in the wake of *Lost* evolved to accelerate the combination of genres, as Hayward suggests is true in the history of seriality, to such an extent that each character may suggest a different genre or a single character may sum up the entire history of multiple subgenres. Thus on *Lost*, the surgeon Jack Shephard's story lines frequently involve the medical profession and suggest the medical series as Shepherd dramatically goes into surgery both on and off the island with lives in the balance. Kate's escape from the marshal she was handcuffed to in the crash and her subsequent flashbacks to how she came to be convicted of murder, which in a sense exonerate her or at least present the "murder" as a justified response to a male abuser, certainly more than suggest the road movie and particularly its manifestation on television in *The Fugitive*. Elsewhere on the series, Charlie's life of sex, drugs, and rock and roll for which he is trying to atone summons up the rock-band variant of that older genre, the unhappy rise of the entertainer, as seen in *A Star Is Born* (1954). One of the key ways of varying genres is by gender-role reversals, as is the case in the last two examples.

Bohannon on *Hell on Wheels* practically crystalizes all the figures of the early television Western. He is an ex-Confederate, Johnny Yuma–type renegade (*The Rebel* [1959–61]), a bounty hunter (*Have Gun—Will Travel* [1957–63]) with a past he seeks to keep hidden (*Branded* [1965–66], in which the Chuck Connors character, in the wake of *The Fugitive*, was labeled a coward in the Civil War and needed each week to prove his bravery). These references to the past not only sum up the genre but also add layers to the character's initial outside-the-law persona, which makes him a stronger critical force in opposing the capitalist master builder.[13]

The combination of teen film and film noir in *Veronica Mars* is particularly striking for what the overlap of the two genres suggests. Rob Thomas, the showrunner, clearly wanted the emphasis on the series to be the mystery / film noir vein and opened the pilot, with Veronica at night on a stakeout but pausing in her lonely vigil outside a seedy hotel to work on an algebra problem (Mittell 2015). The next scene is the typical teen-genre opening, with the long shot of the high school and the introduction of the high school characters as the day begins. The CW network reversed Thomas's initial order in attempting to change the emphasis. However, over the course of the series Thomas prevailed, with the pilot suggesting a number of questions such as "Who killed Veronica's best friend Lily?" and "Was Lily's wealthy computer-company CEO father involved?" that predominated over typical teen-film questions such as "How will the now-shunned Veronica survive the contempt of her classmates?" and "Will she reconcile with her boyfriend?" The overlay of the noir elements and that genre's history of working-class affiliation (Broe 2009) highlights Veronica and her now-ousted-sheriff father's lower-middle-class distance from the wealthier students in a town she describes as not tolerating the nonrich. From *Twin Peaks*, another noir series, is borrowed the questioning of the twin patriarchs, in this case an arrogant actor and a CEO, as possibly implicated in a plot involving teenage sexual abuse. The crossing of what had been contrasting genres imbues the teen series with a more critically inflected and politically charged content as the teen world itself and its privileged characters is directly connected to the world of adult wealth and corruption.

REFLEXIVITY: SELF-CONSCIOUS SERIALITY AS COMMERCIAL TEASE OR AS CRITICAL ALLEGORY

One of the key aspects of the new hyperseriality is dense layers of reflexivity, in which the series proves itself knowingly conscious of the tropes of its medium, of other series, and of its own carefully constructed conventions. The commercial rationale for this layering is the series' double voicing, its appeal to two audiences at once so that those in the know appreciate the reflexive, though nonobtrusive in-jokes and references, which simply go over the heads of casual viewers. The category also encompasses an increased awareness of the social world that borders the series in a deepening of the storyworld by approximating its real-world referents, as *The Larry Sanders Show*, for example, employed actual talk show guests and engaged their personas to enhance its critique of the ethos of the late-night-television universe. Self-referentiality at its best may function to expose aspects of a commodified milieu in complex allegories of production rather than simply serving as fodder for addictive "forensic fandom" (Mittell 2015).

Reflexivity as a serial feature goes back at least to the nineteenth century, when Pierre Bourdieu points out that Flaubert in *Sentimental Education* in describing one of his characters asks the reader to "recall Rastignac in the Human Comedy," referring to Balzac's serial series and particularly to its most famous entry, *Lost Illusions*. That novel centered on Rastignac's losing his way and his morality in a Paris as treacherous as Flaubert's lead character Frederic experiences it in this later period of both Paris's history and of the history of the novel. Bourdieu views the citation, "the allusion to the internal history of the genre," as a major manifestation and declaration within the novel "of the autonomy of the field" (Bordieu 1992, 172). Similarly, in season 4 of the early serial series *The Fugitive*, in the coda, Richard Kimble, wandering alone in a teeming city, walks past Del Floria's Tailor Shop, the cover for the agents in *The Man from U.N.C.L.E.* (1964–68), so that the more-established series in a similar genre acknowledges and legitimizes the other.

There is a kind of reflexivity also in the accrued layers of an actor's star persona, in a field where the boundaries between texts are "shakier and more permeable than is the case with other narrative mediums" (Kozloff 1992, 93). For example, *The Fugitive*'s David Janssen came to the noir series with a hardened persona already developed from his previous series *Richard Diamond, Private Detective* (1957–60). There are also series that self-consciously "refer" to rather than simply copy other series in the way that *Fringe*'s credits use the block-letter categories of heightened consciousness directly in line with *The X-Files* UFO lettering in its title sequence, employing the self-conscious overlay to deepen its own conspiratorial angle.

There are television reflexive endings in the serial era that harken back to earlier series' endings. The conclusion of *Newhart* had Bob waking up and finding the entire series and his life as an innkeeper in Vermont had been a dream, a jokey reference to the *Dallas* debacle where the murder of the patriarch J. R. and an entire season was explained, in a too-obvious writerly ruse, as a dream. This beginning self-consciousness about a series ending leads in the serial era to, for example, *The Sopranos*' utterly ambiguous ending, which may or may not have concluded with the lead-gangster Tony being, in the show's self-conscious term for a gangster-style hit, "whacked." The series may equally be self-conscious about its episode beginnings—as *Six Feet Under* (2001–5), about a family of undertakers, always started with a death.

Finally, the show may expose its own mechanics, as when in a mystery pilot that undertook the work of setting up a series of unresolved happenings, Veronica Mars says, "These questions need answers," pointing self-consciously to the writerly work of creating the basis for the rest of the season.[14] This exposure also includes allegories of production, where the show's writers reflect on the process of construction in a commercial medium. George Cole points to a pivotal scene in the *Mad Men* pilot where the advertising exec Don Draper, having lost face, reclaims his position by invoking both nostalgia and a childhood imaginary ("Everybody else's tobacco is poisonous. Lucky Strike is toasted" [4311]). Both are used to sell tobacco and presented with a kind of pride that also suggests, since nostalgia and the prelinguistic imaginary are also something television plays upon, a moment of laying bare the process of series construction. Unfortunately what the particular moment in this series constitutes is a kind of reveling, as well, in the ability to addict the audience to a form that has become the digital equivalent of Lucky Strikes. Here the reflexive allegory unwittingly sheds light as well on the merciless quality of aesthetic creation fueled by the profit motive.

Fan Participation: Co-creators or Deluded Serial Promoters?

The serial era is spoken of as increasing audience participation through blogs, creating alternate series events and character trajectories, and waging successful campaigns to keep series on the air. This activity has been seen as a new democratic participation in the medium (Jenkins 1999) along the lines of Benjamin's trumpeting in an earlier era of the possibilities of radio, which included him having his own radio show.[15] In the sense that series are now constructed to elicit particular audience responses and then refined based on how successful they are at producing the desired response, this participation is real. Though, there are two salient points to make about "the tyranny of the audience" (Stiegler 2015).

The first is that, like the participants of Facebook and other social-media websites, serial television fans, under the delusion of participating in and sometimes actually creating communities, are nevertheless primarily unpaid workers whose every post increases the value of the site both by drawing new members and by exposing their personal data, which is constantly being mined and sold in order for advertisers to more specifically target them (Wu 2016). Series that address a boutique audience now are also part of the process of "delivering" that audience's preferences to advertisers, one—if not the main— way the internet is now monetizing its content (Wu 2016). In the same way, serial audiences who claim to be influencing series, in a kind of false power, are in effect unpaid workers for the studios, networks, and streaming services whose labor enhances the value of the serial product. However, it must be added that fan passion has contributed to a new monitoring of networks that has shed light on their daily practices and on the merciless quality of their for-profit treatment of serial series.

The second point is the old Adornian adage ("The attitude of the public, which ostensibly and actually favors the system of the culture industry, is a part of the system and not an excuse for it" [122]) that though they may be minutely affecting certain plot lines and may even "save" a series, fans are essentially only responding to an agenda offered by the producers, rather than the producers giving them what they want. They are in no way setting the agenda, and their heated exchanges often foster the delusion that they have some control over the process. Even fan pressure to "save" a series only ultimately rebounds positively on the owners of the mode of production who deign to listen to them and who judge the long-term publicity gain in bringing the series back more profitable than the short-term gain of canceling it. The actual attitude of serial creators to an aspect of this participation where audiences attempt to write their own versions of the series was perhaps revealed when Jenji Kohan described what she conceded was a lackluster season of *Orange Is the New Black* as being akin to "fan fiction."[16]

Tania Modleski (1983), just prior to the onset of the serial era, cautioned feminists against an uncomplicated validation of "female consumers of mass culture" in a rush to achieve and promote "real social change." Her warning still holds true for all those concerned with contemporary television seriality as a force for more than simply regressive viewing: "We have a responsibility to devise ways of meeting these needs [for social equality] that are more creative, honest, and interesting than the ones mass culture has supplied. Otherwise, the search for tomorrow [as rationale for validating consumer fascination] threatens to go on, endlessly."

Justifying Seriality: King Coal, Raylan and Boyd, and the Social Utility of the Serial Form

The FX series *Justified* ran six seasons and began with a rather loose series arc that focused on a camaraderie/antagonism (love/hate) between the lawman Raylan Givens and the outlaw Boyd Crowder. The series had for its storyworld the eastern Kentucky coal county of Harlan. The second season began a more tightly constructed season arc, rather than the first season's looser criminal-of-the-week pattern. This second-season arc concentrated on a coal-mining company, Black Pike, attempting to buy up the community's land, and it detailed the pain and misery in the interconnection of Harlan and coal, centering on its pro/antagonist Mags Bennett. The season was a model not just of contemporary seriality but also of the potentialities of the form to, by employing the array of narratological characteristics discussed above, map social devastation in a way that few series or seasons have and in a way that was only dimly echoed in the remainder of this series.[17]

The second season was the most coherently serially constructed, winning the show a Peabody Prize and its lead Margo Martindale as Mags an Emmy. Perhaps the most salient narratological feature of the series was its Harlan storyworld, and season 2 in particular refracted and referenced the social totality of "Bloody Harlan," the title of the last episode of the season, by appropriating the county's history of dispossession, violence, struggle, and outlaw economy of drugs through successive generations.

Harlan is one of the poorest, if not the poorest, counties in the US: In 2008, 34 percent of the population lived below the poverty line.[18] The poverty is intimately bound up with the history of coal mining, which still accounts for nearly one-half of US energy production. Coal, mined in the county since the nineteenth century, is the source of legitimate livelihood, but in its wake it leaves behind "leveled mountains, abandoned deep pit mines, lung disease, low pay, and dwindling jobs" (Jones 2015, 622). Coal is the subtext of the series with, in the opening of season 2, the outlaw Boyd, who is trying to go straight, emerging from the mine covered in soot and with the marshal Raylan and Boyd's deepest kinship based on the fact that in their teens they mined coal together.

Coal is also intimately connected with the onset of violence in bloody Harlan, an offshoot of the prior structural violence of an industry that devastates the environment and people from which it needs to profit. In private session (S2E7) a judge watches a homemade video of a resident dying when a mountaintop collapses (and then subsequently forbids the jury from watching the video).[19] The Black Pike Mining representative Carol Johnson tells Mags that unless she sells her land on the company's terms it "will take your mountain, blow the top off of it and the Bennett clan will get nothing." Finally, when Mags makes a deal with the company, she is accused by a farmer, Hobart, of being in collusion with a company that would "blow 1000 feet off the top of the mountain, spill it into our creeks, and wipe out our homesteads" (S2E9).

Likewise the criminal Boyd explains in season 5 that his violent ways were cultivated in the army in Iraq, which he joined to avoid the black lung disease of the mines. The county's deep distrust of law enforcement, evidenced throughout the series in its residents' contempt and suspicion of Raylan as a federal marshal, perhaps springs from a decade-long struggle with the Harlan County Coal Operators Association from 1931 to 1939 over the right to unionize, in which the company employed Chicago gangsters, the county sheriff, his deputies, the mayor, and Kentucky's governor in open warfare against the ultimately successful efforts of the United Mine Workers to win collective bargaining rights (Jones 2015, 650).[20] Thus Harlan's originary violence springs not from the residents but from the industry, with Theodore Dreiser's 1939 report, on the year of struggle that earned the county the appellation bloody Harlan, titled *Harlan Miners Speak: Report on Terrorism in the Kentucky Coal Fields*.

The history of the county is one of successive dispossessions, of removal of its peoples from their land and livelihood. Many of the residents are descendants of Scottish and Irish peoples who were brutally torn from that land in the clearances of the seventeenth and eighteenth centuries by absentee landlords (Fosl 2015, 2896) in a way that drove them either into the newly industrialized English factories as wage slaves or, as was the case in Appalachia, into exile. Likewise in the early twentieth century these émigrés from one eviction were then often pushed off their subsistence farms with the arrival of the railroad and pushed into the mines, such that, as was stated in one strike, "the miners were being starved . . . into the pits" (Jones 2015, 653). Thus, the subject of land and dispossession is a hot-button issue in the series as Boyd, sent by the coal company to clear Raylan's father Arlo off his property, is accused by the old man of being a "gun thug for the mining company. You know what your daddy would say about that." Carol Johnson threatens Mags when she refuses the company's initial offer, claiming the company will invoke eminent domain, a more refined twentieth century term for dispossession, alleging that given Mags's criminal family history the seizing of their property is "an inevitability." And, when the community discovers Mags has sold her property, they assault her store, writing "Benedict"—as in Arnold—over the name "Bennett" on the storefront and, Mags reports, with one resident breaking in and "relieving himself on the floor."[21]

The production of coal is also a determining factor in the county's history as producer of illegal substances, a way, perhaps the only way, for impoverished residents to develop a livelihood independent of mining. Kentucky moonshine was the initial flurry into this activity, which is still in the series remembered in antiquity in Mags's "Apple Pie," a sweet form of whiskey "cut with cider and cinnamon" that figures in the season arc's opening and closing. Mags also has a more-lucrative business in marijuana, estimated to be Kentucky's largest cash crop—bigger than corn, soy, or tobacco (Fosl 2015, 2707). But in the neoliberal age of the jobless recovery and the refusal of government services, the much more damaging drugs of choice have become opioids, crystal meth—the series details Raylan busting meth labs in the county—and Oxycontin, a prescription drug that is being used by the victims of neoliberal globalization to destroy themselves. (It was reported in 2016 that one town in neighboring West Virginia of less than four hundred residents was stocked with nine million pills.)[22] Raylan first encounters the Bennetts when Mags's sons Dickie and Coover knock over a stolen supply of oxycontin on its way from Miami to Detroit, stressing the county's role as halfway point in the shipping and distributing of drugs by these cities' respective mafias.

The series' storyworld materially grounds aspects of Harlan's history and does not cast it, as one critic put it, as " 'Otherness' anchoring the region in America's uncivilized past" (Park 2014). Instead, *Justified* explains Harlan's strangeness as anchored in and as a response to poverty and corporate and government exploitation. Thus its concentration on violence and its documenting of a turn toward more harmful means of coping by residents who are the detritus of globalization is not a retreat into a quasi-mystical otherness and a mythologizing of an uncivilized past but rather a charting of the material conditions that have created the collective unconscious of "America's uncivilized present."

JUSTIFIED'S SEASON, EPISODIC, AND CHARACTER ARCS OF EXPLOITATION

The show's extraordinary season 2 works though a blending of a season-long character and story arc whose center is not Raylan Givens, the lead character of the series, but Mags Bennett, the "monstrous but all too human matriarch" (Rothman 2013) whose rise and fall over the course of the season is intimately bound up with the county's and her community's relationship to coal and to the company that means to exploit and lay waste to its land for profit.[23] Mags is in a sense, over the course of the season arc, a tragic hero, but her tragedy, set in motion by her selling out by selling her land to the company, is not hers alone. As her "earlier concerns about maintaining the unique way of life are sacrificed for financial gain" (Mason 2015, 3394), her capitulation to money at the expense of her community symbolizes the death of an Appalachian way of life she had championed where social ties were bound up with the land. She is overcome not only by greed as she proves herself equal to adapting to the neoliberal world where each sells out his brother and sister and where all human ties are broken but also by the tragic history of Harlan's multiple dispossessions and exploitations.

The season opens with Mags poisoning a fellow Harlan landowner, Walter, with her "apple pie" moonshine (her profitable perversion of American motherhood) for "going outside," turning information over to the marshal, as the two sit face to face with Mags in a commanding position to the left of the frame. The season arc ends with Mags poisoning herself with the same apple pie. Now she is sitting face to face with Raylan, who has come to arrest her, and this time she is in a subordinate position to the right of the frame (Park 2014) as her plan to sell her land to the company and leave the county, to "go outside," unravels and results in the scorn of her community, the death of two of her sons, and the alienation of Walter's daughter Loretta whom she had attempted to adopt.

Episodes 1 to 6 of the arc introduce Mags and her sons as both a dominant outlaw force in the county and as admired entrepreneurs, with Mags's general store—where she says she feeds her fellow residents and caters to their food stamps—as well as her marijuana crop symbols of a successful economy outside the coal mines. Her sons Dickie and Coover, though, somewhat cut off from Mags's love and from the family income, attempt to move by theft and violence into the more lucrative market in oxycontin, which attracts Raylan's attention. Episodes 7 to 9 form a mini-arc that introduces the character of the mining company's assistant vice-president Carol Johnson, Mags's opposite, a (thin, young) Ivy League graduate with no family ties sent by the mining company to purchase the land for a form of extraction called mountaintop removal that "destroys homesteads, creeks, and the mountain itself in the process."[24] In this mini-arc Mags at first stands up for the community and then sells it out. Following the sale of her land, when she seems to have secured a future for her family at the price of her community, her empire unravels, beginning at the end of episode 9 when Raylan kills her son Coover who threatens Loretta and ending with the death of another son, Doyle, a lawman, whose family she had wanted to transport out of the county. She then poisons herself, and her death is accompanied by a bluegrass piece about "the deep dark hills of Eastern Kentucky" whose refrain ends with "you'll never leave Harlan alive."

The mini-arc, episodes 7 to 9, involving the coal company is the series' shining moment. The arc begins with Carol Johnson hiring Boyd, the series' perennial villain and Raylan's doppelganger or evil twin, to assist her in pressuring the community to sell its land. Boyd had begun the season back working in the mines but then realized, through a successful heist, that his true talent and calling instead lay in explosives, which he employed in robbing the company in an illegitimate eruption of a violence not unlike the legitimized violence the company though its mining techniques unleashes on the community. Rather than chastising Boyd, Johnson, as representative of the mining company, hires him, telling him she knows his (criminal) background and claiming she "wants one of my own to watch my back." She recognizes then that Boyd's individual street violence is akin to the company's structural violence. Raylan is charged with protecting Carol, and he compares the executive, who Mags says has come to "rape the hills of her hometown," and Boyd, claiming, "Ya'll deserve each other." When Boyd counters with the neoliberal entrepreneurial defense that in working for the mining company he's just doing his job, that is, what Carol is paying him to do, and that he and Raylan are now on the same side, Raylan deflates that claim with a bit of truth telling: "You're a hired gun thug for a crooked company."[25]

The middle of the mini-arc (episode 8, titled "The Spoil") and the midpoint in the season arc focuses on a community debate with the mining company. Carol begins by acknowledging that "coal is dirty, always has been, always will be" but that it will feed the families of this depressed region, and she points to the marshal Raylan as someone with a steady income, which the company will provide for the rest of the community. Raylan quickly counters by contrasting his federal job with the history of the private company's ill treatment of its workers in the county: "We get overtime . . . [and get paid] fifty-two weeks a year. If I take a sick day, I don't get fired." Boyd then provides the classic neoliberal rationale for letting companies (who are partly responsible for creating the desperation and poverty that allow them to make this argument) have free rein: "It's not easy for a man like me to come by honest work. . . . [The company is here to] stimulate the economy, make it fertile in infertile times. What we need is jobs."[26] It is then up to Mags, speaking not as Carol does from the podium but from the center of the meeting hall, as representative of the people, to counter that argument by citing the devastation capitalist extraction has left in its wake and that this new offensive will continue:

> All they're asking us to do is to let them come in and cut the top off our mountains. . . . The big-money men come in, take the timber and coal and the strength of our people. And what do they leave behind? Poundments full of poison slurry and valleys of toxic trash. When five hundred pounds of slurry breaks loose, the gates of hell open . . . and poison rolls down through the hollars and poisons the water, the land and everything it touches. The mining company has a word for those leavings . . . the spoil . . . and that is what our lives will be if Black Pike has its way with our mountain.

Next, she counters Boyd's claim that the county needs jobs at any price by summoning up an impassioned defense of the community. "We got our own way of courting and raising children and our own way of living and dying. And to protect all that, we have got to say 'No thank you to . . . Black Pike Mining.'" Mags's defense of the community is met by a thunderous applause but disrupted by what sounds like shots and turns out to be firecrackers, which Raylan later implies Carol had set off to break the anticorporate momentum. That the most passionate defense of the community comes from Mags, a matriarch but also a gangster, part Mother Teresa, part Ma Barker, is a very (Orson) Wellesian and Brechtian dialectical method of having the truth delivered by morally questionable characters, such as the demagogue Charles Foster Kane in *Citizen Kane* (1941) or the ex-Nazi too easily absorbed into small-town Connecticut life in *The Stranger* (1946), both played by Welles himself.

In the final episode of this mini-arc (S2E9) at the "whoop de doo" to which Mags has invited Carol to see how the community works, the matriarch gives her a lesson in just that by refusing Carol's final offer and ignoring her threat to take the land through eminent domain. Instead Mags counters by asking four times as much and for a share in the company because she and Boyd have figured out that the particular land they each own is necessary for the company to transport the coal. She also claims the company share will help feed the community, but she is seen by her fellows as betraying them after her stunning speech and this betrayal leads to her downfall.

The series delivers a final, more subtle verdict, though, on Carol and the company in this last episode featuring this character. As she is about to leave to "open up a file on the next mountain" she finally directly states what has been an underlying wish; that she and Raylan sleep together. Carol in physical appearance resembles Raylan's ex-wife and romantic interest Winona and displaces her in the mini-arc, but Winona is a court stenographer whose own money problems lead her to pilfer confiscated criminal funds from the marshal's office and thus a more representative member of the county. Raylan refuses Carol's invitation because his, as she says, "soft spot in your heart for those people" will not allow him this tainted pleasure. The way he puts rejecting her offer is in terms of her character as company shill: "In the end you know who you are." This rejection in terms of the tropes of the romantic and erotic thriller is as damning of the company as Mags's condemnation.

JUSTIFIED'S SHUNNING OF THE SERIAL HYPERTROPES

The series as a whole and especially season 2 either does not participate or participates more traditionally in the serial hypertropes of a frenetic acceleration of time and of narrative caesura employed as special effects. Besides the whole history of Harlan, there is also a prolonged backstory in the season arc that details the relationship between Raylan and Mags's crippled son Dickie. Raylan is first referred to by Mags as a great baseball player, is later seen taking batting practice, and then reveals to Carol he had crippled Dickie with a bat in a high school game after Dickie hit him with a pitch. He is finally strung up by Dickie and beaten with a bat until he is rescued by Boyd. The crucial element in the narrative discourse, the way the story is told, though, is that it unfolds entirely without resorting to flashbacks, in an older kind of storytelling that disdains the hyperserial narrative special effect for a more human and related embedding of the backstory.

Similarly, the series and the second season shuns the narrative special effect of "blowing up" or rebooting as a shocking change in that the Mags story is not introduced suddenly but is carefully built over the first six episodes in a way that allows character and story to breathe and develop. Likewise, although there are multiple deaths in the season, mainly those of Mags and her sons, they are not played as surprising special effects but rather are interwoven into the gradual downhill, tragic descent of Mags and her family, which becomes the tragedy of Harlan itself. Narrative special effects in both these cases are sacrificed to the more rewarding, but less intoxicating, slower development unfolding in an almost inevitable, rather than shocking, conclusion to a social tragedy.[27]

As for hypercombinatory genres, in the previous and more especially in later seasons *Justified* alternated between the gangster and Western, but in this extraordinary second season both were plentifully quoted but did not overwhelm and often took a back seat to the social-problem genre in its mapping of the relationship between the land and the mining company. Mags, as the strong leader of a gang of "my boys," recalls Ma Barker from the gangster film, tries to escape the criminal life but keeps being pulled back in a la Michael in *The Godfather Part III* (1990), and sets in motion a plot with an old woman to free Dickie from jail that is intercut with parallel action similar to the final

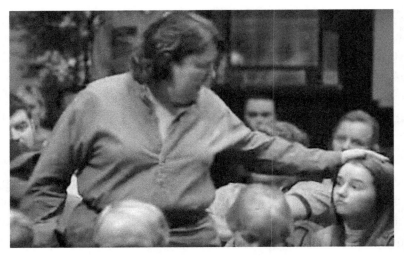
Mags Bennett's defending her community in *Justified*.

revenge montage of *The Godfather* (1972). There is also a gangster-style rise-and-fall aspect to the season arc. However, much of this is subsumed under her role as not just criminal kingpin but as representative of a downtrodden, exploited community, different from the gangster's individual hubris. (The next, more disappointing, season moves full swing into gangster territory, with the main opponent a vicious spurned member of the Detroit wing of the Dixie Mob consigned to Harlan.)

Likewise, this quasi-Western series is replete with shootouts as Doyle, the lawman, after discovering Raylan killed his brother Coover, claims he might want to "O.K. Corral it," suggesting that the feud between the Givenses and Bennetts is building to a final clan shootout (a la the Earps and Clantons). Indeed season 1 did end with an O.K. Corral–type gun battle between Boyd and Raylan and the Dixie Mob. However, season 2 fails to deliver an extended shootout and, with Doyle suddenly shot by Raylan's boss as he is trying to shoot Raylan, instead ends on the more sedate but more tragic, and more tragically linked to the community, demise of Mags.[28]

The series also reflexively refers to *Deadwood*, the series in which Timothy Olyphant, the actor who plays Raylan, previously portrayed a reluctant sheriff in a lawless county with its own exaggerated customs and modes of speaking. But equally it references Barbara Kopple's documentary, *Harlan County USA*

(1976), detailing miners' strikes in the 1970s, yet it seems in some sense to surpass that film, as the title of the last episode, "Bloody Harlan," refers instead to the more crucial period of labor unrest in the 1930s in relating that period to the present. The final bit of reflexivity, that of the series to itself, happens at the conclusion of its final episode in season 6. Raylan has captured Boyd and goes to see him in jail where Boyd asks why he has come and why he did not kill him when he had the chance. The answer Boyd guesses is because "We mined coal together years ago," to which Raylan accedes. In its last and concluding moment, the series recalls its finest moment in season 2 and that season's detailed mapping of the pain and the communal feeling generated around the county's sad, disturbing, and enduring relationship to the extractive industry that has defined it for so long.

In so doing *Justified* deploys the arsenal of serial storytelling techniques but revoices them in a way that allows them to more deeply articulate a social meaning while deemphasizing a number of the more addictive aspects of this new narrative genre.

III

SERIAL AUTEURS AND THE POSSIBILITIES OF INDUSTRIAL RESISTANCE

JOSS WHEDON AND THE
METAPHYSICS OF THE MACHINIC

THIS SECTION EXPLORES THE contradictory but progressive movement of two serial auteurs who challenge the hyperindustrial accumulationist model that has birthed a hyperseriality through television work that is highly critical of American gender politics and a false morality in the wake of 9/11. The section opens with an examination of the way the serial auteur, as an "author in discourse" (Jameson 1998), has carved out, even in a collective and corporate media, a space for challenging authority and commenting on his or her own mode of production.

Andrew Sarris's (1996) famous dictum on the film auteur—the director whose personality, either stylistic or thematic, was supposedly embedded in the film—was that "You must be a good director in order to be a great director," that is, it is necessary to have served time honing one's craft before becoming a film artist. To twist Sarris's dictum in applying it to contemporary television, where the serial explosion has expanded so quickly that even the industry, in its coining of the term "Peak TV" is currently asking if there is a saturation point and perhaps a serial-series "bubble," one could say there are many good series but not many great ones.

What distinguishes one from the other may be the presence of a strong showrunner, the television equivalent of the screen auteur, a sobriquet that suggests a more workaday approach to creativity than the implied notion of the auteur's "genius" in this most commercial of media industries. In discussing the work of these exceptional auteurs we might employ Fredric Jameson's use of the term "author in discourse" to describe those not simply responding to the social world around them but refracting it in ways that suggest a politically progressive filtering of that material that is at the same time based on that showrunner's relationship to the specific discourses that have fashioned his or her experiences. The next two chapters then will explore the work of two television auteurs, Joss Whedon and J. J. Abrams, who following in the wake of the first wave of film auteurs who contributed greatly to establishing the framework of a critical seriality—David Lynch, Lars Von Trier, and Jane Campion—have, through Whedon's commitment to feminism and to locating its struggles within the wider context of changes in the US empire and Abrams's consistent revulsion at the burgeoning US security state, greatly enhanced the medium and challenged its patently accumulationist and militarist ethic. Ironically, while the television work of each has added layers of social sophistication to a medium lacking this quality, their contemporary film work (Whedon's Avengers films [2012, 2016] and Abrams's Star Trek films [2009, 2013, 2016]) have generally participated in a corresponding dumbing down of the film industry through the creation of more sluggish and calculated franchise series that lack the vitality of their long-form work.

Serial Resistance: The Showrunner as Auteur, Author-in-Discourse, and Storyteller

Any discussion of the creative power of a single author in the context of the television industry, to which the showrunner may be both opposed and aligned, must begin with a noting of the limits of that power in an economic sector where "culture is a mere pretext to reach consumers" (Polan 2007, 281). Thus, the "author function" (Foucault 1977) is often used as a device to generate cultural capital to lure viewers and to establish the brand of the network in the way that HBO has employed film auteurs such as Martin Scorsese (*Boardwalk Empire, Vinyl* [2016]) who then make statements claiming the experience was akin to working on a film in order to "amplify a belief in the distinctive creative contribution . . . the company believes it's making to contemporary TV culture based on more established hierarchies of restricted taste and aesthetic appreciation" (McCabe 2013, 4729),[1] in this case, relating the television series to auteur filmmaking.

In addition the showrunner is not only creator but also producer of the series and thus must be extremely conscious of budget and profit margin. In this vein, one of the writers on the series *The Borgias* (2011–13) remarked that "when [showrunner] Tom Fontana writes a line he knows how much it costs."[2] Similarly, Peter Berg, the creator of *Friday Night Lights*, describes the relationship with the network as "about giving them what they need in a way that doesn't violate integrity or offend the audience" (Lotz 2014, 4360). These statements suggest the showrunner is simply a manager who limits the worst instincts of the network to make the show so much about profit and so little about taking risks that it loses its viewers. The showrunner/television auteur is also "produced," through the reception process, that is, created as a "personality" who is the locus of the series with whom fans form a relationship akin to that developed with the series' characters (Mittell 2015, 97).[3]

The showrunner is also constricted by a wide array of industry considerations, many of which involve network negotiations with actors. For Netflix's *Daredevil*, Angela Bassett, who played the lead character's nominal romantic interest, signed on for a limited number of episodes, and her presence had to be inferred in other episodes in a way that seemed to imply she was present. Elsewhere, the perennial prerogative, especially on the teen-oriented CW, of shows to feature younger casts forced Whedon in the fifth season of *Buffy* to materialize out of thin air Buffy's sister Dawn,[4] who through a magic spell had been there all along but was just ignored. Finally, Nicole Belarie was punished by the Fox network for wanting to leave the series *Sleepy Hollow* by being killed in the final episode of season 3 so that she could never return, a demise that her co-lead Tom Hinson reacted to angrily.[5]

All this being said, it is necessary to celebrate the ability of the serial-television auteur, the showrunner, to (a) carve out at least a semblance of an autonomous space, (b) in many cases build a body of work that boasts a consistent progressive engagement with contemporary social discourses, and (c) employ the power of the medium in a way that harkens back to the collective approach of the storyteller, the mythmaker, the griot, and away from the individualized and bourgeois author. It is important likewise, as with the auteur theory, to distinguish those showrunners who simply accelerate the addictive qualities of the serial form, in the auteur theory known as *metteurs-en-scene* or hacks (those who simply put industrial images on screen), what in television what might be called also-rans, from auteur-showrunners who enhance the ability of the form to express a social totality.

A significant contribution of the showrunner is the creation of a (semi-) autonomous space in a medium where this is difficult and where artistic control is transitory and always under attack. Pierre Bourdieu celebrated Flaubert's and Baudelaire's art for art's sake as the necessary groundwork for establishing independence in the cultural realm in the nineteenth century so that the artist is "able to produce themselves as creator . . . as subject of their own creation" and so that their works though constrained by "determinations in the literary field" were "not the pure product of a milieu and a market" but instead contributed to "transforming their milieu" (Bourdieu 1992, 178). They did this by dialectically acknowledging yet transcending this milieu but also by constantly, in the middle of a milieu where "economism," or profit, is all, both refusing in their work to be determined by these demands for profit and embracing and exposing the truths of these economic interests (247). Bourdieu celebrated these artists, as we might celebrate the showrunner, as ultimately in their field subordinating "external hierarchization" that is, the power of blatant commercial interests, to "internal hierarchization" (356), the interests and demands of their own milieu. Bordieu's discussion of the avant-garde literary world might equally apply to the narrative demands of Serial TV.

On television this is accomplished sometimes by sheer weight of story-telling, as Shonda Rhimes was responsible in 2014 for creating an entire night of ABC's prime time with *Grey's Anatomy* (2005–), *Scandal* (2012–2018), and *How to Get Away with Murder* (2014–). At the end of the 2016 season showrunner Rhimes had delivered 588 television episodes at a budget of $350 million reaching globally 300 million households and broadcast in 67 languages.[6] At other times the power to transform the milieu is more limited and is accomplished retroactively, as Rob Thomas's pilot for *Veronica Mars* emphasized the darker noir elements over the teen elements in the pilot for the story of a high school detective, reversed in the broadcast version that made the show look like a standard teen film, but corrected in the director's-cut DVD version, which restored the darker, more somber quality that ultimately deepened the teen angst expressed in the series.

The author is also, as Fredric Jameson notes of Bertolt Brecht, a "site" where various historical discourses meet. Thus Brecht as playwright was a part of German Expressionism in the 1920s, a German refugee from Nazism in the 1930s, a dissident in Hollywood as international refugee in the 1940s, and finally a German Socialist in the GDR in the 1950s. His works encompass, contain, and express these historical periods. The author is then not, as in the original auteur theory, a romantic genius but rather a mediator of overlapping discourses where the individual facts of his or her life involve these imbrications in political, aesthetic, philosophical, and historical representations that are expressed in their work. Thus Orson Welles's *Citizen Kane* is not seen as the work of, as Hollywood had it, a "boy genius," but rather as the coming to Hollywood of a set of discourses from Welles's experience on the New York stage involving experiments in long-take framing and Popular Front political expression.

Joss Whedon's feminism—as it evolves through the periods of the still-hopeful "peace dividend" at the end of the Cold War (*Buffy*), the rebellion against the remasculinization after 9/11 (*Firefly*), and its reinstitution within the framework of a digital militarist economy (*Dollhouse*)—marks various periods of this particular artist in discourse. Likewise, J. J. Abrams's continual opposition to the security state was expressed through his already described transformation of *Person of Interest* from CBS's protofascist police series to contesting new, more encompassing, forms of surveillance. This opposition continued in a serial trilogy that began with his projection of the increasingly conservative American militarism into the future (*Revolution*), continued with his present-day examination of corporate mind control (*Believe*), and concluded with contesting that militarism by returning to the moment it was being installed in a re-evocation of a nostalgic past that analyzed the Kennedy assassination as loss of American innocence (*11.22.63* [2016]).

Finally, the television showrunner works in a collective milieu, which, though he or she is identified as the creator, actually suggests the creation as being closer to what Walter Benjamin (2006) identifies as that of the "storyteller," where the tale in its social origins springs from collective life and its content draws on collective experience (Jameson 1969, 78), though in this instance highly commercially mediated. The television storyteller's primary mode of recounting is not, as in the cinema, visual, but rather is bound up in the story itself. The showrunner is usually not, or not initially, a director but a writer, and television directors are more often hired guns brought onto the show for single episodes whose visual sense is utilized to further the show-runner's concept.[7]

Benjamin contrasted the collective experience of listening to a storyteller to the individual, isolated experience of reading a novel, which might be akin in the media world to the difference between the more personalized avant-garde film versus the more collectively created and received television series. Benjamin also distinguished storytelling from "information," meaning the standard media news, so that information "does not survive [and only lives at] the moment in which it was new. A story is different. It does not expend itself. It preserves and concentrates its strength and is capable of releasing it even after a long time" (Benjamin 2006, 366). Thus Whedon's filtering and transformation of the discourse of feminism as it encounters the various iterations of masculinity over a set period of the evolution of the US empire has a timelessness that is more powerful than both the immediate, though jarring impact of "the news" and perhaps of the aesthetically more refined, yet more-sterile and less-collective forms of a now bourgeoisified and elitist cinematic avant-garde.

Though serial television has now produced its own auteur-storytellers, the form, in its more progressive instantiation, coalesced around the work of three film auteurs on television, and it is important to acknowledge their role. David Lynch in *Twin Peaks* pioneered the hypercombination of genres, particularly the film noir and the soap opera; introduced a visual synchronicity that linked the worlds of a traumatized fantasy and a heightened capitalism; and extended the possibilities of serial critique in his revelation of incest and family violence to be at the center of American middle-class life. Lars Von Trier followed Lynch in *The Kingdom* in confining the action to a single location, a metropolitan hospital, while expanding the time frame to also encompass the previous century's murder of a child who haunts the hospital. Von Trier's series critiques what it views as the horrors of a kind of positivist capitalist spirit of conquest of the physical world. The *Kingdom* also maps the penetration of the neoliberal age into more socialized Scandinavia in the form of the Swedish cost-cutting, godlike but murderous neurosurgeon, who belligerently asks, "In your Danish language, is there a word for budget?" And, finally, there is Jane Campion's later *Top of the Lake*, whose serial mystery of a missing girl is an invitation to investigate the differences between an outside world of a dominant and violent masculinity and an inside world of a contrasting female colony attempting to create new and more open patterns of interaction. These three series in many ways remain the guideposts and touchstones to which all series attempting to trace a social totality in a critical way return.

They, and the series discussed below and in the next chapter, counter, through their critical stance and social commitment, the nihilism of more-standard serial series which simply duplicate hyperindustrial processes in creating new and more detached forms of additive frenzy.

Joss Whedon's Misogynist Menagerie

BUFFY'S SERIAL SLAYING OF COLD WAR MASCULINITY

There are several key characteristics that define Whedon as an auteur-showrunner, all of which come to prominence in his first series, *Buffy the Vampire Slayer*. As often remarked, key to his work is his feminism, and Buffy is first and foremost a "female empowerment saga" where a teenage girl is "not the victim of creatures of horror" (Wilcox 2014, 519) but a superhero capable of defending herself from the increasing aggression of the male order and carving the outline of a liberated world based on a neutralization of that order. Whedon is a third-generation television feminist whose grandfather wrote episodes of *The Donna Reed Show* (1958–66) and *Dick Van Dyke Show*, the former with a female lead and the latter with a strong female co-lead (Laura Petrie). Whedon's father wrote for *The Golden Girls* (1985–92) but more crucially for *Alice* (1976–85), a sitcom about a single mother trying to make it on her own based on Martin Scorsese's *Alice Doesn't Live Here Anymore* (1974). Whedon himself cut his writing teeth on the working-class female sitcom *Roseanne*.[8]

A second characteristic of his television body of work is a predilection for merging his tales of liberation with the genres of science fiction, fantasy, and horror, but deploying these genres often as vehicles for creating a social metaphor rather than just as devices in themselves. *Buffy*, *Firefly*, and *Dollhouse* create specific metaphors that have to do with combatting, surviving, and adapting to new elements of masculinist terror. Thus we have the high-school-as-hell metaphor in *Buffy*, where the school, Sunnydale High, the name seeming to connote bliss, is located literally over the Hellmouth, the gateway to destruction. The metaphor is not just about high school itself but about the male threat to the young girl's path to liberation in that setting. The metaphorical quality is often noted, and one critic wrote of season 1, "Far from being the stuff of fantasy or mere over-the-top satire, [*Buffy*] is the most realistic portrayal of contemporary teenage life on television today" (Kociemba 2014, 689). Whedon often rewrites and reworks the codes of these male genres. *Buffy* opens with the teenage Buffy seemingly followed by the typical horror stalker down an alley, but she turns the tables and bests her attacker rather than, as a female would in a horror film, meekly succumbing to him (644).

To combat the embedded and ancient power of the patriarchy, Whedon, in a third major characteristic of his work, creates groups of women and men, a community of fighters against this tyranny, a community that is also reflected in Whedon's working style, in his consistent reworking of actors from show to show, and in his building of a collaborative team.[9] Whedon referred to the onscreen team of combatants he assembled in *Buffy* as the "Scooby Gang," summoning the childlike world of the *Scooby-Doo* cartoon (1969–70) to battle adult injustice.[10] His sense of community, though, and of the integrity of the collective social world may best be seen in his privileging of the collective settings of each of the three series:[11] the high school in *Buffy*, the marauders' ship in *Firefly*, and the corporate brothel/laboratory in *Dollhouse*.[12]

Finally, Whedon's concern for female empowerment and his position as an author in discourse involves him in particular moments of criticism of patriarchy as it embeds itself historically in US militarism, leading him to take positions on the post–Cold War peace dividend in *Buffy*, the immediate installation of a near–police state after 9/11 in *Firefly*, and the long-term effects of the remilitarization of US society in *Dollhouse*.

This critique might be seen most strongly in the first season of *Buffy*, a season-long duel with the Master, an ancient subterranean vampire whose appearance recalls the earliest cinematic instantiation of that monster in *Nosferatu* (1922). The Master is the locus of patriarchal power who, once destroyed by Buffy in season 1, allows newer, less devastating, more conflicted forms of evil to appear—say in the person of Spike, who Buffy eventually becomes lovers with—and whose vanquishing allows a more free play of sexual and creative possibilities while Buffy's best friend, Willow, becomes in later seasons both a lesbian and a witch. But the Master is something else also. He is the embodiment within US society and within television representation of the Cold War security state. Buffy debuted in 1997 when the idea of a peace dividend at the end of the Cold War and an end to permanent war was not yet squelched.

On popular television, the medium Whedon has chosen rather than the more lofty confines of cable or the pay-per-view HBO, the Cold War patriarch might be epitomized by a character such as Steve McGarrett, the granite-faced, silent, explosively violent and righteous protector of America's outpost (itself a colonized possession) in *Hawaii Five-0* (1968–80, 2010–). That Whedon was cognizant of this connection can be seen in his characterization of the series as "*My So-Called Life* [about teen angst, 1994–95] meets *The X-Files* [and its security state conspiracy]" (Kociemba 2014, 800). Buffy's slaying of this primeval character then opens the path for more complicated versions of femininities and masculinities in both the show itself and in the medium of poplar television in general (For more on *Buffy*'s inheritors see note 8 above).[13]

Whedon claimed he created the show based on the feminist college movement against date rape called "take back the night." In line with this movement, the series generically presents the vampire and demon intrusion on the young girl not, as in for example the Hammer *Dracula* films, as tinged with sexual excitement on the part of the victim but rather as brutal disruption of ordinary life. We see this in the girl who goes for a smoke in the bowels of the high school in "Nightmare" (S1E10) and is brutally beaten (metaphorically raped) by the demon whose masculine power fully manifests itself in the darkness. The dangers of the masculine world are equally apparent in Buffy's relationship with Angel who in season 1 episode 8 she believes is a kind of Prince Charming protector and later discovers is a vampire. In Whedon's metaphor, male power, which seems to be benevolent, may turn violent at any moment. It is only after a good deal of hostility, mutual suspicion, and a prolonged battle in the best male-female Hitchcock tradition (*The Thirty-Nine Steps*) that a tentative relationship is formed.[14]

"Nightmare" (S1E10), which features Buffy's first open confrontation with the Master, who buries her alive, is a highly reflexive exploration of each character's worst nightmare presented as either comic (beauty-queen Cordelia has frizzy hair) or terrifying (Buffy turns into a vampire herself).[15] The nightmares are prompted by the trauma of a boy who is chastised by his baseball coach who rematerializes as a demon. When the demon is vanquished the boy talks back to the coach, who is then put in jail for his cruelty. Buffy's initial nightmare of descending into the Hellmouth to face the Master also seems prompted by the coming visit of her father, who later in another nightmare rejects her, telling her she was "not nearly as bright as I thought you were going to be." Masculine power is everywhere in Whedon's world the agent of hidden traumas that must be confronted and bested before any free or collective life is possible, though in that battle a collective may form.

This auteurist reading of Whedon as author in discourse also highlights the way his commitment to employ the tropes of seriality toward critical and progressive ends counters more-standard uses of hyperserial devices as either merely addictive or as themselves facilitating the fashioning of the hyper-industrial worker.

FIREFLY'S BLOWS AGAINST THE EMPIRE

Whedon's intersection with the world of US empire had only been tangential in *Buffy*, with the show being itself a kind of impassioned plea for new freedoms, collectivities, and sexualities to grow once the Cold War, militarized Master had been vanquished. In his next television effort, *Firefly*—in the immediate aftermath of 9/11 and the imposition of a heightened security and surveillance state—about a ragtag band battling the overwhelming military force of the Alliance, the metaphor becomes more historically specific and contestatory. Here Whedon strikes a blow against the same US empire whose increasing militarization is the obverse and dark side of its supposedly enlightened hyper-industrial innovation.

As *Firefly* was in production in 2001 and 2002, the US had first attacked Afghanistan for vague reasons (since the majority of those perpetrating 9/11 were from Saudi Arabia); had promulgated the Patriot Act, expanding the capacity of the government to carry out domestic surveillance and wiretaps; and had begun, through Judith Miller's "reports" in the *New York Times* and others, beating the drums of war against Iraq. As the show was airing, the first reports emerged of US torture of Taliban prisoners in Afghanistan, and the euphemism "extraordinary rendition" entered the lexicon—this was the practice of illegally kidnapping prisoners and dumping them in foreign jails where they had no right to a trial so, as one military official told the *Washington Post*, "they [the foreign jailors] can kick the [expletive] out of them."[16]

In the series the Alliance is the combined might of the US and China, though US figures dominate. This force, having destroyed the planet referred to as "Earth that was," then projects its power into the universe and into a new galaxy. The Alliance was a term that had been bandied about by the Bush administration to engage in military interventions post-9/11 without the consent of the UN Security Council. When in March 2003, as the *Serenity* film was being conceived (as a way of ending the series after the show had been cancelled), Bush met with the Spanish right-wing leader José Aznar and Tony Blair in the Azores, the name they then used to promote the trio's illegal invasion of Iraq was the "Alliance." That the show was read as an intervention in opposition to a wholesale lifting of democratic rights can be seen in its attracting a new "overtly libertarian . . . fan base, a politically active one at that" (Wilcox 2014, 3167). The Western genre elements of the series are often summoned as a paean to a time when Americans had more freedoms, and this sentiment is voiced in the bluegrass series title song, which ends with the lyric "You can't take the sky from me."[17]

The two leaders of the *Serenity*, the battered cargo ship now used for smuggling, are the captain Mal and his first mate Zoe who, over the course of the series as Fox aired it, are revealed to be soldiers who fought on the losing side of a war against the Alliance and were crucially defeated in the battle of Serenity Valley, from which the ship takes its name. In "Bushwacked" the Alliance commander who has halted *Serenity* says Mal fought on the "wrong side," but Mal corrects him, "The losing side, [I'm] not convinced it was the wrong one." Far from, as some critics maintain in taking the Alliance position, simply being embittered (Buckman 2014), Mal is clinging to the idea of a lost freedom, as many must have felt in the wake of the oppressive Patriot Act, which was seen as limiting their opposition to the real-world Alliance. Whedon stated at the time that the Fox network, which aired the series out of order, was displeased that the show involved "nobodies" who "get squished by policy" instead of siding with the policy makers;[18] that is, the show takes a position opposing the forced consensus of the post-9/11 new Cold War.[19]

The metaphor that Whedon constructs as an author/showrunner-in-discourse includes three main forces: the Alliance (the US and its allies); the independents or dissidents (those opponents within the country); and those outside the Alliance, the Reavers and in another sense the young girl River, both of whom are ultimately revealed to be victims of the Alliance (and in terms of the metaphor stand as third- and first-world casualties of US policies).

The Alliance, as analogous to the US-led global neoliberal empire, is, in the context of the television virtual milieu, both an exterior colonizer (of the worlds of the new star system) but also, in its experimentation on River and the Reavers, an interior colonizer of minds (Buckman 2014, 3580). It is the power at the core of this post–*Star Wars* world illustrated by a static camera, representing "stasis, comfort and lack of mobility" (3600). Meanwhile Whedon employs a more jarring and unstable handheld camera effect to represent those on the periphery, including the *Serenity* crew, as impoverished and under pressure.[20] The Alliance color scheme is the more fascist grays, blues, blacks, and whites; Mal, the independents, and the impoverished worlds they hide out on are swathed in browns, ochres, deep red, and faded red or russet—earth colors identifying them in terms of the codes of the Western with the soil.

The series charts what Marx had termed the "uneven development" of today's neoliberal world as "we move from the advanced, twenty-sixth-century technology of the core planets to the nineteenth-century conditions of the rim" (Buckman 2014, 3512). The Alliance, which proclaims itself the epitome of civilization, is not above petty thievery, as when in "Bushwacked" after Mal has saved the young Alliance commander's life, the *Serenity*'s mercenary Jayne points out that in return the commander then confiscated the goods on the settler ship that Mal and his band had lifted. To let us profit would not be "civilized," Mal retorts, underlining that Alliance civilization, epitomized by the post-9/11 military and financial order, is based on power and profit.

The Reavers, living at the edge of this star system and supposedly random and savage killers, in terms of the Western are Native Americans but in terms of the contemporary metaphor are jihadists. However, it is ultimately revealed that both River's uncontrolled telekinetic powers, which can wreak awesome destruction and the Reavers' unmotivated savagery were created in Alliance laboratories in experiments gone wrong. Thus the violence, internal

Mal faces the Alliance in *Firefly*.

in the case of River and external in the case of the Reavers, unleashed in the world is the result of the Alliance, as it was felt that the US alliance's unleashing of unrestrained force after 9/11 would simply create generations of terrorists, a sentiment that has proved prescient in the wake especially of ISIS being hatched in US prisons in Iraq.[21] There is also a comparison of the Reavers and the Alliance when in "Bushwacked," having seen the destruction of the settlers aboard a floundering ship, when another ship arrives, Mal and his crew are expecting Reavers, but, in a narrative twist, instead are menaced by an Alliance ship. That is, the two are to some extent interchangeable.

Against this harsh world, Whedon constructs the community of the *Serenity*, a group of smugglers and escapees, choosing to live on the fringes of the empire rather than to join it. The ship itself is the physical manifestation of this community, with each room designating a particular aspect of the individual characters. River's room, for example, is replete with Buddhist and Eastern statuary and designs representing her more outsider status vis-à-vis the West. The ship as a whole was designed to emanate "warm, golden light, both in its afterburn and its internal living quarters."[22] The ship is also, following on from *Buffy*, a place where experimentation with sexual roles occurs, with the most masculinist character, the violent mercenary, bearing the feminine sounding name Jayne; the female first mate, Zoe, being a tough, hardened soldier married to the more sensitive and vulnerable male ship's pilot; and the female engineer, Kaylee, the most tech-savvy member of the crew, also an ingénue. The difference between this group and the group in *Buffy*, though, is that in the post-9/11 world all experimentation takes place within a militarized context and the reversal of roles still involves roles subsumed as part of a war machine.

The show then took a position counter to US policy but also counter to US post-9/11 television, where the police procedural now reigned supreme on the "homefront." In the 2001–2 season, *CSI*, with its validation of surveillance in the use of forensics to make the body betray itself, supplanted *ER*, the medical drama about saving lives. The *CSI* format was then replicated by a host of series where the police team supplants Whedon's outsider communities in a harkening back to the implantation of the first Cold War in the 1950s, highlighted by a revival of the McCarthyite procedural *Dragnet*. Whedon's troubles with the Fox network, his first foray into the world of major network television, needs to be seen also in light of these developments and not merely as a problem with the show's confounding of genre expectations and its failure to provide easily franchisable characters and story lines (Pateman 2014). Whedon had produced *Buffy* and its spin-off *Angel* (1999–2004) for the Fox Production Company but that was different from the Fox Network, more actively overseen by the corporation's owner Rupert Murdoch, a 9/11 militarization cheerleader who proclaimed himself a William Randolph Hearst–like champion of war with Iraq, which lifted Fox to number one in cable news, in the way Hearst had championed war with Spain more than a century earlier.

The Fox Network was famous for its welcoming of more *outré* television series with untried formats (the musical series *Glee*) but also famous for canceling or interfering with any series where the *outré* content veered from the merely outrageous to the politically progressive. The network in the 1990s had famously canceled in one fell swoop the majority of its African American programming having used that programming as a lure to attract white middle-class audiences. It had also altered the trajectory of its headline series *24* after 9/11 to make the lead character less a noir outsider and more a vigilante trampling on constitutional rights. Fox had also quickly yanked potentially trend-setting series such as *South Central* (pulled after five episodes) about a black woman's struggle to raise her family alone and *Rake* (seven episodes) a remake of the Australian series about an addicted-to-everything defense attorney with a much more explicit anticorporate law bent than its Aussie original. Fox was fast becoming the network where all good series go to die.

The network ran only eleven of the fourteen *Firefly* episodes and ran the series out of order de-emphasizing Mal and Zoe's roles as opposing The Alliance which is firmly established in the opening of Whedon's original pilot, which was instead the last episode aired before the show was canceled. There is also the possibility that The Alliance as an allegory of production was a stand in for the networks and particularly for Fox and the power they wielded against Whedon himself and his ragtag band, or television repertory of writers, set and production designers, and cinematographers. Whedon and his team had come from the comparatively freer atmosphere of the more distant in the network galaxy fourth and fifth networks the WB and UPN which had run *Buffy* and *Angel*. Universal Studios, not Fox, financed the film *Serenity*, and it is perhaps no mistake that the film opens with a much more explicit condemnation of The Alliance than would have been allowed on Fox. River, in a flashback, is chided for questioning her schoolteacher and told "We're not telling people what to think. We're just trying to show them how." The teacher then stabs at the young girl's head, which, through a cut, becomes a shot of a needle stabbed into her skull by the doctors in the Alliance laboratory, emphasizing that education is part of this indoctrination and that when it fails it is accompanied by more violent repressive techniques. The film's opening then, stresses in terms of the metaphor, the oppressiveness of the brave new post-9/11 world—both in its actuality and as it played out in television representation, which affected Whedon directly.[23] The serial construction of the series, which was aborted and had to be concluded in the subsequent film, nevertheless was designed to counter and critique merely addictive serial and episodic fare that surrounded it at the time.

DOLLHOUSE'S REIMAGINING OF A FRACTURED FEMININITY

Whedon's next series, also for Fox, *Dollhouse*, featured the darker vampire slayer from *Buffy*, Faith (Eliza Dushku), as Echo—here stripped of her mental facilities and confined to a corporation named Rossum that imprints her and other "Dolls" and sends them out for sexual and emotional pleasure. *Dollhouse* approached the subjects of pornography, prostitution, and rape culture but this time in a more hardened form that represented the return of a new aggressive and more open misogyny in the post-9/11 world. The pounding and more liberatory musical theme from *Buffy*'s title sequence was dramatically transformed into a much more passive doll-like chant of "la la la la la la" over images of Dushku naked, flouncing her behind, and prancing as a leather-clad mistress. The series, which at its beginning was not above indulging in the titillation it seemed to be critiquing, did ultimately chart the awakening and difficult flight to a hard-won and compromised freedom of its heroine. The serial aspect of *Dollhouse* traces the obstacles Echo surmounts: a militarized post-9/11 masculinity; the onslaught of the internet porn industry and its attendant fantasy elements—the equivalent in the more digitalized West of human trafficking in the third world; and, a dawning consciousness that the post-feminist position of knowingly enlisting in male fantasy to gain power might be contributing to a new powerlessness.

Whedon's most complicated work laid bare all of these positions while stressing the difficulties for any collective or intimate relationship to form— in the last broadcast episode Echo says, "Call us whatever you want, just not family" after her handler (pimp) Boyd had betrayed her and the group saying, "You're my family, I love you guys." The way out suggested here then is not a simple "return" to a less complicated personhood but an amalgamation of the prosthetic and the real, as Echo combines her Dollhouse personalities with her former self, the political activist Caroline. This liberation is also accomplished formally with the series shedding its more binding and restrictive episodic framework based on the Dolls' different weekly missions of servitude and moving to a kind of pure seriality in which both the female and male Dolls struggle for their freedom. It is in *Dollhouse* that Whedon suggests, a la Stiegler, that the way out of the hyperindustrial binding of consciousness is not by abandoning the digital but by absorbing it and putting its innovations to progressive use. This is a far different conjecture than passively employing the capitalist virtual world as a palliative or simply being molded by it into a better worker or weapon.

In her National Book Award–nominated *The Terror Dream*, published in 2008, the year Whedon was conceptualizing *Dollhouse*, Susan Faludi (2007) laid out the ways the response to the 9/11 attack challenging American global dominance had initiated a new militarism and colonialism in the Middle East and had likewise entailed attempts to recolonize women. These consisted of restoring "traditional manhood, marriage and maternity," complete with "regressive fixation on Doris Day womanhood and John Wayne masculinity," featuring "trembling-lipped 'security moms,' [and] swaggering presidential gunslingers." All this topped off with "old-school sexist headlines such as 'As War Looms, It's OK to Let Boys Be Boys Again,' and 'We're at War, Sweetheart,'" resulted in general in "women marginalized by mainstream media."[24] In like manner, the powerful image of a gradually more liberated Buffy, Willow, and Cordelia is replaced by Echo's forced servitude as we find that because of a past militant action she has been compelled to surrender her mind and her body to the Dollhouse. Similarly, Anthony, the shell-shocked soldier who as a Doll is named Victor, has replaced the trauma of the (post-9/11) battlefield with Dollhouse forgetting.

In the gap between *Buffy* and *Dollhouse*, internet porn and the attendant fantasies it promoted had burgeoned. By 2007 global porn revenues were estimated at $20 billion, with $10 billion of that in the US, and pornography accounted for 62 percent all internet traffic and 69 percent of the total pay-per-view internet-content market, more than news, sports, and video games.[25] The perfect bodies and willingness to serve of the programmed Dolls aped the false emptying of all resistance and phony sense of enjoyment that accompanied porn.[26] The Dolls were ultimate fantasy objects often for corporate "clients" (Johns) as Echo was for the internet baron needing to prove he has not lost his humanity and the extreme-sports fanatic turned deadly in season 1. Victor also was consigned to being a sex slave to the Dollhouse's own corporate manager Adelle. This exploitation is made possible through what in the series is termed "the tech," essentially "the dehumanization of women and the emptying of their bodies for men's pleasure" (Sutherland and Swan 2014, 4715). The equivalent to "the tech" in online porn was the now-powerful digital delivery system that makes easy access possible and almost unavoidable.

The Doll's opening position in the series may also be a result of a post-feminism that had too complacently assumed that playing the male power game, albeit willingly, would yield actual power. British novelist Melissa Harrison (2014) lamented a period in the early 1990s and 2000s when "going to striptease classes, working for a magazine with scantily clad women on the cover and attending lap dancing clubs with my then boyfriend" was a moment when "liberation seemed to mean aping the freedoms of men." Instead she claimed this path resulted in no longer being able to "tell the difference between the satisfaction that came from being approved and true pleasure. . . . Unconsciously playing to a male gallery had obscured my own experience." Echo's journey begins in a kind of postfeminist mind numbing and recounts her awakening to her radical past as an anticorporate activist, but also her being able to incorporate the post-feminist period (her multiple download-ing and missions) into her new identify as she emerges from the confining debacle of post-9/11 masculinity, the predominance of internet porn, and an ultimately confining postfeminism.

This is a harder, harsher world than that of *Buffy* or *Firefly*, one where the damage is more personal. Dushku's persona—and she was co-creator with Whedon of the series—is tougher than Sarah Michelle Gellar's. She radiated bad-girl meanness and underneath hints of past sexual abuse: first as Buffy's evil twin Faith, who had come from a traumatic background; then as the forensic doctor who communed with corpses in her next venture, *Tru Call-ing* (2003–5); and finally as Echo, where in their first meeting she stands in a prototypical fighting pose (the full Dushku) with a knife over the FBI agent, Paul Ballard, who is in love with her. Elsewhere, Boyd describes the commu-nity of the Dollhouse, unlike the flawed but sustainable groups of *Buffy* and *Firefly*, as "broken." Besides the open prostitution perpetrated by the generally rich "clients" on the Dolls, there is a case in the Whedon-authored episode "Man on the Street" (S1E6) where the Doll Sierra is sexually assaulted by a Rossum security official who tells her to be "very quiet during the game"—the closest Whedon has ventured to documenting the moment of sexual abuse.

The Ballard-Echo romance, the fated-to-be-mated series relationship, is more toxic than that of Buffy and Angel. On what Adelle ironically refers to as "their second date," they engage in a no-holds-barred brawl that ends with Echo shooting a cop with Ballard's gun to frame him, though just before running away she tells him she has been programmed by someone in the Doll-house to help him. Ballard is told by Adele early on, "You don't get the girl," and later when Echo fleeing the Dollhouse comes to stay with him, he refuses

Echo "meeting" Ballard on their "second date" in *Dollhouse*.

to have sex with her. Theirs is not even, as with Buffy and Angel, a relationship that can be "worked out" after initial distrust and hostility, though Adelle does recognize about Echo that "she loves him" and that is part of her coming to consciousness.

The forming of both individual couples and of the "family" in the enduring post-9/11 militarized atmosphere is fraught with danger and menace. It must also be added that, for the first time in a Whedon work, the major impediment to personal or collective growth is the corporation, which had not figured in previous works. Behind the new indulgence in these forms of masculinist domination is the profit motive as engineered by Rossum, which is ultimately positioned as the final enemy as the serial aspect of the series dominates in the second season.

Echo and the other Dolls' liberation from this world cannot come from a simple return to who they were. The digital "revolution" has gone too far and often too far in a wrong direction supporting misogyny for there to be an easy solution. Instead, Echo's path to freedom is a dialectical incorporation of her past radical persona, Caroline, with all the programmed experiences she has had as Echo. By the end her transformation has taken her from clean slate to palimpsest (Koontz 2014, 4454), and she has absorbed all that has been written on her. In "Hollow Men," the series' broadcast finale, when asked if she is the Doll Echo (with the name itself implying her lack of being) or the activist Caroline, she replies, "I'm everything you made me." Echo ultimately reverse engineers the Rossum technology, using the commands that wipe her consciousness (Boyd: "Did I fall asleep?" Echo: "For a little while.") to program Boyd, revealed as the Rossum head, to destroy the corporation. Victor/ Anthony attacks Rossum with his enhanced fighting skills engineered by the company, and Ballard and the neighbor who loves him, Mellie, both of whom have now been programmed as Dolls, finally claim about their feelings for each other that their synthetic nature "doesn't matter anymore, we feel what we feel."

Stiegler (2015, 82) describes this ultimate position of the Dolls as succumbing to but then surmounting the (corporate) logic that is aimed at destroying them: "There is no alternative to the destruction of public power, that is to say the unlimited expression of computational logic induced and necessitated by the total market." However, this "technical individual" who "concretizes a work made of psychic energy thus socializes as work a collective energy, that is a collective individuation founded on the dynamic power of transindividuation" (345). Thus in response to the Dolls being told that they are "definitely interesting at least on a microscopic level," that "the mind doesn't matter, it's the body we want," another Doll, Victor's companion, answers "I'm not a doll. I'm Prya." Whedon's dialectical response is that she is both; to battle much more domineering and complex technological market forces necessitates a collective coming to power and understanding while also incorporating this new level of the machinic in any mode of resistance, rather than simply suppressing or transcending it.

Dollhouse also moves from a primarily episodic series to one that is highly serialized. This is a move away from the weekly presentation of the Dolls in compromising situations where they were on the defensive against generally rich, generally male, predators with each episode containing a different situation involving the "Actives," Whedon's ironic name for the programmed Dolls. Gradually then, beginning in season 1 and accelerating in season 2, the focus shifts from the single-episode encounters of the Actives toward their gradual awakening and reclamation in a manner that is less network friendly and that moves away from individual male aggression in the series' episodic mode and begins to highlight the Rossum corporation as the primary enemy in its serial mode. Even the initial more-episodic story lines highlight the fact that relationships are now market commodities, as Mellie tells Ballard early on (S1E7) that in relationship circles she is not considered a "long-term investment" and that previous boyfriends "wanted to dump the stock before it went public."

This gradual awakening is accompanied by a dawning that Rossum, in its drive for profit, does not intend to stop at high-end prostitution but that it plans global market domination with mind-wiping technology and control of the vaccine engineered by charting Echo's own developing immunity to the treatment. As the characters are more under pressure in the second season, Whedon also shifts the shooting mode from 35-millimeter film to grainier high-definition video while employing more handheld camera as used in *Firefly* to similarly give the impression of constant struggle. There was constant struggle offscreen as well. After a second tense interaction with the Fox network, which canceled the series after two abbreviated seasons, the links between Rossum and Fox—with its pattern of profit created though a roboticized episodic format of similar fare every week—strongly suggests an allegory of production.

In this last series of the trilogy, Whedon fashions himself as a true serial auteur in a way that illustrates how seriality itself may be a progressive form used to expose masculinist corporate capital and to also write into the production a critique of the particular industry in which showrunners locate themselves. He follows then the progress and pattern of Echo, critiquing and revitalizing the form even as he engages it, with the engagement itself now written into the critique.

J. J. ABRAMS AND THE SERIAL FRACTURING OF POST-9/11 ENTERTAINMENT MILITARIZATION

IT SEEMS STRANGE TO credit perhaps the most popular and successful entrepreneur in television and film since the new millennium, the establisher of the key network serial television series *Lost* and the reviver of the Star Trek franchise, with, along with Joss Whedon, poking the most significant hole in the post-9/11 military-industrial-entertainment-complex dike. However, it can be argued that a trilogy of series from 2012 to 2014 all executive-produced by Abrams for his company Bad Robot, and all short-lived, consisting of *Revolution, Believe*, and *11.22.63*, each attempted to upend the entertainment model of the *CSI* procedural with its unquestioning presentation of the unerring accuracy of the repressive state apparatus.[1] Each employed a heightened version of the serial model to accomplish this task, and this more progressive version of the model, in its first two iterations, was met with staunch opposition by networks beginning to close ranks against the use of the model for anything but further enslaving an audience.

Abrams's company employed the serial format in this questioning and in so doing helped redefine the serial auteur. First it must be noted that, unlike the puffery about a new golden age of television, television remains, as Antonio Gramsci (2012) defined culture in general, a series of maddening openings and closings and a continual and persistent "site of struggle." The abstract quality of television narrative may "complexify," but that hardly means the form needs move to any more depth of meaning or committed programming in an arena in which as the profits increase the ability to challenge the new serial norm becomes as difficult as challenging the episodic framework of the network era. However, as this book has been at pains to point out, the serial opening does offer the possibility of expressing a totality, rather than merely engulfing viewers in an addictive return.

Series, like most forms of capitalist entertainment, are incapable of resolving the now-heightened contradictions of the system that is in the process of (a) destroying the planet environmentally, (b) unemploying over half of the world's workforce though automation,[2] and (c) continually building economies through financial speculation that eventually will crash. Some of the most interesting series on television, though, have attempted to deal with these contradictions in various ways, but it is a truism in the network, cable, and streaming eras that the best series, and often ones that in some way highlight these contradictions, are often quickly canceled.[3] *Revolution*, especially in its second season revolving around the "Patriots," challenged the distorted view of the US promulgated by the Patriot Act while *Believe* portrayed official US agencies as maniacally devoted to weaponizing all types of physical and psychic energy. *Revolution* only survived two seasons, with its conclusion coming not on television but in a four-part graphic novel, and *Believe* was quickly canceled, retired in the US, after twelve episodes. Both series bucked the imposed post-9/11 "consensus," fashioning at their core rebel bands pursued by those in power.[4]

Television's challenging of cultural norms is often a response to social openings in the society, with these series responding perhaps to a never-ending war on terror that in effect seemed instead to be promoting terror, and with the American public beginning to favor an end to ever more involving wars in the Middle East as Iraq, Libya, and Syria followed Afghanistan as combat zones, each seeming to lead to more virulent forms of violence that increasingly targeted the West. Bad Robot's attempt to undermine these policies, though ultimately not successful by commercial standards, led to compelling and more committed television. As an auteur, in this instance, Abrams, unlike Whedon with his hands-on approach, functioned more like Renaissance artists such as Tintoretto, who laid down the initial plan for the work and then had those in the studio execute it. Abrams was executive producer of all three series but not writer and director, with Eric Kripke and the film director Alfonso Cuarón handling those duties for *Revolution* and *Believe* respectively.

REVOLUTION: THE END OF PATRIOT GAMES

In the wake of the persistent recession in the American economy from the crash of 2008 and the failure of the 2009 Copenhagen climate conference to halt global warming, American television series, following cable's most popular series, *The Walking Dead*, began to experiment with various present and future dystopias.[5] *Revolution* was NBC's entry in that cycle in the 2012 season. The series is set fifteen years in the future, after a mysterious blackout in 2012 permanently cuts all electricity. *Revolution*'s character structure centers around one jaded family, the Mathesons and particularly teenage Charlie, who sees her father, Ben, killed in front of her. The show also features Charlie's uncle Miles, an ex-mercenary and deserter who joins Charlie after being cofounder of the warlord-run "Monroe Republic," and her mother, Rachel, who with her dead husband, Ben, is revealed to have designed the technology that caused the blackout.

Both seasons are highly serialized, with one built around bringing down the East Coast warlord empire Miles cofounded and the second with the band out west battling the Patriots, a brown-suited (suggesting Hitler's SA) group formerly quartered in Guantanamo Bay, where so much US torture had taken place. The Patriots are led by an ex-US Secretary of Defense who deployed nuclear missiles against the republics of Georgia and Philadelphia in the first season and who returns to the mainland to pit the areas of Texas and California against each other in reconquering the country.[6]

The structure of the two seasons follows the cable structure of the first two seasons of *The Walking Dead*. Season 1 has more of a road-movie-type layout, featuring the resistant group each week retaking areas of the republic and constantly on the run as is the group in the cable series. The second season situates them in a single location in Texas being assaulted each week by the Patriots as the group from *The Walking Dead* settle in the farmhouse in its second season. The episodic quality of the series, where a set pattern evolves for each episode, is replaced by a serial development of character and a continually evolving challenge of the band to their opponents. However, especially in the first season, this constant moving and being in danger does have a patterned feel to it, the result of a twenty-episode run, which is more difficult to sustain without some form of patterned repetition than cable's thirteen-episode, less-standard season.[7]

The Rebels threatened with "Patriot games" in *Revolution*.

While progressive in its choice of enemy, the show's energy politics were highly suspect, since at the time of the initial broadcast NBC was still owned by General Electric and the idea of focusing a series around all that was lost by electricity deprivation was a direct benefit to the network's corporate owner. In the second season the producers partnered with a United Nations task force, focusing attention on the world's "energy poor" in promoting its message,[8] while also calling attention to the possibility of running out of energy, a "concern" that helps promote subsidies for GE and the rest of the energy industry. On the other hand, the postapocalyptic world where resources are thin and where there is a return to more primitive forms of subsistence functions more critically as the imagining of a world impoverished through automation and an income gap that has continued to widen after what many Americans outside Wall Street experienced as a permanent economic "blackout" following the 2008 Great Recession.

There is also a knowledge among the series' lead characters that they have played a part in the destruction of the world, just as the US, historically the world's largest carbon emitter, in 2017 having dropped out of the Paris Accords, has played a devastating part in bringing the Earth to the brink of catastrophe. Near the end of the series (S2E20) Miles professes his love for Rachel by tacitly acknowledging this guilt: "You're a miserable person. We both are. You ended the world. I put a nail in its coffin. Hell of a pair." This is perhaps the first acknowledgment in American television of the guilt of a privileged American middle class in continuing to maintain its right to widen the carbon footprint in order to maintain its lifestyle.

The second-season villains, the Patriots, are clearly similar to the George W. Bush neocons and stalwarts of the security state. This final season before the show was cancelled emphasized the fascism concealed under the American flag and other patriotic paraphernalia. The contrast is revealed even in the titles of the first two episodes, with "Born in the U.S.A.," recalling the Springsteen song used by the Reagan campaign, giving way to "There Will Be Blood," a recollection of the Paul Thomas Anderson film about the viciousness of the oil industry concealed under the patriotic patina of corporate power. In the series mythology, the Patriots, led by "President" Jack Davis—who, after the blackout had staged a coup, assassinating the vice president and wrapping himself in a legal mantle that concealed the fact that the democracy was now being run on a warlike basis by the ex-Secretary of Defense—evoked Bush's cabinet as it was run by Defense's Donald Rumsfeld and the energy czar Vice President Dick Cheney. To install himself in power this dictator dropped nuclear bombs on Atlanta and Philadelphia. He is presented as a sociopath who murders those around him who disobey his orders and plans to install a "new order for the ages," whose "brand" is drawn from the insignia on the US presidential seal, implying that this order which Davis refers to as "manifest destiny" may be arriving in the present.

In "Tomorrowland," the penultimate episode before the two-part, series-ending finale, Ed Truman (whose name is that of the president who began the post–World War II military buildup), carries out Davis's orders deploying mustard gas to stamp out the opposition, with the Patriots then entering the town Charlie, Miles, and Rachel inhabit wearing gas masks and brutally murdering the townspeople. The idea of chemical-weapons use wrapped in the US flag is a direct reversal of the Bush- and Obama-era claims about Saddam Hussein, Muammar Gaddafi, and Bashar Assad's use of chemical weapons used as a pretext to invade Iraq, Libya, and Syria for colonial and energy gain. The band survives the attack by burying themselves in a storage tank. They demonstrate the effects of the gas and the fact that the Patriots are using it to Truman's girlfriend to get her to spy on him, with Miles telling her, "They're not the squeaky clean US you think they are." She then becomes convinced and agrees to act against Truman—as a result of a scene that is a reversal of the many US appearances in world forums claiming that its destruction of the

Middle East is justified by a moral high ground. Abrams's apocalyptic future broaches a nearly direct critique of an American present.

The serial aspect in the second season accelerates as the stakes become greater in the battle against the Patriots. The first season—where the enemy was the more mundane and simply openly mercenary Monroe Empire led by Miles's former partner—employed as its serial structuring device a series of constant attacks and retreats staged on the warlord's fortress in a repetitive pattern. The second season had far less repetition as the now-defeated Monroe joined the battle against a more formidable and ideologically specific opponent. That season was structured on the ever more menacing threat of the Patriots as they attempted to consolidate power and on the response of the band to those threats.

As the series became more critical of contemporary US power in its reflection in this apocalyptic future, the serial element increased as well, overflowing the restraints in the way the network episodic format attempted to confine the story. The transgression was rewarded with the show being unceremoniously canceled without resolving its series-long questions about the possibility of restoring power. The series finally came to an end in a four-part digital comic book that tied up loose ends from the second season. The series especially in its more strongly serialized second season proved too critical for network television.

BELIEVE'S ASSAULT ON THE CONTEMPORARY SECURITY STATE: WHO'S YOUR DADDY?

Believe continues the assault on the post -/11 military-industrial-entertainment complex by summoning up two resistant popular works with roots in the 1960s. The first is Stephen King's *Firestarter*, in which the daughter of parents experimented on by the CIA, in a way that recalls the MKUltra CIA mind-control experiments, is endowed with destructive psychic powers. In the series, this character is reborn as Bo, separated at birth from her parents, with her psychic powers coveted by a corporate and government Dr. Mengele–type scientist, Roman Skouras. The second series quoted is *The Fugitive* with Bo's actual father, Tate, a falsely convicted murderer rescued from death row, though after spending seven years in prison, by a renegade scientist from Skouras's Orchestra project, Dr. Milton Winter. Bo and Tate then go on the run, aided by Winter and pursued by local police but more stridently by Skouras, who employs a group of government assassins as well as other psychics he has been grooming in his program sanctioned by the FBI head to whom he reports.[9] The series was developed with Abrams by Alphonso Cuarón, the Mexican director whose *Y Tu Mamá También* (2001) was a critical look at an impoverished Mexico through the eyes of its elite scions.

The primary action of the series is the serial pursuit of Bo, Tate, Winter, and his associates by Skouras and various government assassins. However, there is an episodic element as well, since each week Bo meets someone on their travels whom she helps with her abilities, the opposite of the destructive use the corporate and government Skouras is employing those same abilities for in weaponizing other psychics. Bo is a beguiling combination of precocious seven-year-old and advanced soothsayer. In "White Noise" (S1E5) she tells the pregnant wife of a blogger who is trying to reveal the truth about Orchestra, "You have everything to offer." Then she quickly adds, "I have to pee." The way that Skouras harnesses psychic abilities for destruction in his laboratory, as opposed to Bo's benevolent use of her talents, seems to duplicate the power of digital technology, ever advancing and ever fluctuating between benefitting the populace and being weaponized and employed against the same populace, as the revelations of Edward Snowden and WikiLeaks have demonstrated.[10]

Like the brown-suited Patriots of *Revolution*, the Dr. Mengele–like psychic-experimenter Skouras summons up fascist connotations.[11] That he is backed and encouraged by and has at his disposal the resources of the FBI, which includes access to various off-the-books government assassins, is a statement of the show's belief that these maverick (and digital?) forces are being subsumed under a military-corporate state. In that sense the show is bolder in its condemnation of Skouras and his bosses than *The X-Files* is of its antagonists, with the conspiracy here not just hinted at but an open part of the show's mythology. The conspiratorial elements are also present from the beginning and openly acknowledged rather than being slowly revealed as in *The X-Files*.

Skouras is played by Kyle MacLachlan, whose persona, as he and the country have aged, has evolved from an ingénue introduced into the ways of the world in *Blue Velvet*, to a still-innocent but obsessed detective in *Twin*

Bo with her father in *Believe*.

Peaks, to a deceitful husband in *Desperate Housewives*, and to the security-state villain of choice in *Believe* and *Agents of S.H.I.E.L.D.* (2013–). His innocence is tarnished, as is the country's, in his post-9/11 casting. Skouras cultivates psychics, such as Joshua who can target and destroy memory cells, as ultimate weapons and also sends rogue mercenaries to "plug" Orchestra leaks. In "White Noise" (S1E5) his torture expert Zepeda (a Cuarón Mexican concoction, perhaps the perversion of the revolutionary Zapata?) threatens to scald the pregnant Taryn to get information about a source her blogger husband is using to expose Orchestra. *Believe* rewrites the *24* rationalization of torture as necessary in the war on terror to instead make it a terrifying adjunct to the maintenance of power and control by the security state.

Finally, the central relationship in the series, and the primary conflict, is who will reclaim Bo as a father figure, her actual father, Tate, or her surrogate father, Skouras. The developing key relationship in the series involves Tate's acceptance of Bo. In "White Noise" Taryn tells Tate that "Bo is special," to which Tate replies, "She's just a kid." For any father good parenting may involve the feeling that their child is special, which Tate, the reluctant father, at this point denies. Taryn then admonishes him: "What are you running from? Most people spend their whole lives looking for a connection like that." But Tate denies it, "She doesn't need me." To which Taryn responds that it is he Bo asked to bring her rag-doll turtle Stanley, indicating, though neither knows it, their actual relationship at this point—that Bo is thinking of him already as a father.

Tate's growing love for Bo contrasts sharply with Skouras's simple fascination with her as a weapon. His reaction to her display of power in the same episode, is simply an awed "she's getting stronger."

Believe ends with a wishy-washy conclusion where Bo and Tate flee to Mexico and Skouras destroys Orchestra but then stays to delay his higher-ups from finding the two, this rapid turn perhaps occasioned by the need to wrap up after a half-season cancellation. *Believe* was a vehicle that used the serial form in a way that was highly critical of the confluence of the US security state and its corporate backers. Like many other series that questioned the supposed security-state consensus and employed a heightened seriality to lodge their critiques—including ABC's *Last Resort* (2012–13), about the US starting a nuclear war and *Traveller* (2007), which had American middle-class students pursued as terrorists by the military—*Believe*'s dissident view was quickly halted, with NBC so eager to get it off the air that the network only ran twelve of thirteen episodes that were produced.

Abrams' executive-produced trilogy ends with *11.22.63*, an imagination of the world on the brink of the JFK assassination, before the imposition of the security state—that is, the continuation of imagining the devastating effects of its imposition in the present and the future in *Believe* and *Revolution*. All three highly serialized series poke holes in the security-state entertainment establishment and, given their short runs, illustrate the tentative, constantly appearing and disappearing, quality of resistance to that seemingly impregnable wall. However, the continual appearance of such series, all of which employed a highly serialized mode, suggests that the contradictions of the system continue to erupt. *Believe* in particular suggests that, given Tate's underclass fellow feeling versus Skouras's elite exploitation, behind these eruptions still lies the always hidden specter, especially in American entertainment where it is so thoroughly repressed, of class.

CONCLUSION

The King Is Dead, Long Live the King: US Serial TV "Peaks" while Global TV Soars

THE FUTURE OF US Serial TV, it would seem, could not be rosier. In 2017 there were 487 new series available to American viewers, with the streaming services alone accounting for 117 of them, a massive increase from the 24 series those services offered in 2013. Netflix boasts of allocating $8 billion for new content in 2018, with presumably much of that being for series.[1] Yet, the phrase that has risen to prominence in this period is "Peak TV," implying there may be a saturation and a sameness about the production that will eventually result in a drying up of the form.

It is very possible that what the industry terms the second golden age of television, in the US at least, may be over. A recounting of one hundred seminal series for the appendix of this book makes it clear that the "classical" period of US seriality, where the form coalesced, from 1990 to 2000, was perhaps the most inspired period, while the "mature" serial period that followed it far exceeded the earlier period in number of shows produced but perhaps not in quality.

There is another development that may hasten the flattening of American Serial TV, and that is the overthrowing of net neutrality so that companies that control access to the home, in what was in previous models called distribution, may now charge more for the streaming and network services. This development has already had the effect of hastening all kinds of mergers and consolidations as producers of content attempt to bond with distributors or internet providers (Time Warner and AT&T) or secure their own means of distribution (as Comcast has now managed successfully to buy the majority share in Sky TV) or lock up such a huge swath of content that distributors will have to come to them (Disney's recent purchase of the Fox cable channels and production studio). With the absorption by ever-larger conglomerates will come more pressures for standardization, and there is also the possibility that these mergers and the increased charges may limit the effectiveness of Netflix, Amazon, and Hulu, the streaming leaders who at present are without providers. (NSA) AT&T has already attempted to remake HBO from a quality boutique producer to a Netflix producer of quantity.[2]

This "mature" period of American seriality, though, has seen the form spread across the globe, with Netflix itself now available in the majority of countries. The result has been a blending of established patterns of cultural history and storytelling in each of these countries with aspects of the American model with which they now attempt to compete. Each "takes what they like and leaves the rest" from that model, modifying, contesting, and disrupting it to produce their own distinctive series. Germany, with the Netflix series *Dark* (2017–) but more prominently with *Berlin Babylon* (2017–), which presents a full-scale Weimar Berlin, is now challenging the production values of series such as *Game of Thrones* and *Westworld* (2016–). The Germans are also proving capable of providing their own specific content with a relevant global appeal, as the series *Bad Banks* is a characterization of the ruthless nature of the German banks that, in the age of austerity, have been terrorizing the rest of continent.

Another example of this incorporation is a Scandinavian trilogy of series that each deal with the energy industry as it affects those countries, Norway's *Occupied* (2015–) and *Acquitted* (2015–) and Denmark's *Follow the Money* (2016–). *Occupied* borrows negatively from the US, imagining a Russian invasion of Norway because of the country's refusal to drill for oil in a heightening of the new Cold War fashionable on US network TV, where the Russians are appearing more and more as villains. The other two series though engage corporate neoliberal locking up of energy in a highly thoughtful way. *Acquitted* tracks the personal and professional story of an executive in a Chinese investment firm's return to his native village. On the personal level he has to clear himself from a murder the townspeople suspect he committed twenty years before, in a serial trope particularly popular in Scandinavia of an anxious return to a birthplace. On the professional level he has to counter the efforts of his company to absorb and then liquidate the town's attempt to develop a more encompassing energy-storage battery that will challenge the development of oil and natural gas. *Follow the Money* concerns an Enron-like company that

Challenging American television hegemony in re-creating Weimar in *Berlin Babylon*.

claims to be selling energy but is in fact a shell company with almost no assets. The series focuses on the efforts of a male cop outside the company looking to topple it and a female lawyer inside who is continually corrupted by her charismatic CEO.

Both series owe much to US shows such as *House of Cards* in their examination of ruthlessness, but both, unlike that series and Showtime's *Billions*, do not simply wallow in the extravagance of corruption but detail its effects—in the first instance on the townspeople who are victims of corporate neglect and in the second on the interior lives of those swept into the maelstrom of greed. It is important to note that the American influence and success of *House of Cards* may be partly responsible for these countries altering the standard "Scandi Noir" series format, which has become too often about a cop's anxious return to a remote birthplace to track the disappearance of a child or another townsperson and the bleak landscape surrounding the disappearance (*Jordskott* [2015–], *Norskov* [2015–17], *Monster* [2017–]). The three American-influenced series mentioned above have adapted the corrupt-corporation fable to their own economies—with energy production being crucial to each of these countries—while emphasizing its truth-telling ability.

The next interesting moment, then, in the development of Serial TV is its decentered spreading across the globe and the changes that world distribution and that decentering are prompting. The form continues to prosper and grow

Corporate investors versus Norwegian locals in *Acquitted*.

not only as capitalist center of profit but also and equally at the same time as part of a resistance to that mode of production and as continual harbinger of a brighter future than the one that economy can imagine.

This book began, though, with the question of whether Serial TV was simply part of new accelerated forms of symbolic accumulation in the hyperindustrial era or whether it challenged those precepts. Is the form simply a key palliative that capital is offering to numb us as it proceeds on its path of accelerated unemployment through automation, global devastation of the environment, and a reengagement—in the form of a reconstructed Russian and Chinese menace—with the possibility of nuclear destruction? Or could this most-seductive element of the digital economy in its new mode of transmission as constantly available streaming and in its heightened narrative devices that duplicate the mobility of that economy also be the purveyor and even harbinger within the belly of the beast of a more enlightened mode of being?

The answer that this book has proposed to both questions is yes. Serial TV is both a palliative and a progressive force, and both at the same time.

This new form of television fits into the overall ever-burgeoning media landscape of what has become an industry crucial to the continual growth and perhaps even survival of capitalism. Serial TV is itself a part of an industry that is patterning and forming consciousness at least partially in order to fashion workers suitable to the symbolic economy. The mode of delivery of this new form, rather than simply freeing up the audience or giving them greater control, is also emblematic of a sociological change in the workforce in the neoliberal economy where leisure is fast vanishing. Television has now accommodated to a beleaguered workforce that must simply grab bits of time when it can.

In addition, the accumulationist aspect of this digital and symbolic economy that has in part patterned the development of Serial TV has furthered new accelerated forms of acceptable addiction centered on the mode of delivery ("binge watching") and promotion of a social autism that devalues social relations and overvalues pure productivity. In the contemporary capitalist economy, which, through Bernard Stiegler, we have labeled *hyperindustrial* rather than, post-industrial, serial-era production practices as well as narrative patterning may be viewed not as an extraordinary break from the profit system of network television but as an accelerated continuation of that system. The wave of mergers now affecting the television industry are only increasing this centralization at a time when production supposedly addresses more fragmented audiences while potentially molding them into one audience.

This dystopic view of Serial TV however is countered by the way that the form itself and its creators contest the constraints of this ever more commercialized process, as the final episode of *Lost* questioned the perfection of the digital world by countering it with a more bleak description of the "desert of the real." The form itself continually challenges network profit motives in the way it has thwarted the cost-cutting mediocrity of Reality TV and continually overflowed the boundaries of the made-for-syndication single episode. Emblematic of this struggle was the way that *Fringe* battled those dictates in attempting to break free of the monster-of-the-week restriction to more prominently feature its mythology. The series attempted then to develop a whole that was more than a fragmented, difficult-to-reconstruct memory of its parts. The very attempt at the construction of a totality challenges the fragmentation and atomizing that is the basis of media production where snippets of an incoherent, constantly-shifting new or next big thing substitute for understanding.

The history of seriality as a persistent element of art, music, and literature and in the media forms of comics, radio, cinema, and early television (and particularly the genre of soap opera, which was endemic to all three media forms) suggests the debt today's creators owe to the past and also suggests the persistence and continuity of this popular form from the nineteenth to the twenty-first centuries. This history itself often mirrored the situation today, with a Nietzschean serial current moving toward perpetual (and addictive) repetition and a Hegelian current moving toward a more progressive definition of a totality for the purpose of understanding. The narratological aspects of the serial form (multiple characters and story lines, socially oriented storyworld, dazzling narrative "special effects") suggest as well the way these characteristics may be employed to create series that are addictive or elucidating or both.

The possibility for a progressive use of the form may center on the newly increased power of the serial showrunner to resist and fashion critical texts. This possibility in a highly commercial medium lies not in viewing the auteur-showrunner as an otherworldly genius but rather as an "author in discourse," that is progressively related to and fashioned by his or her social moment, which includes his or her experiences within the industry as well as socially critical currents outside the industry.

What do we take from this uneven picture of the potential of the medium? First that it is struggling, by fits and starts, toward a more social and more coherent representation of an ever more perilous reality. Second, it is this struggle that needs to be affirmed and validated rather than simply ever more frantic addictive practices such as "forensic fandom," which are really simply byproducts of the drive of the medium and of the capitalist economy to enlist its audience in the creation of its own profit while elsewhere promoting their demise.

Appendix

One Hundred Seminal Serial Series

Many of the series listed here had short runs, an indication that on television longevity may have little to do with quality, but also an acknowledgment that some limited series runs significantly advanced the form.

Pre-Serial TV

Maverick (1957–62) Both Mavericks in same "special" episode presaged *X-Files* mythology.

The Fugitive (1963–67)

Branded (1965–66)

The Prisoner (1967–68)

The Invaders (1967–68)

Coronet Blue (1967) CBS post *Secret Agent / Prisoner* summer series about amnesiac spy with summer run enabling network to experiment.

Alias Smith and Jones (1971–73)

Seventeen Moments of Spring (1973) Russian serial series about a Russian spy in the Gestapo.

Early Serial TV

Mary Hartman, Mary Hartman (1976–77)

Hill Street Blues (1981–87)

St. Elsewhere (1982–88)

Cheers (1982–93)

Miami Vice (1984–90)

Moonlighting (1985–89)

Crime Story (1986–88)

Wiseguy (1987–90)

1990s: The Actual Golden Age?

Twin Peaks (1990–91)

Seinfeld (1990–98) Pioneered the season arc in George's "engagement" to Susan.

The Larry Sanders Show (1992–98)

The X-Files (1993–2002)

The Kingdom / Riget (1994–97) *Twin Peaks* in a Danish hospital, directed by Lars Von Trier.

South Central (1994) Groundbreaking series about a single African American mother, quickly canceled by Fox.

Friends (1994–2004)

Nowhere Man (1995–96)

Buffy the Vampire Slayer (1997–2003)

Oz (1997–2003)

The Sopranos (1999–2007)

Deadwood (2004–6) Though chronologically later, retains form and thematics of this earlier era.

"Mature" Serial Era

24 (2001–10)

The Wire (2002–8)

Firefly (2002–3)

Lost (2004–10)

Desperate Housewives (2004–12)

Veronica Mars (2004–7)

Battlestar Galactica (2004–9)

The Office (2005–13)

Weeds (2005–12)

Burn Notice (2007–13)

Big Bang Theory (2007–)

Fringe (2008–13)

Glee (2009–15)

Dollhouse (2009–10)

Fast Forward (2009–10)

Justified (2010–15)

The Walking Dead (2010–)

Revenge (2011–15)

Homeland (2011–)

Hell on Wheels (Season 1) (2011–16)

The Hollow Crown (2012–16) Shakespeare as the original serializer. *Game of Thrones* (2011–) with the actual, not pseudo, Shakespearean language.

Once Upon a Time (2011–)

Person of Interest (2011–16)

Episodes (2011–17)

Revolution (2012–14)

Last Resort (2012–13)

Longmire (2012–17) Much more firmly grounded in tribal dynamics in its first two, pre-Netflix seasons.

Arrow (Season 1) (2012–)

Dracula (2013) The vampire challenges a British energy cartel in this short-lived but luscious series.

Top of the Lake (2013, 2017)

Desperate Maids (2013–16)

Rectify (2013–16)

The Bridge (2013–14) Particularly the second season. Adaptation of the Danish-Swedish series *Bron* (2011–18).

Mom (2013–)

Orange Is the New Black (2013–)

Sleepy Hollow (2013–17)

The Americans (2013–18)

Selfie (2014) Short-lived but striking satire of digital obsession.

Believe (2014)

Silicon Valley (2014–)

Gotham (2014–)

Mr. Robot (2015–)

Jessica Jones (2015–) Best of the Marvel series.

Agent Carter (2015–16)

Goliath (2016–)

11.22.63 (2016)

Damnation (2017)

Serial TV Global Era

Varg Veum (2005–12) Norwegian series with strong social content whose lead detective's name translates as "wild wolf."

Intelligence (2006–7) Canada. Best post-9/11 spy series, by serial auteur Chris Haddock.

Un Village Français (2009–17) France.

Rake (2010–16) Australia. Beguiling quasi legal drama, but the US version on Fox (2014), which only aired one season, was sharper.

The Hour (2011–12) Britain. Second and last season on the chicaneries of Cold War Britain as they influence the media is one of the best in the serial era.

Ripper Street (2012–16) Britain.

Shokuzai (English Title: *Penance*) (2012) Japan. Murder in a girl's school with future ramifications for its witnesses by film director Kiyoshi Kurosawa.

Peaky Blinders (2013–) Britain.

Strange Empire (2014) Canada. With *Deadwood*, best Western of the Serial Era.

Halfworlds (2015–) Indonesia.

Narcos (2015–) Set in Columbia with an international cast, but the real "country of origin" is Netflix.

London Spy (2015) Britain.

The Romeo Section (2015–16) Canada.

Wasteland (2016) Czech Republic.

Night Manager (2016) Britain. The thinking person's *24*.

Rebellion (2016) Ireland.

K2 (2016–) Korea.

Salaam Moscou (2016) Russia. Brutally honest and jaundiced appraisal of contemporary ethnic relations in Russia.

You Are Wanted (2017) Germany.

In the Name of the People (2017). Chinese series about corruption that broke all single-episode records for viewership.

Taboo (2017–) Britain.

Berlin Babylon (2017–). German re-creation of the already fascist tendencies of the Weimar Period with production that rivals series such as HBO's *Game of Thrones*.

Bad Banks (2018–) Germany.

NOTES

Preface

With apologies to Bob Sklar's "Oh! Althusser!: Historiography and the Rise of Cinema Studies," *Radical History Review*, no. 41 (Spring 1988): 11–36, https://doi.org/10.1215/01636545-1988-41-11.

1. This book attempts to be more holistic, to encompass what Hegel calls the totality—in this case the totality of capitalist relations that surround serial television. Its perspective is emphatically not that of media futurists such as Amanda Lotz, who in a revealing passage in *The Television Will Be Revolutionized*, in discussing cord cutting from cable TV, says, "I don't want the whole *New York Times*, I want articles about television" (2014, 6003).

2. Press release, Ernst and Young, November 23, 2015, https://www.ey.com/ru/en/newsroom/news-releases/news-ey-media-and-entertainment-industry-poised-to-generate-one-of-the-best-profit-margins-in-2015-compared-to-leading-stock-market-indices.

3. "2017 Top Markets Report, Media and Entertainment," US Department of Commerce, http://www.trade.gov/topmarkets/pdf/Top%20Markets%20Media%20and%20Entertinment%202017.pdf.

4. An example is the Carsey-Wolf Center at the University of California at Santa Barbara and its Media Industries Project (set up and partially funded by *Friends* creator Martha Carsey and *Law and Order* franchise director Dick Wolf), which does indeed provide analysis of the industry but filtered through a purely analytical, that is, noncritical, lens. The project tracks such subjects as "branded entertainment" (complete with "ironic" website photo of *Modern Family*'s Phil Dunphy holding a tablet) and "comics orientated screen adaptations" in a supposedly neutral manner where objectivity serves not as a component of a critical perspective but as a useful research tool for the industry.

Introduction

1. See the excellent description in Todd Gitlin's (1985) *Inside Prime Time* of the origins of seriality in *Hill Street Blues* in what its creators simply referred to as "realism." Gitlin ties the overlapping sound and narratives to Robert Altman's stylistics, and the show itself was done not so long after Altman's most prominent foray into multicharacter plotting, *Nashville* (1975).

2. The name itself, "hyperindustrialism," suggests that in the digital realm the frantic attempt to monetize attention is being pursued with the same vigor, and perhaps the same caustic side effects, as the textile manufacturers pursued profit and created slums in the north of England beginning just under two centuries ago in the original era of industrial capital. (For the best description of the triumphs and tragedies of this era see Hobsbawm, *Industry and Empire: The Birth of the Industrial Revolution.*)

3. This new "flow" also includes internet and mobile activity that takes place while the viewer is watching the series that may enhance or disrupt the viewing.

4. It has in some cases also allowed their critique to penetrate into the heart of the bourgeois family, through the sanctified site of the television as modern hearth.

5. For example, Quentin Tarantino's division of his '50s-style Western *The Hateful Eight* (2015) into five parts could be thought of as a narrative experiment, but the "experiment" seems much influenced by contemporary television, with each of the parts roughly equivalent to a television episode. The same pattern is at play in the undervalued Dutch Western *Brimstone* (2016) and in the Cohen Brothers' *Ballad of Buster Scruggs* (2018).

Chapter 1

1. J. J. Abrams produced *11.22.63* (2016) based on a Stephen King novel about a time traveler who attempts to stop the Kennedy assassination, and Amy Poehler produced *Difficult People* (2015–), a sort of quirkier *Friends* (1994–2004), about—what-else?—best friends living in New York. Emily Steele, "Aiming to Break Out of a Crowded Landscape," *New York Times,* January 22, 2015.

2. Thus, a limit of a rise of 2 degrees Celsius, which scientists predicted would still "devastate the environment and endanger humanity" is now being talked of as no longer feasible, and instead a technical fix is presupposed as the solution that allows the technical frenzy to continue. Faced with this predicament there is also the more deadly head-in-the-sand approach of Donald Trump's climate denial. Renee Lewis, "Capping Warming at 2 C not Enough to Avert Disaster, Climate Experts Warn," Al Jazeera America, November 8, 2014, http://america.aljazeera.com/articles/2014/11/8/climate-change-temperature.html.

3. Shawn Donnan and Sam Fleming, "America's Middle-class Meltdown: Fifth of US Adults Live in or near to Poverty," *Financial Times,* December 11,

2015, http:// www.ft.com/cms/s/0/c3de7f66-9f96-11e5-beba-5e33e2b79e46
.html#axzz3xso8yY35.

4. This is to say nothing of the new threat to US global hegemony posed by
    the continuing economic development of China, which is now surpassing
    the US even in many technological fields to the point where the Pentagon
    is hatching contingency plans for wars with both Russia and China. Aaron
    Mehta, "The Pentagon is Planning for War with China and Russia—Can It
    Handle Both?," *DefenseNews*, January 30, 2018, http://www.defensenews
    .com/pentagon/2018/01/30/the-pentagon-is-planning-for-war-with-china
    -and-russia-can-it-handle-both/.

5. Anglo-American capital now extends its bloody tribal wars in the Balkans
    and the Middle East to the rest of Europe where Fox News, in the vanguard
    of US policy, attempted in the wake of the French *Charlie Hebdo* assassi-
    nations and the Bataclan attacks to provoke a religious civil war, claiming
    Muslim neighborhoods were "no go zones" to go along with the new Cold
    War with Russia, so that in one scenario Europe ends up looking like war-
    torn Syria or Libya, whose devastated and divided economies are still being
    touted as a NATO success story.

6. Although, it has been pointed out that the abundance of the virtual world
    in its significant technological leaps forward is countered by a real-world
    technology plateau in which hoped-for technological changes have not
    materialized. This contradiction is manifest in PayPal founder Peter Theil's
    famous comment: "We were promised flying cars, and instead what we got
    was 140 characters" (quoted in Ford, 64–65).

7. Anne Lowry, "Changed Life of the Poor: Better Off, but Far Behind." *New
    York Times*, April 30, 2014.

8. As Naomi Klein observes in *No Logo*, this is now directly acknowledged by
    corporate advertising, which places far more emphasis on the imaginary
    that is activated by the brand name than on the product itself. In this context
    Nike's "Just Do It" sounds not like a call to action but a demand for loboto-
    mizing or obliteration.

9. This initial onslaught on consciousness is celebrated in *Mad Men* (2007–15),
    where advertising is deficient not because it encroaches on subjectivity
    tout court but because it appears to be oblivious to minority and female
    consciousness, inadvertently proposing that the solution is to pay more
    attention to exploiting their consciousness as well.

10. "Wall Street joue et gagne," *L'Anticapitaliste*, March 10, 2016, https://www
    .npa2009.org/agir/entreprises/lanticapitaliste-ndeg327-en-pdf-couleurs.

11. Thomas Piketty in *Capital in the 21st Century* demonstrates how income distribution and inequality, rather stable from 1950 to 1980, begins to rise in 1980, peaking for a first time in 2007, the year before the Great Recession. New data added by Piketty's cohort Emmanuel Saez show that peak was exceeded in 2012 when 10 percent of the US population owned 50 percent of US wealth. John Cassidy, "Piketty's Inequality Story in Six Charts," *New Yorker*, March 26, 2014, http://www.newyorker.com/news/john-cassidy/pikettys-inequality-story-in-six-charts.

12. The exact quote is "Give me the child for the first seven years and I give you the man," possibly attributed to Ignatius by Voltaire but not an unfair characterization of the aim of the Jesuits' own technologies of control.

13. The conception is from Bergson's *The Creative Mind: An Introduction to Metaphysics* but was pioneered in a series of lectures just after the turn of the century now published as *Histoire de l'idee de temps, Cours au College de France 1902–1903* in 2016 by Universitaire Press de France.

14. In the 2015 South Carolina primary a Black Lives Matter activist confronted Clinton with a phrase she had used in 1994 about bringing at-risk youth, whom she termed "superpredators," "to heel." "#WhichHillary? #BlackLivesMatter Activist Demands Apology from Clinton for 'Superpredator' Comments," *Democracy Now*, February 26, 2016, https://www.democracynow.org/2016/2/26/whichhillary_blacklivesmatter_activist_demands_apology_from.

15. Binge watching is being promoted as an answer to limited worker downtime, with sites suggesting binge watching for Thanksgiving, New Years, and during snow storms. Eliana Dockterman, "Here's what You Should Binge-Watch while It's Snowing," *Time*, January 22, 2016, http://time.com/4190251/binge-watch-stream-shows-snowstorm-blizzard/.

16. And also more costly forms of, as the French say, divertissement, or diversion so that the book provided hours of entertainment in a more active reading experience for a lower cost whereas the film or television series is a more passive and far more expensive experience. (Let's say a novel, which you can still buy in France for eight euros takes twelve hours to read so the cost is 1.50 euros per hour. A film at even two hours, a slightly longer running time than most, at twelve euros, costs six euros per hour.)

17. To which Jameson's proposed solution at the end of *Postmodernism or the Cultural Logic of Late Capitalism* is "cognitive mapping."

18. Aaron Smith, "Public Predictions for the Future of Workforce Automation," Pew Research Center, March 10, 2016, http://www.pewinternet.org/2016/03/10/public-predictions-for-the-future-of-workforce-automation/.

19. *Limits to Growth*, "Jeff Bezos Predicts Amazon Drones Will Be as Common as Delivery Trucks," August 16, 2015, http://www.limitstogrowth.org/articles/2015/08/16/jeff-bezos-predicts-amazon-drones-will-be-as-common-as-delivery-trucks/.

20. Regarding climate change, 2016 was the hottest year on record in the Industrial Age, and for the first time since the beginning of the neoliberal era, 1969, the life expectancy in one of the world's leading industrial countries, France, has fallen, with the decline due partly to changes in climate, which also promote disease. "L'espérance de vie en France recule pour le premiere fois depuis 1969," *Le Monde*, January 19, 2016, http://www.lemonde.fr/societe/article/2016/01/19/l-esperance-de-vie-en-france-recule-pour-la-premiere-fois-depuis-1969_4849747_3224.html.

21. Though this is a particularly French inflection of individualism as intellectuality that seems to eliminate the presence and power of various collectives (workers, various ethnicities, women) in themselves forming an "I" that is already turned toward a collective "we."

22. "Écrans bleus et nuits blanches," *Le Monde*, March 16, 2016.

23. For a powerful description of the inception of this process see Charles Eckert, "The Carole Lombard in Macy's Window," *Quarterly Review of Film Studies* 3, no. 1: 1–21.

24. Johnson admits that in fact gaming is not leisure but rather hyperindustrial work in the guise of leisure: "In a sense, the closest analogue to the way gamers are thinking is the way programmers think when they write code: a nested series of instructions with multiple layers, some focused on the basic tasks of getting information in and out of memory, some focused on higher-level functions like how to represent the program's activity to the user" (2006, 702–4).

25. Susan Silverman's famous line questioning, yet again, another white male "hero" was, "You know what's really interesting about Matthew Fox (the actor who plays Jack)? Nothing."

26. The opening and closing itself resonate cinematically in references from Luis Buñuel and Salvador Dali's cutting of the eye to introduce a new way of seeing in *Un Chien Andalou* (1929) as this series will introduce a new way of constructing television, to David Lynch's featuring of Jeffrey's finding of the ear that will plunge him into the secret world in *Blue Velvet* (1986), and Marion Crane's vacant eye that accusingly aligns with the violence of the voyeuristic and nihilistic spectator in *Psycho* (1960) and that disrupts the identification process in a way that resounds with Jack's loneliness at the end of the series and the shock of his death.

27. Jen Chaney, "Talking *Lost* with Damon Lindelof and Carlton Cuse," *Washington Post*, May 23, 2010.

28. There is of course the possibility that this is also an allegory of production; that what is being described here is the world of the production of the series itself and the line is a summing of the work, labor, and affiliations created during the six years of filming.

Chapter 2

This chapter is particularly indebted to the work of activist economists Rick Woolf and Robert Reich who are in their own right also expert sociologists.

1. Michael Snyder, "Goodbye Middle Class: 51 of All American Workers Make less than 30, Dollars a Year," Washington's Blog, October 21, 2015, http://www.washingtonsblog.com/2015/10/goodbye-middle-class-51-percent-of-all-american-workers-make-less-than-30000-dollars-a-year.html.

2. The episodic format was also an expression of the rigidity of the factory system, a product as well of Frederick Taylor's streamlined work atmosphere, called Taylorism, predicated on the assumptions that "the primary, if not the only, goal of human labor and thought is efficiency; that technical calculation is in all respects superior to human judgment; that in fact human judgment cannot be trusted, because it is plagued by laxity" (Carr 2011, 151–52).

3. Amadine Cailhol, "Reconnaître le burn-out, un travail de longue haleine," *Liberation*, May 26, 2015.

4. Leo Lewis, "Japanese still Suffer 'Death by Overwork' as Long Hours Persist," *Financial Times*, October 8, 2016, https://www.ft.com/content/0cd29210-8dd1-11e6-a72e-b428cb934b78.

5. Leo Lewis, "Slumber Data Adds to Fears Japan is Sleepwalking into Overwork," *Financial Times*, November 19, 2016.

6. Richard Wolff and Max Wolff, "Economic Update," WBAI Radio, October 5, 2009, http://www.rdwolff.com/content/1-hour-radio-special-richard-wolff-995-wbai-nyc-0.

7. The writer was Ali Walker from *Late Night with Jimmy Fallon*. Eunkyo Rosa Lee, "Criticism," Productive Couch Potato blog, May 24, 2015, http://productivecouchpotato.weebly.com/blog/modern-family.

8. Money did become an extratextual concern in the *Modern Family* artistic household when four years into what was a very profitable run the six adult principals banded together to successfully sue their production company, Twentieth Century Fox, resulting in a tripling of their salaries for each

episode and receiving a share of the back end or syndication profits, which is where money is made on most network television series. Matthew Belloni, "'Modern Family' Cast Reaches Deal to End Salary Standoff," Deadline.com, Hollywood Reporter, July 27, 2012, https://www.hollywoodreporter.com/thr-esq/modern-family-cast-deal-salary-355527.

9. This is a quote from an article about a 2015 year-end study by the Pew Foundation, which found 20 percent of Americans at or near the poverty line and a majority having a fear of falling into that 20 percent. Sean Donnan and Sam Fleming, "America's Middle-Class Meltdown: Fifth of US Adults Live in or near Poverty," *Financial Times*, December 11, 2015, http://www.ft.com/cms/s/2/c3de7f66-9f96-11e5-beba-5e33e2b79e46.html#axzz47r2JjLf5.

10. The sexism of the moment really goes without saying, as Trish, the spectacled art patron on the board of Christie's reveals herself in "reality" to be utterly jealous of Gloria's body and supposed proficiency in bed. Gloria's answer to Trish's insecurities is to raise her arms to embrace her and say, "Welcome to the family."

11. Part of this pressure is not to be labeled, in the American parlance, "losers," that is, those who usually through no fault of their own fall down into a different layer or income bracket (Wolff 2012, 1867–69).

12. Bureau of Labor statistics (quoted in Reich 2010).

13. The figure is from a 2016 Oxfam Study. "La justice americaine s'intéresse aux fichiers," *Le Monde*, April 22, 2016.

14. The surveys were from Deloitte and Defy Media. Marketing Charts Staff, "The State of Traditional TV: Updated with Q2 1017 Data," December 13, 2017, http://www.marketingcharts.com/television/are-young-people-watching-less-tv-24817/.

15. "The Worksong Naoncluster" (S2E18).

16. Jonathan Crary discusses experiments led by the Pentagon's research division DARPA to "create the sleepless soldier," the forerunner of "the sleepless worker or consumer" in a "global infrastructure for continuous work and consumption" (2013, 1–3).

17. Stacy Liberatore, "Watch in Real Time how Much Money Apple, Google and Facebook are Making every Second," Daily Mail, February 5, 2017, http://www.dailymail.co.uk/sciencetech/article-3434290/Watch-money-Apple-Google-Facebook-making-SECOND-Graphic-reveals-worth-internet-giants.html.

18. Steven Leckart, "Mike Judge Skewers Silicon Valley with the Satire of Our Dreams," *Wired*, April 2, 2014.

19. The series that dethroned *Modern Family* for the Emmy as Outstanding Comedy Series in 2015 after that series' fifth win in a row.

20. Richard Wolff and Max Wolff, "Economic Update," WBAI Radio, October 5, 2009, accessed April 14, 2016, http://www.rdwolff.com/content/1-hour-radio -special-richard-wolff-995-wbai-nyc-0.

21. "1936 Quand La Gauche Faisait Encore Rever," *Marianne*, Hors-Serie, March 2016, 33.

22. This evisceration comes at the same time as many, after losing their homes, were forced to live in their cars with automobiles themselves also becoming last-resort mortgage objects in what constituted the building of a new subprime bubble. Claudia Assis and Rachel Koning Beals, "Subprime Car Loans Aren't Subprime Mortgages yet Still Worry Jamie Dimon, and, now, John Oliver," Market Watch, August, 15, 2016, http://www.marketwatch .com/story/could-subprime-auto-loans-lead-to-same-economic-catastrophe -as-risky-mortgages-2016-07-27.

23. In the second season the "evil" corporate head Gavin Belson makes the same argument to Richard, claiming that Pied Piper, though smaller, will, like any company, scale upward (and become more heartless) in its goal of reaching the start-up jackpot of being a publicly traded company.

24. Nathaniel Popper and Conor Dougherty, "Wall St. Stars Join Silicon Valley Gold Rush," *New York Times*, March, 24, 2015, http://www.nytimes.com/ 2015/03/25/business/wall-st-stars-join-silicon-valley-gold-rush.html.

25. Limits to Growth (website), "Jeff Bezos Predicts Amazon Drones Will be as Common as Delivery Trucks," August 16, 2015, http://www.limitstogrowth .org/articles/2015/08/16/jeff-bezos-predicts-amazon-drones-will-be-as -common-as-delivery-trucks/.

26. The situation in terms of recruiting for Wall Street is worsening. Only 10 percent of MIT graduates, a major source of programmers, enlisted in finance in 2014, while 28 percent flocked to software companies (Popper and Dougherty 2015). Gorman's reply to the *FT*'s suggestion that, given the corruption associated with his industry in the wake of the 2008 financial crisis, graduates are going elsewhere and only seeking banking because of the monetary compensation is fairly hilarious and belongs on an episode of *Silicon Valley*: "I think it's still a fabulous industry. . . . We had something like 92,000 résumés from kids this year. If you're just interested in the prestige of banking, that's not what's going to sustain you. You have to be interested in what we do: Managing and originating capital, helping issuers and investors come together is great, bringing these companies to life." "Lunch with the

FT: James Gorman," *Financial Times*, May 22, 2015, http://www.ft.com/intl/cms/s/0/e1c68512-ffa7-11e4-bc30-00144feabdc0.html.

27. Evgeny Morzov interview, *Liberation*, May 14, 2016.

28. Robert Refkin, who left Goldman in 2012 for the real estate start-up Compass (Popper and Dougherty 2015).

29. This view, satirized in *Silicon Valley*, is the dominant mode in another genre of serial series, the series about power. Thus for example, *Wolf Hall*, with a neoliberal view of history, celebrates Thomas Cromwell for his efficiency in managing Henry VIII's court and marriages while the villain of the piece is Thomas Moore, whose ethical opposition to Henry's divorces is viewed as a pitiful delaying of progress. In this view of history, the realist Henry Kissinger / Cromwell is not a war criminal who for example overthrew Allende in Chile or in the case of the latter extended the powers of the king and encroached on Parliament but a realpolitik, neoliberal hero lauded for his efficiency. The contemporary version of *Wolf Hall* is Showtime's *Billions* where Paul Giamatti's Eliot Spitzer–like attorney, complete with sadomasochistic sex life, comes off as equally or more power grabbing than Damian Lewis's constantly on-the-go investor and innovator. Thus, crusading attorneys like Spitzer, despite his personal faults, and the new "Sheriff of Wall Street," Preet Bharara, are seen as headline-grubbing impediments to the free flow of capital: Those who cheat the system for gain and those who pursue them are equally corrupt and self-serving, a very neoliberal, utterly probusiness position posing in the series as a neutral look at "corruption" in high places.

30. This is the backbiting core of the D.A. Pennebaker and Chris Hedges documentary *Startup.Com* (2001), where one childhood friend fires the other from the company they both created.

31. There is in the show also a lively allegory of production about the entertainment industry. Richard's ouster as creator of his own company suggests the moment in early cinema where D. W. Griffith, the Lumière brothers, and Georges Méliès were all sidelined as leaders of their own productions as their catalogs were taken over by more corporate entities. Griffith's financial decline and loss of independence, to the point where he is told by a bank governing his funds that they could make more profits on him (through his back catalog) if he were dead, is detailed in Janet Wasco's *Movies and Money*.

32. More contemporary protests in San Francisco have centered around antagonism over automation with citizens defecating on a robot that was supposed to be monitoring them. Leslie Hook, "How San Francisco turned

against robots." *Financial Times*, January 3, 2018, http://www.ft.com/content/e11e9394-f012-11e7-ac08-07c3086a2625.

Chapter 3

1. Sheldon's reflection can also be observed in *Fringe's* schizophrenic scientist Doctor Bishop.
2. John Plunkett and Mark Sweney, "Kevin Spacey's MacTaggart Lecture Prompts Defence of Traditional TV," *Guardian*, April 21, 2015.
3. "We discovered the network—the world of connectivity—to be uniquely suited to the overworked and overscheduled life it makes possible," is the way Sherry Turkle (2012, 13) describes this convenient overlap.
4. "US Antidepressant Use Jumps 65 Percent," *Healthday*, August 15, 2017, https://medicalxpress.com/news/2017-08-antidepressant-percent-years.html.
5. As series become more popular they often feel the competitive need to indulge in more violence. Thus, season 4 of *Peaky Blinders* (2013–), a return plot-wise to a more traditional gangster narrative, also featured an uptake in bloody beatings and murders, no doubt in a move to extend its growing popularity.
6. This is what Richard Florida refers to as the "creative class," who, after a day of conceptual labor, wish to indulge in the physicality of cooking (Polan 2007, 274).
7. A complimentary addiction is food, from which the term "binge watching" takes its name. Long a problem in the US, overeating has now reached epidemic proportions in France where one in two are now overweight and where the hardest-hit areas economically are the areas with the most obesity. Pierre Le Hir, "Un Français sur deux est en surpoids," *Le Monde*, October 26, 2016.
8. Wang Bing in *Bitter Money* (2016) traces this physical exploitation where life is utterly precarious and workers, with no medical benefits, are replaced as soon as they cannot match the daily speed required in the sweatshops of the areas outlying Shanghai.
9. Thus, for example, in the *DSM-5* impaired language communication is dropped from the list of characteristics defining the autism spectrum, and Sheldon's use of language on *Big Bang* is indeed enhanced not impaired, but also often unrelated and in the end validated as clever.
10. Turkle also describes the contemporary landscape as one where people are present but disappearing, with train stations, airports, cafés, and parks no longer a "communal space" of "social collection," but rather individually autistic places where "each is tethered to a mobile device" (2012, 155).

11. This relationship has been developed in the course of the history of seriality, with Dickens noting that (his) novels provided a community of "friends," which mitigated the fact that in his view in London "99 percent were strangers to everybody" (quoted in Hayward 1997, 44). While a French critic described Americans as spending their whole life "in the company of the same heroes . . . they are his oldest friends . . . and . . . the most stable elements of his existence" (Pierre Coupery quoted in Hayward 1997, 137).

12. James Chamberlin, review of "The Friendship Algorithm," *IGN*, January 20, 2009, http://www.ign.com/articles/2009/01/21/the-big-bang-theory-the -friendship-algorithm-review.

13. Barry Kramer and Michael J. Patrick, "Venture Capital Survey Silicon Valley Fourth Quarter 2011," Fenwick and West LLP, February 23, 2012, http:// www.fenwick.com/publications/pages/venture-capital-survey-silicon-valley -fourth-quarter-2011.aspx.

14. "JPL Small-Body Database," retrieved September 1, 2012, https://ssd.jpl.nasa .gov/sbdb.cgi?sstr=246247;orb=0;cov=0;log=0;cad=0#discovery.

15. Rose Eveleth, "A Brand New Bee Was Just Named after Sheldon from *The Big Bang Theory*," Smithsonian.com, Smart News, December 17, 2012, https://www.smithsonianmag.com/smart-news/a-brand-new-bee-was-just -named-after-sheldon-from-the-big-bang-theory-165898757/.

16. Though Sheldon himself has escaped a working-class Texas background, which he disavows.

17. Of course network-television series are integrating this more intensely assaulted viewer by constantly referring to social media and more spectacularly with ABC during the run of *Lost* featuring hyperlinked episodes explaining the arcane references to previous shows for viewers to catch up and to catch on to the show's referential construction.

18. Martin Delahaye, "Les scénaristes français sortent de l'ombre," *Le Monde*, October 30, 2016.

19. Dave Itzkoff, "Netflix Builds Its Own Superteam," *New York Times*, April 7, 2015.

20. Jason Mittell describes the series as "the televisual equivalent of a can of Pringles" (2015, 210).

21. David Lambert, "24's TV-on-DVD success leads to new DVD concepts," TVShowsOnDVD, 2003, accessed December 15, 2016, http://www.tvshows ondvd.com/news/24/764.

22. Kyle Smith, "Triumph of the Normal," *New York Post*, September 11, 2011.

23. Less terror-stricken series such as *Glee* and *Once Upon a Time* emphasize

this break; *Glee* with its characters often entering their first singing competition, and *Once* which has two arcs per season with the second beginning after the Christmas break.

24. The show's legacy continued with the lead actor, Kiefer Sutherland, no longer protecting the president but now in that role himself in ABC's *Designated Survivor* (2016–8), an adrenaline rush suitable for the age of Trump.

25. Andrew Buncombe, "US military tells Jack Bauer: Cut out the torture scenes . . . or else!," *Independent*, February 13, 2007.

26. The ending was argued over in the writer's room, and the show went so far as to film another ending where Teri is alive and she and Jack reunite. There is also some hint in early reports in the British press when the show aired there that the actress who played Teri, Leslie Hope, had wanted a salary increase for the next season and was openly critical of aspects of the show's politics and of Rupert Murdoch's policies in general, with her murder being a symbolic chastising or elimination of a critical and outspoken woman from the masculinist world of the (televisual) War on Terror.

Chapter 4

1. Todd Spangler, "Netflix eyeing total of about 700 original series in 2018," *Variety*, February 27, 2018, https://variety.com/2018/digital/news/netflix-700 -original-series-2018–1202711940/; Jerome Marin "Amazon se prépare á attaquer frontalement Netflix," *Le Monde*, November 20, 2016.

2. Alain Constant, "Ecran Total," *Le Monde*, January 8, 2017.

3. Rick Moriarty, "Spectrum-Time Warner Cable 'Ripping You Off' with Slow Internet Speeds: New York AG," NYup.com, February 1, 2017, http://www. newyorkupstate.com/news/2017/02/spectrum-time_warner_cable_rip- ping_you_off_with_slow_internet_speeds_new_york_ag.html.

4. For a detailed account of studio monopoly practices see Tino Balio, *Grand Design: Hollywood as a Modern Business Enterprise, 1930–39* (Berkeley: University of California Press, 1996).

5. The profits for both network and studio though could be enormous. *I Love Lucy* (1951–57), a show whose run ended in 1957, was still producing profits of $20 *million* in 2012 (Lotz 2014, 2301), and in 2005 a single network prime-time-ratings point was worth $400 million per year (4803).

6. This they accomplished by nullifying of the "fin-syn" rules, finally over- thrown in 1994, forbidding networks from creating their own series. These regulations were seen as partly responsible for the creation of a first golden age of independent production in the 1970s with most prominently the

Norman Lear (*All in the Family* [1971–79]) and MTM (*Mary Tyler Moore* [1970–77], *Lou Grant* [1977–82]) studios bringing progressive content to television (Lotz 2014, 2346). The overthrowing of the rules began when the Fox Network, because it did not broadcast a full prime-time schedule, was decreed to not be subject to the rules (Lotz 2014, 2354).

7. And on a previously highly devalued form of prime-time seriality in the 1970s, the nighttime soaps *Dallas, Dynasty*, and *Knots Landing*. For a detailed examination of the relation between that earlier period and contemporary seriality see Mittell (2015), chapter 7, "Serial Melodrama."

8. Lutz, Ashley. 2012. "These 6 Corporations Control 90% of the Media in America." http://www.businessinsider.com/these-6-corporations-control-90-of-the-media-in-america-2012-6. The six have since narrowed to five.

9. The merger of content providers and delivery systems has also continued apace, as Time Warner is now applying to merge with AT&T and Fox was narrowly thwarted from owning a majority share in Sky TV.

10. Advertisers also followed the trend toward mergers and conglomeration, as by the mid-2000s four holding companies (Omnicom Group, WPP Group, Interpublic Group, and Publicis Groupe) owned forty of the top fifty US agencies, earned $31 billion, and controlled the majority of the industry's business. In 2013 the big four became the big three with the merger of Publicis and Omnicom (Lotz 2014, 4200).

11. Thus Disney's Touchstone studios produced *Once and Again* (1999–2002), which aired on Disney-owned ABC and was then syndicated to Lifetime, half-owned by Disney (Lotz 2014, 3243).

12. In exchange for not charging cable operators a fee for including their network station, the conglomerates demanded that the companies carry their cable channels and in this way launched at least thirty-five channels by 2003 (Peers 2003).

13. And that is not even to mention the digital-corporate satire *Silicon Valley*.

14. Thus cable channels have experimented with a pattern of scheduling ten sitcom episodes as a test run, which, if the run is successful, then necessitates the channel produce ninety more episodes so the sitcom can later be syndicated (Lotz 2014, 2545). This has generally produced, at least in the case of TBS, knock-off, subpar network sitcoms catering to specialized audiences, and in many cases it is where African-American programming and programming blocks, formerly on the major networks, have migrated to with a corresponding loss of quality.

15. Many students no longer say they watch television, meaning the TV box,

since they are most likely streaming, but instead talk about the particular series they watch, of which they are avid fans.

16. Alain Constant, "Ecran Total," *Le Monde*, January 8, 2017.

17. In addition, the company claimed that in peak download time in 2015, it accounted for 37 percent of all internet traffic. Farhad Manjoo, "State of the Art: Why Media Titans Would Be Wise not to Overlook Netflix." *New York Times*, Jan 13, 2016, http://www.nytimes.com/2016/01/14/technology/why-media-titans-need-to-worry-about-netflix.html. Neil Hughes, "Netflix boasts 37% Share of Internet Traffic in North America, Compared with 3% for Apple's iTunes," Apple Insider, January 20, 2016, http://appleinsider.com/articles/16/01/20/netflix-boasts-37-share-of-internet-traffic-in-north-america-compared-with-3-for-apples-itunes.

18. Alain Constant, "Ecran Total," *Le Monde*, January 8, 2017.

19. Anna Nicolaou, "Netflix on Track to Hit 100 Million Customers after Record Growth," *Financial Times*, January 19, 2017, http://www.ft.com/content/8859f16e-ddcf-11e6-9d7c-be108f1c1dce.

20. Patty Domm, "Netflix shares rise after video streamer hits 100 million subscriber milestone." CNBC Market Insider, April 24, 2017, https://www.cnbc.com/2017/04/24/netflix-shares-rise-after-video-streamer-hits-100-million-subscriber-milestone.html.

21. Jerome Marin, "Amazon se prépare á attaquer frontalement Netflix," *Le Monde*, November 20, 2016.

22. Just as the film industry in many instances now distributes and exhibits films digitally, saving the cost of transporting the cans of celluloid.

23. Pierre Serisier, Blog, *Le Monde*, April 28. http://seriestv.blog.lemonde.fr/2016/04/28/marseille-et-soudain-cest-le-drame/; James Ponlowezik, "Khan Job: Netflix's Ludicrous Marco Polo," Time, December 11, 2014, http://time.com/3626227/netflix-marco-polo-review/.

24. For detailed accounts of the industrialization of series production by Warner Bros. see Christopher Anderson, *Hollywood TV: The Studio System in the Fifties* (Austin: University of Texas Press, 1994), and Dennis Broe, *Maverick* (Detroit: Wayne State University Press, 2015).

25. Jason Mittell counters this mechanistic view with the joys of "forensic fandom" (2015, 288) whereby the complex series challenges fans to find connections between episodes. However, the Netflix model, by releasing one season in toto at a time in a plea for binge watching routinizes this clue detecting that was a factor of week-by-week production to simply tracking the onslaught of the series in continuous episode after episode.

26. The creators of each of the three series come from a network television sitcom background. Ricky Gervais, the British creator of the then Americanized *The Office*, worked on a number of British network sitcoms. Garry Shandling famously was a writer on *Welcome Back Kotter* (1975–79), and Jenji Kohan before *Orange* worked on *Mad About You* (1992–99) and *Friends* before creating the Showtime sitcom *Weeds* (2005–12).

27. The episode aired February 23, 2011.

28. "Take Your Daughter to Work Day" (S2E18) aired on NBC March 16, 2006, and was written by Mindy Kaling.

29. Neither does *Orange* disdain traditional joke structure, often built on the "rule of three," as witness Crazy Eyes' desire in front of the delinquents to "play a role, like Desdemona or Ophelia, or Claire Huxtable."

30. The most vulgar manifestation of Reality TV, the Trump TV of *The Apprentice* (2004—), is now being writ large in the nation as a whole.

31. The survey is from Deloitte, 2017. "The State of Traditional TV: Updated with Q3 2016 Data," Marketing Charts, December 13, 2017, http://www.marketingcharts.com/television/are-young-people-watching-less-tv-24817/.

32. The article describes *The Bridge* (2011) creators', Måns Mårlind and Björn Stein, series *Midnight Sun* (2016), a French-Swedish coproduction, which in its detailing of the Laplanders "evokes the question of origins and racism in today's Europe." Daniel Psenny, "Jour Polar', noirceurs en plein lumiere," *Le Monde*, November 27, 2016.

33. The idea of a strong script compensating for lower production values was pioneered in the RKO socially conscious noir films (*Crossfire* [1947], *Out of the Past* [1947], *The Window* [1949]) of the postwar 1940s of then studio head Dore Schary. For a detailed description see Dennis Broe, *Film Noir, American Workers and Postwar Hollywood* (Gainesville: University of Florida Press, 2009).

34. Mustapha Kessous, "M6 rate sa rentrée," *Le Monde*, September 20, 2015.

35. The other industrial sector in which the US maintains this kind of dominance is the arms industry, where US arms sales accounted for more than half, $40 billion, of all global sales, with its nearest competitor, France, accounting for $15 billion. Tom Shanker, "US. Sold $40 Billion in Weapons in 2015, Topping Global Markets," *New York Times*, December 26, 2016, http://www.nytimes.com/2016/12/26/us/politics/united-states-global-weapons-sales.html.

36. Rani Molla, "Netflix now Has nearly 118 Million Streaming Subscribers

Globally," Recode, January 22, 2018, https://www.recode.net/2018/1/22/16920150/netflix-q4-2017-earnings-subscribers.

37. Vincent Giret and Alexandre Piquard, "Les plates-formes numériques seront bientot nos premiers concurrents," *Le Monde*, January 22, 2016.

38. Oliveri Abecassis, Director General of France's TF1. Olivier Dumons, "Les chaînes françaises se cherchent un avenir." *Le Monde*, July 7, 2014.

39. Reed Hastings, the network head, presented the show as a true international production with Netflix in partnership with the French company Gaumont in a series shot in Bogota by a Brazilian, José Padilha, with Columbian, Chilean, Brazilian, and American actors, and the language three-quarters Spanish to one-quarter English. Bruno Icher, "Nous Vaulons Plus," *Le Monde*, November 11, 2015.

40. A recent issue of the journal *Television* titled "Rethinking story in the television series" (2016, no. 7) involves a high degree of complexity of analysis regarding serial narrative patterns but far less consideration of the series' imbrication in American commercial production.

41. In 2018 the French Theater owners reasserted themselves and ordered the festival's director to forbid Netflix films in competition, but this seems a losing battle. It would be far wiser to tax Netflix and use the money for French production. For a recounting, see Dennis Broe, "Art Versus Commerce at Cannes 2018," Culture Matters, May 15, 2018, http://www.culturematters.org.uk/index.php/arts/films/item/2816-art-versus-commerce-at-cannes-2018.

42. Robert Briel, "Canal+ France Continues to Lose Subscribers," Broadband TV News, December 5, 2017, http://www.broadbandtvnews.com/2017/05/12/canal-france-continues-to-lose-subscribers/.

43. Matt Fowler, Review of "If-Then-Else," *IGN* January 6, 2015, http://www.ign.com/articles/2015/01/07/person-of-interest-if-then-else-review-2.

44. "Person of Interest Cancellation Explained by CBS Chief," Renewcanceltv, May 19, 2016, http://renewcanceltv.com/person-interest-cancellation-explained-cbs-chief/.

45. In a penetrating analysis titled "How Fox is killing *Sleepy Hollow*," Kaitlin Thomas claims that "What the network didn't seem to understand was that *Sleepy Hollow*'s highly serialized nature was largely what resulted in its early success." Kaitlin Thomas, "How Fox is Killing *Sleepy Hollow*," TV.com, January 18, 2015, http://www.tv.com/shows/sleepy-hollow/community/post/sleepy-hollow-season-2-problems-142152185812/.

46. David Itzkoff, "Complexity Without Commitment," *New York Times*, August

22, 2008, http://www.nytimes.com/2008/08/24/arts/television/24itzk.html ?_r=1&pagewanted=all.

47. Kathie Huddleston, "J. J. Abrams, Alex Kurtzman and Roberto Orci Dig Deep to Discover 'the Pattern' in their New Fox Series, *Fringe*," *Science Fiction Weekly*. March 19, 2008, http://archive.li/aJUDt.

48. Adam-Troy Castro, "J. J. Abrams' Reaction to Fox Moving *Fringe* to Fridays: 'Sh*t!'," Syfy Wire, December 14, 2012, http://www.blastr.com/2011/01/ jj_abrams_reaction_to_fox.php.

49. The image was starkly portrayed in the 1990 Hal Hartley film *Trust* (2010), where the teenage girl looks for a certain individual at the LIRR train station but can't distinguish him from the rest of the look-alike businessmen.

50. Another difference is the genre itself, or perhaps the approach to the genre. For all its purported rationality, *The X-Files* was a science-fiction/horror series with the emphasis on the latter. *Fringe* is a horror/science-fiction series with the emphasis on the science, or rather, in *Fringe*, the monstrous effects the team investigates all have, however far-fetched, a scientific explanation provided by the scientist Walter, which is a key component of the episode, but which in no way prevents the series from graphically emphasizing the horrific aspects of its errant science. While the detecting in *The X-Files* involves more straightforward FBI work, the "detecting" in *Fringe* often instead centers on Walter's scientific explanation of the graphic events, suggesting that in the almost two decades between the two series the calculable had reached into more aspects of life, seemingly explaining the irrational.

51. In this rather sneaky way in the parallel world the show returns to the Big Pharma critique it had abandoned in our world. In that way the parallel world represents a world without corporate network interference.

Chapter 5

1. Call for papers for New York University Deutsches Haus Conference on Seriality, held September 13, 2014, Elisabeth Bronfen and Christiane Frey.

2. The series is subtitled *Natural and Social History of a Family under the Second Empire*.

3. Hagedorn's characterization is from 1988, but the prescription, which forecasts today's television seriality, has proved prescient.

4. See Frank Krutnik, *In a Lonely Street: Genre, Film Noir, Masculinity* (London: Routledge, 1991). Krutnik and Neale both stress the ways that genre is designed to contain, channel and diffuse dissent.

5. Edward Gross, "Writing *Fringe*—The Evolution of a Series, Interview with

J. H. Wyman and Jeff Pinkner," Comicbookmovie.com, September 23, 2010, http://www.comicbookmovie.com/sci-fi/exclusive-interviews-writing-fringe-the-evolution-of-a-series-a22972.

6. Eugene Hirschfeld, "Totality," Marxist Theory of Art, March 27, 2011, http://marxist-theory-of-art.blogspot.fr/2011/03/totality.html.

7. Olga Petrova, "On Seriality" (program notes for Cornell University Conference on Seriality, May 1–2, 2015).

8. Christine Schrei, "Minimal" (PhD thesis, University of Applied Design, Graz, Austria), http://www.nook.at/minimal/en/repetition/.

9. Blanqui proposed that since there were sixty-four known elements in the periodic table the world in consequence was finite and time was not a progression but a continual repetition of these finite elements. Blanqui's proposal, like Nietzsche's, eliminated any creator, afterlife, and heaven or hell and substituted for a belief in advancement toward equality a version of Nietzsche's *amour fati*, love and acceptance of fate as continual repetition (Dombrowski).

10. This was the organizing principle of an exhibition at Rouen's Beaux Art Museum in the summer of 2014.

11. What Andy Warhol will later add in a far more serialized-for-its-own-sake version of Monet's project in his Campbell Soup Can series of thirty-two paintings, where the element that changes is not light, but the kind of soup and which along with his Marilyn silk screens convey the sense of how industrial production has by the mid-1960s usurped nature as the producer of phenomena in series—the soup cans replacing Monet's wheat stacks and Marilyn replacing the Cathedral as a cultural icon.

12. Quoted in Herman Sabbe, *Het muzikale serialisme als techniek en als denkmethode: Een onderzoek naar de logische en historische samenhang van de onderscheiden toepassingen van het seriërend beginsel in de muziek van de periode 1950–1975* (Ghent: Rijksuniversiteit te Ghent, 1977), 114.

13. Quotedin Jonathan Cott, *Stockhausen; Conversations with the Composer* (New York: Simon & Schuster, 1973), 101.

14. For the 2007 version on xylophone see https://www.youtube.com/watch?v=ntfdmh5laTc.

15. Émile Zola, Thérèse Raquin, preface to 2nd edition, in *Les Œuvres complètes*, Paris: International Library, vol. 34, 1928, xiv.

16. Jack J. Woehr, "The Rougon-Macquart Novels of Émile Zola (for English-speaking Readers)," Well.com, 2004, https://www.well.com/~jax/literature/Rougon-Macquart.html.

17. *The Wire* each season attempted to map a different aspect of the decaying infrastructure of Baltimore, with seasons dedicated to education, the press, and city government. *Un Village Français* each season dealt with an aspect of World War II in a village on the Franco-German border, covering topics such as the temporary stationing of a group of Jews on their way to the deportation camp at Dracy; the right-wing French militias at the end of the war; and the issue of collaboration at war's end.

18. One of the primary reasons for the expansion of the boulevards was to thwart the kind of uprisings where narrow streets could be easily commandeered by workers that had led to the revolutions of 1789, 1830, 1832, and 1848 and which Louis Napoleon feared would return to haunt his reign. A 2016 exhibition on Haussmann at the Cite de l'Architecture in Paris ignored this aspect of the building project and simply celebrated its execution.

19. Or rather that the father has corrupted the son's initial attraction to his stepmother and turned it to speculation by offering to deal him in on the appropriation after Maxime and Renee have been sexual.

20. The novel was made into a film, *The Game Is Over*, in 1966 by Roger Vadim starring Jane Fonda and stressing the lascivious qualities of the illicit relationship. A more apt re-adaptation, though, might be *Chinatown* with its concern for the appropriation of the water supply of Los Angeles and its combination in one person, Noah Cross, of both personal (in his raping of his daughter) and social (in his laying waste to the city) evil.

21. It is also important that the term "transmediality" not be fetishized and that its adoption as a critical device be seen in relation to the industry term "synergy," that is, relations across media platforms, so that the critical term does not obscure the purely commercial nature of these relationships. Thus, for example, *Terry and the Pirates*, made its debut as the tenth Columbia film serial in 1940 during a successful daily newspaper-comic run that began in 1934 and that was then followed by the property appearing on the radio.

22. Paolo Virno (2001) among others, taking their cue from Marx's phrase in *The Grundrisse*, "the general intellect" has explained how collective consciousness is furthered as a socialist development within the heart of capitalism.

23. Though the expressionist form of comedy strips like those of Winsor McKay also interacted with more experimental contemporary cinema as well.

24. Caniff was a child actor in Hollywood in 1916 at the height of silent serials such as *The Perils of Pauline* (Hayward, 100).

25. This production was drawn upon in the 2017 Shakespeare in the Park *Julius Caesar*, which resulted in the graphic knifing of Trump, a latter-day fascist.

26. Omnipresent in the 1930s, the Shadow no doubt influenced Bob Kane's creation of *Batman* in late 1939.

27. A radio drama titled *Lights Out* by Arch Obler in 1934 had helped pioneer these techniques, making use of "multiple first-person narrators, stream of consciousness monologues, and scripts that contrasted a duplicitous character's internal monologue and his spoken words." "Windy Kilocycles: Arch Obler's Description of Radio Drama in Chicago," *Theatre Arts,* July 1951. Retrieved March 23, 2016, from www.richsamuels.com/nbcmm/windy.html.

28. https://archive.org/details/RkoOrsonWelles-TheShadow-RadioRecodings/TheShadow38-01-23TheSocietyOfTheLivingDead.mp3.

29. David Chase, who created *The Sopranos*, was a writer on Cannell's *The Rockford Files* (1974–90).

30. Related by series producer Leonard Goldberg to Dan Pasternak in 2004. Leonard Goldberg, interview by Dan Pasternak, Television Academy Foundation, October 21 and December 7, 2004, http://www.emmytvlegends .org/blog/?p=6545.

31. This too-abrupt change of character, with Gerard's even-more-blatant change in allowing Kimble twenty-four hours to find the one-armed man once they get to his hometown, is somewhat mitigated in the epilogue, where Gerard approaches Kimble on the street in a patrol car and Kimble blanches at the sight of it and we realize because of this man's pursuit he will never be the same again. Being declared innocent does not wash away the years of paranoia Gerard's maniacal pursuit helped induce.

32. Huggins, a member of the Communist Party in 1939, was called to testify before the House Un-American Activities Committee and did in his words "'reel off about twenty names' but later renounced his testimony, often hiring blacklisted actors, writers and technicians and in his television work remained remarkably true to the ideals of the Popular Front period" (Broe 2015, 90).

33. In "World's End" a stone-faced Gerard arriving at a Chicago airport to conduct a manhunt with the techniques that are the equivalent of a two-way wrist radio cartoonishly resembles Dick Tracy.

34. Conversely, Gerard in "End Game" in the midst of his self-righteous manhunt and in his best Joe Friday fashion refers to those who would help Kimble as "dupes."

Chapter 6

1. Seymour Chatman distinguishes between narrative "kernels" that are scattered in the story that will be returned to later in the season or series

arc (Chekhov's gun in the first act that must be fired by the end) versus "satellites" which hover around the character only for the moment of their existence or for the episode (Kozloff 1992, 70).

2. Network season-long arcs are often constructed in six to eight episode sub-arcs built around ratings periods consisting of fall, fall sweeps (mid-November), Christmas holiday (mid-December), winter sweeps (February), and spring sweeps (May) (Newman 2006, 24).

3. The season arc can also have positive effects on progressive storytelling as witness season two of the FX series *The Bridge* which overcame its slavish copying of the Scandinavian original's concentration on a serial killer in season 1 to explore in more depth US-Mexico border inequalities in season 2. There is also the example of the Canadian Broadcasting Company series *The Romeo Section* (2015–16), created by Chris Haddock, about a Canadian intelligence unit, which in season 1 pulled its punches in its detailing of the security state, post Haddock's involvement with American TV as producer on *Boardwalk Empire* (2010–14). However, in season 2 the series returned to Haddock's major theme, the corruption of security services in the wake of 9/11, which he had previously explored in the neglected and masterful Canadian series *Intelligence* (2006–7).

4. Indeed contemporary daytime and weekend cable is still a police procedural graveyard with day and evening blocks of *Law and Order, NCIS* (2003–) and the various *CSI*s defining many cable schedules.

5. These moments may also be musical in the way, as Faye Woods points out, that *The O.C.* drew on the "emotional resonance" of Jeff Buckley's cover of Leonard Cohen's "Hallelujah," which appeared at three different moments in the series, with the last appearance of the song overlapping the death of one of the lead characters, Marissa, and being used to recall previous moments on the series (2013, 5098).

6. A series such as *Goliath*, which in the past would have been much more strongly focused on the star turn of Billy Bob Thornton as an alcoholic lawyer with a chance for redemption, in the serial mode is now much more focused on the case itself, its corporate-law firm and defense-industry defenders, and the team of women the lawyer assembles, which like him are in various states of disrepair, with Thornton downplaying the character's alcoholism and dramatic turnaround.

7. These "languages" are what the Russian literary theorist Bakhtin (1981) referred to as multivoicing and as "language systems."

8. *Crossfire* in particular was targeted by the House Un-American Activities

Committee, with its producer Adrian Scott and its director Edward Dmytryk being the only nonwriters in the initial group, later named the Hollywood Ten, to be called before the chamber.

9. In February sweeps in season 2, Emily's double Amanda, who had hijacked her childhood boyfriend Jack, dies as Emily tries to save her. For the season-3 Christmas break, Emily, having marrying Daniel, the scion of the family she seeks revenge upon for setting up and then betraying her father, is shot by Daniel and appears to be dead. Most startling of all, at the end of season 3, Conrad, the patriarch of the family Emily is out to destroy, dies at the hands of a disgruntled writer (although it can be argued that all of these characters are dying at the hands of disgruntled writers, but that's another story).

10. This use of the device goes back at least to the 1940s, when it was employed in exactly the same way in the prison escape noir *Brute Force* (1947).

11. The trope has become so dominant that the narrative special effect on the courtroom series *Goliath*, which has a major backstory based on the lead lawyer's founding and then being ousted from his own firm, is to *not* use flashbacks to tell its backstory but to have it told only through character references in the present.

12. For a thorough critique of the *CSI* forensic techniques see the PBS *Frontline* documentary *The Real CSI* (2012).

13. With such rapid and overlapping combinations then, one of the functions of the pilot is to set the generic rules often in a genre hierarchy that allows us to read the series. For example, *Sleepy Hollow* was a complex mix of the supernatural and detective series but one in which supernatural events have the force of actuality. *Fringe*, on the other hand, a series that could be seen as supernatural, instead was at pains to remain within the science-fiction realm, with elaborate rational (scientific) explanations offered for visual events straight out of the horror genre.

14. Series may also refer to their own level of referential complexity, as John Locke in the ever-thickening framework of *Lost* says nominally about a video of the mysterious Dharma Group that was found in the Hatch, "We're going to have to watch that again," a statement that also suggests to viewers what is necessary to grasp the density of the series (Mittell 2013, 46).

15. For a description of the shows see *Radio Benjamin*, edited by Lucia Rosenthal, Verso Press, 2014.

16. Laura Bradley, "Jenji Kohan Knows *Orange is the New Black* Season 5 Wasn't Very Good," *Vanity Fair*, August 28, 2017, https://www.vanityfair.com/hollywood/2017/08/orange-is-the-new-black-season-5-jenji-kohan.

17. The next season was probably the show's least interesting, employing perennial genre-TV "bad guy" Neal McDonough (who reprised the same role later on *Arrow* as the season-3 villain) in a reversion to strict gangster mode, as a mobster exiled from Detroit who schemes to return to the mob's good graces.

18. "Mapping Poverty in the Appalachian Region," Community Commons, August 9, 2016, https://www.communitycommons.org/2016/08/mapping -poverty-in-the-appalachian-region/.

19. The judge's callousness, which seems to result in the coal company winning the case and being absolved of legal responsibility for the death of the resident is perhaps an allusion to the 2000 Martin County coal slurry spill, a disaster thirty times larger than the *Exxon Valdez* spill and for which, due to the influence of Senator Mitch McConnell, the company Massey Energy was fined only $100,000 (Fosl, 2921).

20. Prior to that, in 1921 in the Blair Mountain uprising, the US army bombed the rebels from the air in what was called the most serious confrontation in the US since the Civil War and in what may be the only time, prior to the bombing of the MOVE movement in Philadelphia in 1985, that the US has publicly bombed its own citizens on its soil (Fosl, 2913).

21. This shared experience and an insularity encouraged by the mining companies also creates a singular culture as Mags describes in her opposing Carol's intersession: "We got our own kind of food, music, liquor." The series is replete with these customs, as we see Mags's son, the lawman Doyle, is also a bluegrass musician at Mags's "whoop-de-doo" or Sunday picnic and later, when the Bennetts and Crowders meet for a parlay, it takes place inside a church, arranged by the reverend.

22. Frances Langum, "Nine Million Oxy Pills to One Pharmacy in Town of 392 People," Crooks and Liars, December 20, 2016, http://crooksandliars .com/2016/12/nine-million-oxy-pills-one-pharmacy-town.

23. William Rothman's (2013) pun indeed links the character and the economic situation: "With Mags, the series hits the mother lode" (4495).

24. David Thier, "On 'Justified,' Coal Politics Hit Primetime," *Atlantic*, April 13, 20111, https://www.theatlantic.com/entertainment/archive/2011/04/ on-justified-coal-politics-hit-primetime/237083/.

25. In this mini arc, the Raylan-Boyd dichotomy, which fuels the series, is merged with the opposition community/corporation and the character antipathy Mags/Carol in the way that Raylan, supposedly neutral as a lawman, takes the side of Mags in defending the community against the

small-time pilfering of Boyd and the more grand theft and destruction being engineered by Carol in buying up the land. Carol calls attention to the Raylan-Boyd love/hate relationship saying it "sounds like a love affair" but in the season, and especially in this mini-arc, the series long doppelganger and homoerotic sides of the opposition are absorbed into the larger community/corporation antipathy.

26. This is exactly the argument ExxonMobil is now making in its advertisements about the "gift" of natural gas to the Louisiana bayou. In the wake of the devastation caused by the BP oil spill, it shows young, happy members of the community gainfully employed in "healthy" extraction, ignoring the damage this will do to the water supply and what these now-employed careerists will look like after a decade of extraction.

27. There is a surprise death of a series character, and that is Raylan's surrogate mother Helen, who dies at the hands of Dickie as casualty of the Raylan-Dickie feud. However, even this sudden death is foreshadowed in a previous episode, when Helen and Arlo, Raylan's father, are fired upon for selling their land and Helen stands almost as a target at the window.

28. Perhaps the most jarring generic combination the series effects is its musical theme, "Long Hard Times to Come" by Ganstagrass and T.O.N.E-z, which lays hip-hop beats over bluegrass guitar and banjo. Matt Zoller Seitz, "*Justified*'s Unexpected Social Commentary Propels the Show to TV's Elite Ranks," Vulture, March 24, 2015, https://www.vulture.com/2015/03/tv-review-justified-final-season.html.

Chapter 7

1. The contemporary commercial use of the author function often excludes the person of the author while trading on their name. Thus DC Comics emphasizes that *Batman* was created by Bob Kane while the company, not the author, owns the rights to the strip. The Star Trek franchise often cites the name of Gene Roddenberry after he sold the rights to the production. The afterlife of the franchise has so far exceeded its creator and is so enmeshed in corporate maneuvering, for example, that Fox Broadcasting needed to specify that its "Bob Kane" *Batman* prequel *Gotham* would not "impinge upon the narrative continuity of the Warner Bros. *Batman* films" (Pearson 2017, 120).

2. At the French television-convention Series Mania in 2016 *Sopranos*' creator David Chase was asked what he remembered about the deceased star of the series, James Gandolfini. Chase first replied that the actor would show

up late on the set when everyone was waiting for him and they would lose a day of shooting. He then talked about Gandolfini as being a remarkable natural actor capable of extraordinary spontaneity whose "sad eyes" conveyed something crucial about the character. The response indicates perfectly the two hats that the showrunner as accountant and creator wears simultaneously.

3. The famous fan phrase about Whedon when network or other considerations seemed to be steering his shows in a more blatantly commercial path is "Trust Joss" (Mittell 2015, 112).

4. The name itself is Whedon's pun on the fact that her presence is thrust upon him as the character suddenly materializes or dawns.

5. Her death hung over the entire third season with the character at the midpoint being consigned to hell, returning and then dying again at the end of the season. Kimberly Roots, "*Sleepy Hollow*'s Tom Mison Talks Abbie-less Season 4 for First Time Since Nicole Beharie's Exit." TV Line, May 31, 2016, http://tvline.com/2016/05/31/sleepy-hollow-season-4-tom-mison-nicole -beharie-exit-abbie-death.

6. Mustapha Kessous, "Le monde selon Shonda Rhimes," *Le Monde*, October 22, 2016, https://www.lemonde.fr/televisions-radio/article/2016/10/22/ le-monde-selon-shonda-rhimes_5018448_1655027.html.

7. Showrunners who do not want to get involved in the on-set production of the show now have a "concept director" who makes sure the look of the show corresponds to the showrunner's idea and who coordinate the show's multiple hired-gun directors.

8. Whedon's own feminist legacy can be seen in *Veronica Mars* and *Alias*, with the wise-cracking female threatened by the male order also emerging in *Once Upon a Time, Revenge*, and *Quantico* (2015–), which is *Buffy*'s Scooby Gang under pressure from the security state as each betrays the other and as they try to cling to some semblance of a now much more battered community—*The Fugitive* meets *Police Academy* (1984).

9. In his serial casting, the *Serenity* ship's pilot and docile husband Hoban Washburne, Alan Tudyk, in *Firefly* becomes the murderous Alpha in *Dollhouse* and Summer Glau as the mercurial River in *Firefly* reappears as a duplicitous doctor in the second season of *Dollhouse. Buffy*'s season-1 finale featured the coalescing of a collaborative production group that included cinematographer Michael Gershman, Emmy-winning makeup artists Todd McIntosh and John Vulich, set designer Carey Meyer, and *Angel* co-creator David Greenwalt (Kociemba 2014, 908).

10. Whedon's own "team" also includes his self-professed mentor the film scholar Jeanine Basinger, whom he studied with at Wesleyan and whom, just as Buffy does with the erudite librarian Giles, he has made pilgrimages to when he is starting a new project. Her work on the noirish Western director Anthony Mann and her more recent work on the war film and the Hollywood platoon film influenced *Firefly* and *The Avengers*.

11. The "team" element though has been somewhat questioned by reports that Whedon himself seduced and intimidated actresses in his "collective." Andrea Mandel, "Director Joss Whedon's Ex-Wife Alleges Serial Cheating in Scathing essay," *USA Today*, August 21, 2017, https://www.usatoday.com/ story/life/people/2017/08/21/director-joss-whedons-ex-wife-alleges-serial -cheating-scathing-essay/587978001/.

12. For *Dollhouse*, Whedon chose to allocate a high percentage of the budget to the construction of this set, feeling that the collective space of the captivity of the Dolls itself was a most crucial element in the unfolding of his story/ metaphor about a femininity now returned to slavery in the post-9/11 militarized and utterly corporatized world.

13. The engagement with the security state becomes more literal, less metaphorical in the season-4 villainous conclave the Initiative, a secret military-scientific group whose methods and ethos in experimenting with demons pose them as a threat to Buffy and her group equal to that of the demons themselves.

14. Hitchcock's most prescient presentation of the difficulty outlines how after much mutual suspicion the formation of the couple ends with a strong note of ambiguity as the last shot has them holding hands but lingers on the handcuffs that still bind them.

15. There is also an early foreshadowing of Echo in *Dollhouse* as Buffy as a vampire, that is, one who has lost herself, is able to defeat the demon who terrorized her as the Slayer.

16. Investigating Power, "Post 9/11," https://www.investigatingpower.org/ timelines/9-11/.

17. The Western identification with freedom also counters George W. Bush's Texan use of the Western codes for conquest where the War on Terror becomes an extension of Manifest Destiny as when Bush stated he wanted Osama Bin Laden "dead or alive."

18. Joss Whedon, "Commentary," *Firefly*: The Complete Series, DVD, 20th Century Fox, January 1, 2008.

19. Fox's airing the series out of order, with the pilot emphasizing Mal and Zoe's

opposition to the Alliance in the opening losing-battle sequence in Serenity Valley, also obscures their commitment by only revealing it sporadically, parceling their backstory out over several episodes rather than opening with it, as Whedon had done.

20. He incorporates into this scheme computer-generated images to apply an older "documentary" look to a quintessentially modern array of special effects.

21. Martin Chulov, "ISIS the inside story." *Guardian*, December 11, 2014, https://www.theguardian.com/world/2014/dec/11/-sp-isis-the-inside-story.

22. Hillary A. Jones, " 'Them as Feel the Need to Be Free': Reworking the Western Myth," *Southern Communications Journal* 76, no. 3 (2011): 230–47, https://www.tandfonline.com/doi/abs/10.1080/1041794x.2010.507109?src =recsys&journalCode=rsjc20.

23. That Whedon was capable of constructing these kind of allegories is illustrated in Elizabeth Rambo's explication of a funeral scene in "The Message"—the last episode written for the series—and in the course of which the series was canceled. The scene has Zoe and Mal hilariously describing a dead comrade in a way that honored their battle time together and that seemed to stand in for the cast and crew's experience of shooting the series.

24. Sarah Churchill, "We're at War, Sweetheart," *Guardian*, March 22, 2008.

25. Michale Arrington, "Internet Pornography Stats," May 12, 2007, https:// techcrunch.com/2007/05/12/internet-pornography-stats/?guccounter=1.

26. Critics (Sutherland and Swan) have compared the Dolls to the underdeveloped world's problem of sex slaves and human trafficking, but there is equally a comparison to the developed world's problem of online porn, which promotes the same activity but since its victims are paid seems to be a different problem all together.

Chapter 8

1. The last of the three, which I will not consider here, attempts to return to a moment supposedly before that state was permanently installed as a kind of questioning of its origin in an examination of the Kennedy assassination.

2. According to an Oxford study this figure is realizable by 2050. Carl Benedikt Frey and Michael A. Osborne, "The Future of Employment: How Susceptible are Jobs to Computerisation," *Technological Forecasting and Social Change* 114, no. C: 254–80.

3. Witness the canceling by USA and Netflix after one short season of *Damnation* (2017), a series set in the Depression based around a farmer's strike in

Iowa that attempted to express the resentment and unease of rural communities not only in the 1930s but in the present as well.

4. Another series that challenged the national-security caveat was ABC's *Last Resort* (2012–13), where forces within the US government launch a nuclear first strike and the crew of one nuclear submarine rebels and refuses to launch. The series lasted thirteen episodes and was allowed to wrap up but was quickly pulled after it seemed to appeal too much to a male audience on ABC's more female-oriented lineup.

5. Network series built on apocalyptic events, with a high degree of seriality, included *Flashforward*, with the whole world moved ahead an hour; *Heroes*, a kind of *X-Men* (2000) for the small screen with the mutants combining to stop a world-domination plot; and NBC's own *The Event* (2010–11), a military-disaster series, which partially because of its wishy-washy politics turned out to be a nonevent for audiences.

6. Conceived long before his ascension, the red state/blue state rivalry of Texas and California sounds more prescient than ever with Trump barely able to set foot in California and only able in his appearances in the state to appear before armed-forces gatherings.

7. There is in fact a new network pattern of repetition within seriality much in evidence in the first (2015–16) season of ABC's *Quantico*. Each week appears different in its pursuit of the terrorist threat that haunts the lead recruit Alex and her FBI cohorts, however in truth there is also a sameness about the constant revelations built around determining which is the terrorist and a simple shifting of focus throughout the twenty-two-episode series from one character to another in a way that recalls film serials from the 1940s such as *Captain Marvel*.

8. Brian Cozen, "Facting Fiction: *Revolution*, the United Nations, and Cultural Politics of Electricity," *Critical Studies in Communication* 34, no.4 (May 2017): 329–43, http://www.tandfonline.com/doi/abs/10.1080/15295036.2017.1325510?journalCode=rcsm20.

9. Episode 6 recalls the final episode of *The Fugitive* where Tate returns to his home town, confronts his false accusers, and forgives them with Bo's intercedence.

10. The psychics, following in the line of Whedon's Dolls, both succumb to this power and attempt to wake from it.

11. Skouras's precursor in *Revolution* was the Patriots' Dr. Calvin Horn, who exerted control on the town of Willoughby, the Patriots' headquarters, by inflicting various diseases on the inhabitants while ruling with an iron fist.

Conclusion

1. John Koblin "487 Original Programs Aired in 2017. Bet You Didn't Watch Them All," *New York Times*, January 5, 2018, http://www.nytimes.com/2018/01/05/business/media/487-original-programs-aired-in-2017.html.

2. See the *Intercept* report detailing how the conservative company from Texas has loaned its facilities in buildings in several major American cities to the National Security Agency for surveillance. Ryan Gallagher and Henry Moltke, "The Wiretap Rooms: The NSA's Hidden Spy Hubs in Eight U.S. Cities," *Intercept*, June 25, 2018, https://theintercept.com/2018/06/25/att-internet-nsa-spy-hubs/. Edmund Lee and John Coblin, "HBO Must Get Bigger and Broader, Says Its New Overseer, *New York Times,* July 8, 2018, https://www.nytimes.com/2018/07/08/business/media/hbo-att-merger.html.

BIBLIOGRAPHY

Adorno, Theodor, and Max Horkheimer. 1972. "The Culture Industry: Enlightenment as Mass Deception." In *Dialectic of Enlightenment*. New York: Seabury Press.

Alliez, Eric, and Maurizio Lazzarato. 2016. *Guerres et capital*. Paris: Éditions Amsterdam.

Althusser, Louis. 1971. "Ideology and Ideological State Apparatus." In *Lenin and Philosophy and Other Essays*, 127–186. New York: Monthly Review Press.

American Psychiatric Association. 2000. *Diagnostic and Statistical Manual of Mental Disorders*. 4th ed. Washington, DC: American Psychiatric Association.

———. 2013. *Diagnostic and Statistical Manual of Mental Disorders*. 5th ed. Washington, DC: American Psychiatric Association.

Anderson, Christopher. 2005. "Television Networks and the Uses of Drama." In *Thinking Outside the Box: Television Genres in Transition*, edited by G. Edgerton and B. Rose, 65–87. Lexington: University Press of Kentucky.

Athanassoglou-Kallmyer, Nina. 2015. "Le Grand Tout: Monet on Belle-Île and the Impulse toward Unity." *Art Bulletin* 97, no. 3: 323–41. https://www.tandfonline.com/doi/abs/10.1080/00043079.2015.1023158?src=recsys&journalCode=rcab20.

Bakhtin, Mikhail. 1981. *The Dialogic Imagination: Four Essays*, edited by Michael Holquist. Translated by Caryl Emerson and Michael Holquist. Austin: University of Texas Press.

Barthes, Roland. 1974. *S/Z: An Essay*. New York: Farrar, Straus and Giroux.

Belcher, Christina, and Kimberly Maich. 2014. "Autism Spectrum Disorder in Popular Media: Storied Reflections of Societal Views." *Brock Education* 23, 97–115.

Bell, Stuart. 2016. " 'Don't Stop': Re-Thinking the Function of Endings in Narrative Television." PhD thesis, University of Glasgow. http://theses.gla.ac.uk/7282.

Beller, Jonathan. 1994. *The Cinematic Mode of Production*. Lebanon, NH: Dartmouth College Press.

Benjamin, Walter. 2006. "The Storyteller." In *The Novel: An Anthology of Criticism and Theory 1900–2000*, edited by Dorothy J. Hale. Malden, MA: Blackwell.

Bergson, Henri. 2001. *Time and Free Will : An Essay on the Immediate Data of Consciousness*. London: Dover Publications.

Bordieu, Pierre. 1992. *Les règles de l'art: Genèse et structure du champ littéraire*. Paris: Editions du Seuil.

Bordwell, David. 1989. *Making Meaning: Inference and Rhetoric in the Interpretation of Cinema*. Cambridge, MA: Harvard University Press.

Broe, Dennis. 2009. *Film Noir, American Workers and Postwar Hollywood*. Gainesville: University Press of Florida.

———. 2015. *Maverick*. Detroit: Wayne State University Press.

Buckman, Alyson, R. 2014. "'Wheel Never Stops Turning': Space and Time in *Firefly* and *Serenity*." In *Reading Joss Whedon*, edited by Rhonda V. Wilcox, Tanya R. Cochran, Cynthea Masson, and David Lavery. Syracuse, NY: Syracuse University Press. Kindle.

Calvet, Louis-Jean. 1990. *Roland Barthes 1915–1980*. Paris: Flammarion.

Cardwell, Sarah E. 2007. "Is Quality Television Any Good? Generic Distinctions, Evaluations and the Troubling Matter of Critical Judgement." In *Quality TV: Contemporary American Television and Beyond*, edited by Janet McCabe and Kim Akass, 19–34. London: IB Tauris.

Carr, Nicholas. 2011. *The Shallows: What the Internet Is Doing to Our Brains*. New York: Norton. Kindle.

Cash, Conall. 2015. "Sartrean Seriality and Nietzschean Heroism in Serial Killer Narratives." Paper presented at Institute for German Cultural Studies, Cornell University, Ithaca, NY.

Chabris, Christopher F. 2008. "You Have Too Much Mail," *Wall Street Journal*, December 15, 2008. https://www.wsj.com/articles/SB122930180757905529.

Crary, Jonathan. 2013. *24/7: Late Capitalism and the Ends of Sleep*. London: Verso. Kindle.

Culler, Jonathan. 1976. *Structuralist Poetics: Structuralism, Linguistics and the Study of LIterature*. Ithaca: Cornell University Press.

Deleuze, Gilles. 1992. "Postscript on Societies of Control." In *October*, no. 59 (Winter): 3–7.

Denning, Michael. 1998. *The Cultural Front: The Laboring of American Culture*. New York: Verso.

Derrida, Jacques. 1981. "Plato's Pharmacy." In *Dissemination*, 61–172. London: Athlone Press.

Derrida, Jacques, and Bernard Stiegler. 2007. *Echographies of Television.* Cambridge, UK: Polity Press.

Dombrowski, Andre. 2015. "Monet and the Wreckage of History." Paper delivered at Terra Foundation conference on politics and impressionism. http://www.terraamericanart.org/what-we-offer/american-art-resources/limpressionnisme-et-la-politique/.

Elsaesser, Thomas. 2009. "The Mind-Game Film." In *Puzzle Films—Complex Storytelling in Contemporary Cinema*, edited by Warren Buckland, 13–41. Oxford: Wiley-Blackwell.

Faludi, Susan. 2007. *The Terror Dream: Fear and Fantasy in Post-9/11 America*. New York: Metropolitan Books.

Favard, Florent. 2016. "La sèrie et un récit (improvisé): L'articulation de d'intrigue a long terme et la notion de 'mythologie.'" In *Television, Dossier Repenser le récit avec les séries télevisées*, 49–64. Paris: CNRS Editions.

Ford, Martin. 2015. *Rise of the Robots: Technology and the Threat of a Jobless Future*. Basic Books. Kindle.

Fosl, Peter. 2015. "Motherhood and Apple Pie." In *Justified and Philosophy: Shoot First, Think Later*, edited by Rod Carvath and Robert Arp. Chicago: Open Court. Kindle.

Foucault, Michel. 1977. "What is an Author." In *Language, Counter-Memory, Practice: Selected Essays and Interviews*, edited by Donald F. Bouchard, 113–38. Ithaca, NY: Cornell University Press.

García, Alberto N. 2016. "A Storytelling Machine: The Complexity and Revolution of Narrative Television." *Between* 6, no. 11. http://ojs.unica.it/index.php/between/article/view/2081.

Gindin, Sam, and Leo Panitch. 2012. *The Making of Global Capitalism: The Political Economy of American Empire*. London: Verso.

Gitlin, Todd. 1985. *Inside Prime Time*. New York: Pantheon.

Gramsci, Antonio. 1971. *The Prison Notebooks*. London: Lawrence and Wishart.

———. 2012. *Selections from Cultural Writings*, edited by David Forgacs and Geoffrey Nowell-Smith. London: Lawrence and Wishart.

Grumley, John. 1986. "Adventures of the Concept of Totality: Thoughts on Martin Jay's *Marxism and Totality*." *Thesis Eleven* 15, no. 1: 111–21. http://journals.sagepub.com/doi/abs/10.1177/072551368601500111.

Guilluy, Christophe. 2014. *La France périphérique*: *Comment on a sacrifié les classes popularizes*. Paris: Flammarion.

Hagedorn, Roger. 1988. "Technology and Economic Exploitation: The Serial as a Form of Narrative Presentation." *Wide Angle* 10, no. 4: 4–12.

Harrison, Melissa. 2014. "Generation XX: Feminism Reinvented." *Financial Times*, Life and Arts, July 5, 2014. https://www.ft.com/content/32497422 -012f-11e4-a938-00144feab7de.

Hassan, Robert. 2009. *Empires of Speed: Time and the Acceleration of Politics and Society*. Boston: Brill.

Hatab, Lawrence. 2015. "Time Is a Flat Circle: The Doctrine of Eternal Recurrence." The Critique. http://peter-tang.com/critique-test/2015/07/15/no -exit-from-darkness-the-philosophy-of-true-detective/.

Hayward, Jennifer. 1997. *Consuming Pleasures: Active Audiences and Serial Fictions from Dickens to Soap Opera*. Lexington: University Press of Kentucky.

Heidegger, Martin. 1954. *The Question Concerning Technology, and Other Essays*. New York: Garland Publications.

Herman, David. 2002. *Story Logic: Problems and Possibilities of Narrative*. Lincoln: University of Nebraska Press.

Hobsbawm, Eric. 1999. *Industrial Revolution. Industry and Empire: The Birth of the Industrial Revolution*. New York: New Press.

Howells, Christina, and Gerald Moore. 2013. *Stiegler and Technics*. Edinburgh: Edinburgh University Press.

Huws, Ursula. 2014. *Labor in the Global Digital Economy: The Cybertariat Comes of Age*. New York: Monthly Review Press.

Jameson, Fredric. 1969. "Walter Benjamin, or Nostalgia." *Salmagundi*, no. 10–11: 52–68.

———. 1991. *Postmodernism, or, The Cultural Logic of Late Capitalism*. London: Verso.

———. 1998. *Brecht and Method*. London: Verso.

———. 2004. Foreword to *Critique of Dialectical Reason Volume 1*. London: Verso.

Jenkins, Henry. 1999. "The Work of Theory in the Age of Digital Transformation." In *Film Theory*, edited by Toby Miller and Robert Stam. Wiley Online Library.

Johnson, Steven. 2006. *Everything Bad Is Good for You*. Penguin Group US. Kindle.

Johnston, Kyle. 2014. "True Detective's Moral Occult." Realism and Seriality. http://serialvampire.blogspot.fr/2014/09/kyle-johnston-true-detectives -moral.html.

Jones, Clint. 2015. "The Crimes of Old King Coal." In *Justified and Philosophy: Shoot First, Think Later*, edited by Rod Carvath and Robert Arp. Chicago: Open Court. Kindle.

Kelleter, Frank. 2017. "From Recursive Progression to Systemic Self-Observation: Elements of a Theory of Seriality." *The Velvet Light Trap*, no. 79: 99–104.

Kociemba, David. 2014. "From Beneath You, It Forever Foreshadows: Why *Buffy*'s First Season Matters." In *Reading Joss Whedon*, edited by Rhonda V. Wilcox, Tanya R. Cochran, Cynthea Masson, and David Lavery. Syracuse, NY: Syracuse University Press. Kindle.

Koontz, David. 2014. "Reflections in the Pool: Echo, Narcissus, and the Male Gaze in *Dollhouse*." In *Reading Joss Whedon*, edited by Rhonda V. Wilcox, Tanya R. Cochran, Cynthea Masson, and David Lavery. Syracuse, NY: Syracuse University Press. Kindle.

Kozloff, Sarah. 1992 "Narrative Theory." In *Channels of Discourse Reassembled: Television and Contemporary Criticism*, edited by Robert Allen and Robert Cylde, 67–100. Chapel Hill: University of North Carolina Press.

Kracauer, Siegfried and Thomas Y. Levin. 1995. *The Mass Ornament: Weimar Essays*. Cambridge, MA: Harvard University Press.

Krauss, Rosalind. 1986. "Grids." In *The Originality of the Avant-Garde and Other Modernist Myths*. Cambridge, MA: MIT Press.

Leroi-Gourhan, André. 1945. *Milieu et techniques*. Paris: Albin Michel.

Lesage, Julia. 1977. "*S/Z* and *Rules of the Game*." *Jump Cut: A Review of Contemporary Media*, nos. 12–13 (Winter): 45–51. http://pages.uoregon.edu/ jlesage/Juliafolder/RULESOFGAME.HTML.

Levine, Elana. 2017. "Historicizing the Influence of Soap Opera." *The Velvet Light Trap*, no. 79: 105–9.

Lipovetsky, Gilles, and Jean Serroy. 2013. *L'esthétisation du monde*. Paris: Gallimard.

Lotz, Amanda D. 2014. *The Television Will Be Revolutionized*. 2nd ed. New York: NYU Press. Kindle.

Mar Azcona, Maria del. 2010. *The Multi-Protagonist Film*. Hoboken, NJ: John Wiley and Sons.

Marschall, Richard, John Paul Adams, and T. Nantier. 1981. *Milton Caniff: Rembrandt of the Comic Strip*. New York: Flying Buttress Publications.

Marx, Karl. 1977. "A Contribution to the Critique of Political Economy." Moscow: Progress Publishers. https://www.marxists.org/archive/marx/works/1859/critique-pol-economy/preface.htm.

Marx, Karl, and Frederick Engels. 2015. *The Holy Family: Critique of Critical Critique*. Amazon Digital Services. Kindle.

Mason, Julia. 2015. "Mags Bennett—Outlaw Mother." In *Justified and Philosophy: Shoot First, Think Later*, edited by Rod Carvath and Robert Arp. Chicago: Open Court. Kindle.

Mayer, Ruth. 2017. "In the Nick of Time? Detective Film Serials, Temporality, and Contingency Management, 1919–1926." *The Velvet Light Trap*, no. 79: 21–35.

McCabe, Janet. 2013. "HBO Aesthetics, Quality Television and *Boardwalk Empire*." In *Television Aesthetics and Style*, edited by Steven Peacock and Jason Jacobs, 185–98. New York: Bloomsbury. Kindle.

McDonald, Kevin P. 2013. "Digital Dreams in a Material World: The Rise of Netflix and Its Impact on Changing Distribution and Exhibition Patterns." *Jump Cut: A Review of Contemporary Media*, no. 55. https://www.ejumpcut.org/archive/jc55.2013/McDonaldNetflix/index.html.

McGuire, Ann. 2016. *War on Autism: On the Cultural Logic of Normative Violence*. Ann Arbor: University of Michigan Press.

Mical, Thomas. 1998. "The Eternal Recurrence of 'l'effroyablement ancien.'" http://noel.pd.org/Perforations/perf20/mical.html. Blog.

Mittell, Jason. 2006. "Narrative Complexity in Contemporary American Television." *The Velvet Light Trap* 58, no. 1: 29–40.

———. 2009. "Lost in a Great Story: Evaluation in Narrative Television and Television Studies." In *Reading Lost: Perspectives on a Hit Television Show*, edited by Roberta Pearson, 119–38. London: I. B. Tauris.

———. 2010. "Previously On: Prime Time Serials and the Mechanics of Memory." In *Intermediality and Storytelling*, edited by Marina Grishakova, 78–98. Boston, MA: DeGruyter.

———. 2015. *Complex TV: The Poetics of Contemporary Television Storytelling*. New York: New York University Press.

Modleski, Tanya. 1983. "The Rhythms of Reception: Daytime Television and Women's Work." In *Regarding Television: Critical Approaches—*

An Anthology, 67–75. Frederick, MD: University Publications of America.

Moffett, Craig. 2011. *US Telecommunications and Cable & Satellite: The Poverty Problem*. New York: AllianceBernstein.

Moran, Meghan B., and Steve Sussman. 2013. "Hidden Addiction: Television." *Journal of Behavioral Addiction* 2, no. 3: 125–32.

Morris, Justin. 2017. "Ace Drummond, Buck Rogers, and the Sustained Desires of Seriality." *Velvet Light Trap*, no. 79, 67–80.

Mumford, Lewis. 1934. *Technics and Civilization*. New York: Harcourt, Brace, and Company.

Neale, Steve. 1980. *Genre*. London: BFI.

Nelson, Joyce. 1979. "Caught in the Webs: Political Economy of TV." *Jump Cut* 20, no. 1: 31–33.

Newman, Michael. 2006. "From Beats to Arcs: Towards a Poetics of Television Narrative." *The Velvet Light Trap*, no. 58: 16–28.

Nietzsche, Friedrich. 1974. *The Gay Science*. Translated by Walter Kaufmann. New York: Random House.

Owen, Rob. 2011. "Cable Networks Brand Themselves through the Look and Feel of Programs." *Pittsburgh Post-Gazette*, July 24, 2011. http://www.post-gazette.com/ae/tv-radio/2011/07/24/Cable-networks-brand-themselves-through-the-look-and-feel-of-programs/stories/201107240141.

Packard, Vance. 1959. *The Hidden Persuaders*. New York: Pocket Books.

Paquet-Deyris, Anne-Marie, et al., 2016. Call for papers for a conference on "Series and Addiction." Nanterre, France.

Park, JaeYoon. 2014. "The Unruly Woman in FX's *Justified*." *Americana: The Journal of American Popular Culture*, 13, no. 2. http://www.americanpopularculture.com/journal/articles/fall_2014/park.htm.

Pateman, Matthew. 2014 "*Firefly*: Of Formats, Franchises and Fox." In *Reading Joss Whedon*, edited by Rhonda V. Wilcox, Tanya R. Cochran, Cynthea Masson, and Davide Lavery. Syracuse, NY. Syracuse University Press. Kindle.

Peacock, Steven. 2007. *Reading 24: TV Against the Clock*. London: I. B. Tauris.

Peacock, Steven, and Jason Jacobs. 2013. *Television Aesthetics and Style*. Bloomsbury. Kindle.

Pearson, Roberta. 2007. "Anatomising Gilbert Grissom. The Structure and Function of the Televisual Character." In *Reading CSI: Crime TV under the Microscope*, edited by Michael Allen, 39–56. London: I.B. Tauris.

———. 2017. "Additionality and Cohesion in Transfictional Worlds." *The Velvet Light Trap* no. 79, 113–20.

Peers, Martin. 2003. "How Media Giants Are Reassembling the Old Oligopoly." *Wall Street Journal*, September 15, 2003.

Pierson, David. 2011. *The Fugitive*. Detroit: Wayne State University Press. Kindle.

Piketty, Thomas. 2014. *Capital in the Twenty-First Century*. Cambridge, MA: Harvard University Press.

Polan, Dana. 2007. "Cable Watching: HBO, *The Sopranos* and Discourses of Distinction." In *Cable Visions: Television Beyond Broadcasting*, edited by Sarah Banet-Weisler, Cynthia Chris, and Anthony Freitas, 261–83. New York: New York University Press.

Popper, Ben. 2014. "Class Tensions Build in San Francisco as Protestors Target TechCrunch Awards." Verge, February 12, 2014. http://www.theverge .com/2014/2/12/5404190/crunchies-become-crappies-as-protestors -blame-tech-industry-for.

Popper, Nathaniel, and Conor Dougherty. 2015. "Wall St. Stars Join Silicon Valley Gold Rush." *New York Times*, March, 24, 2015. http://www .nytimes.com/2015/03/25/business/wall-st-stars-join-silicon-valley-gold -rush.html.

Raphael, Chad. 1997. "Political economy of Reali-TV." *Jump Cut*, no. 41:102–9.

Reich, Robert B. 2010. *Aftershock: The Next Economy and America's Future*. Knopf Doubleday Publishing Group. Kindle.

Rose, Tricia. 1994. "A Style Nobody Can Deal With: Politics, Style and the Postindustrial City in Hip Hop." In *Microphone Fiends, Youth Music, Youth Culture*, edited by Andrew Ross and Tricia Rose, 71–88. New York: Routledge.

Rothman, William. 2013. "Justifying *Justified*." In *Television Aesthetics and Style*, edited by Steven Peacock and Jason Jacobs, 175–584. Bloomsbury. Kindle.

Rottman, Zachary. 2014. "Two Objects that Are One Object: Roni Horn's Androgynous Minimalism." Master's thesis, UCLA. http://escholarship .org/uc/item/4524q4p4.

Salt, Barry. 1992. *Film Style and Technology: History and Analysis*. 3rd ed. London: Starworld.

Sarris, Andrew. 1996. *The American Cinema: Directors and Directions, 1929–1968*. Boston, MA: Da Capo Press.

Sartre, Jean-Paul. 1984. *Critique of Dialectical Reason Volume 1*. London: Verso.

Shelley, Peter. 2013. "Rethinking Minimalism: At the Intersection of Music Theory and Art Criticism." PhD thesis, University of Washington. https://digital.lib.washington.edu/researchworks/bitstream/handle/1773/24092/Shelley_washington_0250E_12317.pdf?sequence=1.

Shortall, Felton. 2005. "Totality and Dialectic in Hegel and Marx." Libcom .org. https://libcom.org/library/incomplete-marx-felton-c-shorthall-4.

Smith, Greg M. 2013. "Caught Between Cliffhanger and Closure: Potential Cancellation and the TV Season Ending." Paper delivered at SCMS Conference.

Stiegler, Bernard. 1998. *Technics and Time: The Fault of Epimetheus*. Redwood City, CA: Stanford University Press.

———. 2008a. *La télécratie contre la democratie*. Paris: Flammarion.

———. 2008b. *Technics and Time, 2: Disorientation*. Redwood City, CA: Stanford University Press.

———. 2013. *De la misère symbolique*. Paris: Flammarion.

———. 2015. *La société automatique: Volume 1, L'avenir du travail*. Paris: Fayard.

Sutherland, Sharon, and Sarah Swan. 2014. " 'There Is No Me; I'm Just a Container': Law and the Loss of Personhood in *Dollhouse*." In *Reading Joss Whedon*, edited by Rhonda V. Wilcox, Tanya R. Cochran, Cynthea Masson, and David Lavery, 221–33. Syracuse University Press. Kindle.

Tischleder, Babette. 2017. "Thickening Seriality: A Chronotopic View of World Building in Contemporary Television Narrative." *The Velvet Light Trap* no. 79: 120–25.

Toles, George. 2013. "Don Draper and the Promises of Life." In *Television Aesthetics and Style*, edited by Steven Peacock and Jason Jacobs. Bloomsbury. Kindle.

Tunstall, Jeremy. 1977. *The Media Are American: Anglo-American Media in the World*. London: Constable.

Turkle, Sherry. 2012. *Alone Together: Why We Expect More from Technology and Less from Each Other*. New York: Basic Books. Kindle.

Ursini, James. 1996. "Angst at Sixty Fields Per Second." In *Film Noir Reader*, edited by Alain Silver and James Ursini, 275–88. New York: Limelight Editions.

Virno, Paolo. 2001. "General Intellect." Generation Online. http://www .generation-online.org/p/fpvirno10.htm.

Vivanti, Giacomo, Olga Tennison, and Donata Pagetti Vivanti. 2016. "Improving the Quality of Life for People with Autism." Autism Europe. http://www.autismeurope.org/wp-content/uploads/2017/08/Diagnostic -criteria-for-autism-under-the-DSM-5.pdf.

Wasko, Janet. 1982. *Movies and Money: Financing the American Film Industry*. London: Praeger.

———. 1994. *Hollywood in the Information Age: Beyond the Silver Screen*. Cambridge, MA: Polity Press.

Wilcox, Rhonda V. 2014. "Introduction: Much Ado About Whedon" and "*Buffy the Vampire Slayer*: An Introduction." In *Reading Joss Whedon*, edited by Rhonda V. Wilcox, Tanya R. Cochran, Cynthea Masson, and David Lavery. Syracuse University Press. Kindle.

Williams, Raymond. 1974. *Television: Technology and Cultural Form*. London: Fontana.

Wolff, Richard D. 2012. *Capitalism Hits the Fan*. Interlink Publishing. Kindle.

Woods, Faye. 2013. "Storytelling in Song: Television Music, Narrative and Alusion in *The O.C.*" In *Television Aesthetics and Style*, edited by Steven Peacock and Jason Jacobs. Bloomsbury. Kindle.

Wu, Tim. 2016. *The Attention Merchants: The Epic Scramble to Get Inside Our Heads*. New York: Knopf.

Zane, Peder J. 2007. "Kimble, Nation Went on the Run." Knight Ridder Tribune News Service, August 28, 2007.

Žižek, Slavoj. 2002. *Welcome to the Desert of the Real*. New York: Verso.

Zola, Émile. 2016. *The Rougon-Macquart Cycle: Complete Collection*. e-artnow. Kindle.

INDEX OF TV SERIES MENTIONED

935-0994

GENERAL INDEX

Fortune of the Rougons, 138, 149

Fosl, Peter, 197–98

Foucault, Michel, 144, 210

Fowler, Amy Farrah, 81

Gaddafi, Muammar, 235

García, Alberto, 153, 163

Geffroy, Gustave, 145

Gellar, Sarah Michelle, 226

Giamatti, Paul, 183

Gindin, Sam, 14

Glass, Philip, 137, 144, 147

Godfather, The, 203–4

Goonies, The, 110

Gorman, James, 66

Gosford Park, 180

Gramsci, Antonio, 120, 126, 153, 231

Griffith, D. W., 94, 155

Grumley, John, 143

Guilluy, Christophe, 124

Hagedorn, Roger, 138

Hangmen also Die, 167

Harrison, Melissa, 225

Hassan, Robert, 80

Hatab, Lawrence, 139

Hayward, Jennifer, 137–40, 148–49, 153–57, 160–61, 179–81, 186, 190–91

Heidegger, Martin, 19

Herman, David, 183

Horkheimer, Max, 14, 28

Horne, Ben, 179

Howells, Christina, 18

Hussein, Saddam, 235

Husserl, Edmund, 17

Huws, Ursula, 56

Intolerance, 94

Island of Lost Souls, 103

Jameson, Fredric, 25, 209, 212–13

Janssen, David, 193

Jenkins, Henry, 194

Johnson, Carol, 197–98, 200–203

Johnson, Steven, 29, 58, 95

Jones, Jessica, 112–13, 139, 175

Judd, Donald, 144

Judex, 158

Kant, Immanuel, 73

Kelleter, Frank, 153

Kelley, David E., 146, 175

Keynes, John Maynard, 42

Kimble, Richard, 137, 164–71, 193

Kirby, Jack, 156

Kociemba, David, 216–17

Kohan, Jenji, 17, 186, 195

Koontz, David, 227

Kozloff, Sarah, 174, 177, 180, 193

Kracauer, Siegfried, 28, 159

Krauss, Rosalind, 145

Kripke, Eric, 232

Lacan, Jacques, 14

Lazzarato, Maurizio, 94

Leroi-Gourhan, André, 22

Lesage, Julia, 88, 90, 96

Lewis, Damian, 183

Lindelhof, Damon, 36

Lipovetsky, Gilles, 120, 124–25

Lotz, Amanda, 100

Lynch, David, 138, 143, 161, 210, 214

MacLachlan, Kyle, 237

Margaret, Mary, 189

Marschall, Richard, 155

McCabe, Janet, 210

McGarrett, Steve, 217

McGuire, Ann, 76–77

Mical, Thomas, 139–40

Milch, David, 149

Minority Report, 127

Mittell, Jason, 13, 21, 23, 88, 112, 124, 178, 182, 186, 191–92, 211

Modleski, Tania, 195

Monster, 243

Murdoch, Rupert, 89, 108, 222

Myers, Nina, 93, 97

Nashville, 180

Neale, Steve, 142

New World, 183

Nietzsche, 139–41, 144

Nosferatu, 216

CPSIA information can be obtained
at www.ICGtesting.com
Printed in the USA
LVHW081955150219
607737LV00012B/53/P